Girls Guide to Aging

with Grit and Gusto

A Memoir & Six Interviews

by

Linda Benjamin, LCSW

Black Rose Writing | Texas

First printing

Some names and identifying details have been changed to protect the
privacy of individuals.

ISBN: 978-1-68433-828-3
PUBLISHED BY BLACK ROSE WRITING
www.blackrosewriting.com

Printed in the United States of America
Suggested Retail Price (SRP) $20.95

Girls' Guide to Aging with Grit and Gusto is printed in Plantagenet Cherokee

*As a planet-friendly publisher, Black Rose Writing does its best to eliminate
unnecessary waste to reduce paper usage and energy costs, while never
compromising the reading experience. As a result, the final word count vs. page
count may not meet common expectations.

For My Family
Mom and Dad, Josh, Flore & Jojo, Dan & Chiara, Sue & Barry and (couldn't have done it without you) Ron.

And My Cheerleaders
Mary and Kathie and AllWriters' Workplace and Workshop LLC

APOLOGIES

This book is part memoir part self-help book, maybe even a political manifesto. It includes a series of interviews with role models. But back to the memoir part—It's how I remember things. Most names are changed, just to keep other lives private, but I'm pretty open about mine.

Dr. Olivski, one of my clinical social work professors, used to hand out a Xeroxed sheet (as photocopying was called back then). The printouts held several stories told in pictures. He said, "I've given you each the same printout. You have ten minutes to write the story you see." When our ten minutes were up, he asked the class members, "Now, who wants to tell us what the first story is about?" This first story was a series of pictures. The first picture had a woman walking with a large pocketbook hanging off her shoulder and a man walking behind her.

In the class, a young man's hand shot up, "They've had a fight," he said. "The man is trying to talk to her and the woman won't give him the time of day!"

Another class member, a woman, called out, "That man is trying to steal the woman's pocketbook!"

The professor went on to tell us that each of us interprets what we see differently, based on our own take on things—past experiences, associations, moods, and maybe whether or not we had our coffee that day. "None of you is lying. Each person just sees things differently," he said.

My point is, I have stories in my head and memories about my feelings and my life and the timing of things. But perhaps someone else, even someone who was there with me at the same time, experiencing the event alongside me, might see it very differently. So to anyone who has a problem with my book and its characters and events, I just want to say, as gently as possible, "Go write your own friggin' book!"

Girls'
Guide to
Aging
with
Grit and Gusto

CONTENTS

Introduction: Getting Your Grit and Gusto Ready

The Journey Begins

Chapter One: Two Orange Shirts: The Dream That Became a Prophecy

Chapter Two: Backstory: *That Girl* and This Girl

Chapter Three: Backstory: I Believe in Miracles

Chapter Four: Backstory: A Cardinal in Queens

Chapter Five: What Do You Do When You Know You Are F**ked?

Chapter Six: There's No Place Like Home

Chapter Seven: The Itsy Bitsy Spider

Chapter Eight: Waiting in the Hall

Chapter Nine: On Milwaukee/Finding My Inner Cowgirl

Chapter Ten: You Are Getting Sleepy: The Hypnotherapy People

Chapter Eleven: Healing by Magic or Meditation?

Chapter Twelve: Interview with The Green Juice Guy

Chapter Thirteen: Serialkillers.com: The Over-Sixty Dating Site

Psychobabbling

Chapter Fourteen: The Simple Secret to Being Attractive

Chapter Fifteen: It is What It Is: The Kreplach Story

Chapter Sixteen: You Talk Too Much

Chapter Seventeen: Flexibility

Chapter Eighteen: Chick Flicks: My Go-To for Tough Times

Finding My Way: Lessons From the Road

Chapter Nineteen: Stuck in the Snow
Chapter Twenty: Soul Dating in My Sixties: I Finally Meet My Better Half
Chapter Twenty-one: Perhaps You Can Go Home Again
Chapter Twenty-two: Invited with my "And Guest" to a Wedding
Chapter Twenty-three: 'Tis My Class Reunion
Chapter Twenty-four: Heart Attack First Date
Chapter Twenty-five: Happy Trails to Me
Chapter Twenty-six: The Queen of Failure
Chapter Twenty-seven: A Tale of Two Sisters
Chapter Twenty-eight: Homage to a Bodhisattva
Chapter Twenty-nine: I'll, Yes, I'll Always Have Paris!
Chapter Thirty: Face Work
Chapter Thirty-one: I Lied to Mary: Or the Shame that Kills
Chapter Thirty-two: Two Orange Coats: Not Every Dream is a Nightmare
Chapter Thirty-three: A Much, Much Younger Man (And French)!
Chapter Thirty-four: Writing for My Life: Synchronicity

But Enough About Me: Surviving the Challenges of Growing Older

Chapter Thirty-five: Elaine Soloway: Caregiving, Widowhood and Risk-Taking
Chapter Thirty-six: Mary Miller: Life After Grief Tsunami
Chapter Thirty-seven: Dr. Renee Garrick: The Healing Power of Spirituality and Community
Chapter Thirty-eight: Barbara Leigh: Hard Times Are Lessons
Chapter Thirty-nine: Mary Pender Greene: Re-Wiring and Balancing
Chapter Forty: Elinor Tolpin: Age is Just A Number

Epilogue

Chapter Forty-one: Thank You For Coming. . . .

INTRODUCTION

Getting Your Grit and Gusto Ready

Just at the end of my Middle Age, and about to dip my toes into what psychological theorists Erik and Joan Erikson dubbed the Maturity phase of life, I found myself up a creek and having to, not just find, but invent my own paddle. In *Girls' Guide*, I share my journey and those of a handful of other women, hoping that these will inspire you to be more prepared than I was, to look at aging differently and, rather than fearing it, enjoy it, even look forward to it.

It's a simple fact that we will all age. So far, we have found no cure for it, other than death. (Though, even as I write these pages, I'm sure there are millions of researchers furiously working on it.)

Like the pearl that develops within an oyster, our younger life-crises contain the sands of deepening. Experience buoys up our courage, teaches us the arts of negotiation and survival. At this point, we have survived some difficult challenges. We can use that learned wisdom to improve our later years.

Aren't most of us in denial that we will ever age? I believed that if only I took the right precautions—ate right, exercised, visited my doctor, took my supplements, got botoxed— all of the negatives associated with aging would not affect me! As a younger woman, witnessing the decline in some of my female relatives and friends, I assumed the depression and decline of self-esteem would bypass me, due to my healthy choices.

I hoped I would age like Dame Helen Mirren or Tina Turner, with wisdom and humor and my own quirky kind of attractiveness, continuing the work and the life I'd always known. Undefined by increasing years.

In the naivety of youth, I wanted to know what the older women I knew were doing *wrong*, so that I could protect myself, in the way you might inoculate yourself from an otherwise inevitable disease.

At thirty-two, browsing in a little bookstore in a mall, I found *Always A Woman,* by Kaylan Pickford. It was a book of musings, accompanied by beautiful black and white photographs of mid-fifties Kaylan. Her age and her short, gray hair made her unique in those times, even though she was tall and shaped like a model.

In her book, Kaylan was photographed dancing on a beach in a diaphanous gown; wearing riding clothes as she groomed a horse; lost deep in thought at her desk; and stretched out on a divan in a peignoir, as if she were awaiting a lover. And, though the pictures were of her alone, she never looked lonely.

I was so excited to manifest a Kaylan way of growing older that I gave her book as birthday gifts to many of my friends. But I was shocked by the responses I got to what I saw as an age-embracing book. Several of my Kaylan-gifted friends reacted with, "Sure, it's easy to be happy when you're thin, rich and beautiful."

Surely, I thought, *there must be happy older women who are not necessarily thin, rich, or even physically beautiful at all. Certainly there must be books with such women in them.*

Of course, this was in 1985, before Dr. Google could instantly access anything we might wish to know. Even if such a book existed, I was unable to find it. And, since I was the one who needed positive older woman role models, I came to realize that if I wanted to see such a book, *I* would have to be the one to write it. From age thirty-seven through fifty, I set about interviewing women who defy the negative cultural images of older women as unattractive, irrelevant, disempowered, and ultimately invisible. To counter these stereotypes, I sought out women who were growing, alive and content in their sixties, seventies, eighties and beyond. Most of the women I included were ordinary women, like me but older. However, I did ultimately meet and interview Kaylan Pickford and Olympia Dukakis, then the Oscar winner for Best Supporting Actress for the film, *Moonstruck.* I called my book, *Better Late: Conversations with Women of a Good Age.*

The one quality each woman had in common was a certain joyfulness of spirit; each was a positive example of what a woman's sager years could be. I use the words "sage" or "sager," because, as Gail Sheehy wrote in her revised *Passages*, called *The New Passages*, "sage" seems a word more associated with wisdom, experience, and a certain kind of loveliness, as compared to the commonly used "senior," which conjures more negative images, along the lines of what we would *not* be able to do or be. I did get some interest from publishers, but ultimately my book never got published.

Though I was recording these interviews with inspirational women, I wasn't actually preparing for aging in the ways these women had advised me to do. I was more like Scarlett O'Hara in *Gone with the Wind*, thinking, as Scarlett might say, "I'll think about that tomorrow, at Tara."

Now, in my seventies, I am an older woman myself. And when I tell friends that I'm writing a book, many respond in the amused-sounding voices that tell you they think you are, at the very least, adorably delusional. Darling! You've never published a book before! And now you think you can write and publish one in your seventies?

Married women of my generation put our "work" in a secondary position to our husbands.' The assumption was, if we cared for our families, our husbands and children would also care for us as we grew older. In the past and still today, men receive higher incomes than most women. In previous generations, women stayed home to parent while their children were young. Women who worked outside of the home had to deduct a sizable amount from their paychecks for childcare. Or they took jobs that didn't pay much, but which kept their creativity or skills fresh. Others took jobs they hoped could train them well enough to develop a career when their children were grown.

When I was married with young children, I always had a "jobette," either a job which could assist my husband to get on his feet, or a creative, fulfilling job which might give me the training and experience to get myself a real job with real pay once my children were grown.

As for my children, how could I not be there for them? I wanted to guide their lives; who better than I to do it? I saw my parenting role as advocate, emotional support and guide for my children and I felt that they needed me. How could I have known that I should have, at that time, been amassing my fortune, laser-focused on finding a way to sustain <u>myself</u> in my older years?

That's the rub. In later life, many women find that there is no system in place to care for us. Pensions or alimony plus social security are not enough to provide us with lives of security and dignity.

In my own life as a clinical social worker, I've done some serious introspection about what works for me and for the people I see in my practice. Ultimately, I have come to believe that Ageism is a widespread form of discrimination that seems invisible to political correctness. Those who suffered racial discrimination successfully asserted themselves and demanded justice and equality. We must do the same.

The aging population of women often experience tremendous loss at the same time: perceived loss of beauty, loss of income and thus choice and freedom, possible loss of health (whether our own or a partner's), loss of husbands who may leave for someone younger or treat us with diminishing respect, the death of friends and family. It's natural to feel depressed in the face of these losses. The future looks bleak when you are disempowered. You lose confidence when your social status plummets. You feel trapped.

All of us, but especially women, whatever our choices, who have been valued for beauty (and in this culture, beauty and youth are synonymous) need to prepare for growing older, readying ways of thinking, behaviors and resources that prepare us for our own coming years in a life-affirming way.

After all, you and I and very likely our younger sisters, when we are seventy, may have twenty years, give or take, left to live. Do we really want to spend them kvetching about being no-longer-young?

An INCH (acronym for "I'm-Not-Coming-Home") bag is a toolkit for emergencies, such as tornados, floods, fires, and wars. We need our own INCH bags in order to sustain us for the years ahead. Had I prepared my INCH bag for growing older twenty years ago, I might have had more of a guidebook for my older years.

Aging is not a personal failure. It is a natural part of life, one which those of us who live long enough get to enjoy.

However, within a youth culture like our own, *femmes d'age incertain* (as the French describe women of a certain age) become invisible to the mainstream. Being invisible, we also lose our power.

And here, a shout-out to Jane Fonda and Lily Tomlin of Netflix's "Grace and Frankie" for telling the story of sager women like it really is in our culture. Though not all of us have the resources, the beach houses, the caring children nearby, or the love interests of the two seventy-something Grace and Frankie characters. Neither do many of us have husbands who are law partners who have fallen in love with one another.

But even before Jane and Lily, I was thrilled to see English character actresses Dames Maggie Smith and Judi Dench and Penelope Wilton featured in British films and television, not as silly old albatrosses, but as wise, vibrant, growing characters important to their families and friends. Their lives were not over. They were crucial to the younger generation who actually sought their advice and assistance. They were helping one another. They were even falling in love.

In *Girls' Guide*, I reveal the lessons, some painful, of my own older woman's journey. But, also, I include inspiring interviews with six women living positive, fulfilling lives, despite crises and loss.

How can we fix this? I know, I know, there are always a lot of things to fix. Women are frequently right on the front lines of the battlefields for equality for all. But we must not forget *ourselves* along the way.

Although we in the Western world are more fortunate than many of our sisters from other cultures, we still need to fight for financial resources, respect, and equality for ourselves. Our younger years are often spent caring for children and parents and partners and bosses and institutions. Now, we need to become advocates for ourselves.

Some of our age-related changes involve huge modifications to our lifestyle. Regardless of our incomes, we wonder, "What will happen to me if I outlive my money?" Social Security can't be counted on to keep us going. And there are those in government who seek to eliminate it altogether.

Our country gives lip-service to education and family values, but then look at what we do! We cut education, don't pay or give benefits to mothers for the most important service our society requires—bringing up and teaching the next generation. We don't provide childcare, adequate health care, or a decent retirement income. And no woman I know plans to get divorced.

So, what can we do? Where can we go? If we can't take care of ourselves and there's nobody to take care of us, and no place we belong—how do we manage? Are we going to be like lemmings and just jump off a cliff together? No way, I say!

Here is my experience, one that I could only have known by living it—as well as the experiences of a handful of ordinary, yet extraordinary women who are living it, too. I give you *A Girls' Guide to Aging with Grit and Gusto* in the hope that it may serve as a guide for you in your own life's journey.

Linda Benjamin

CHAPTER ONE

Two Orange Shirts:
The Dream That Became A Prophecy

I was sixty-two. My husband, Noel, was seven years younger. I was sitting at the big clunky computer, working on a screenplay for my NYU film school class. Out of the blue, I remembered a dream I'd had the night before. It was one of those dreams that you sense means something, but is particularly crazy-making, because you can't for the life of you figure out what.

In the dream, I was packing not one, but two of the orange blouses I bought in the Garment District of New York because they were cheap. I recall that I didn't even like those blouses and their Dreamsicle color when I brought them home. Why would I pack one, let alone two? The dream had to mean something, didn't it? But what?

My husband Noel and I met in New York. We moved to Milwaukee following a great job offer for him. He worked as a hospital administrator and medical doctor. But though this work paid well, it also meant that whenever a hospital got incorporated into another system, all new staff were brought in, leaving Noel looking for a new job. I was still happy to be in the Midwest since I had family and friends there. I was able to join a psychotherapy practice in Milwaukee. We also found a charming apartment for about a quarter of what we would have paid in New York.

The move to Milwaukee precipitated a series of personal losses for me. My oldest son, Sam, who was near Ground Zero at the time of 9/11, survived the blast. (I am forever grateful for that!) But his work dried up in New York so he moved to Europe. Friends there found him a job and were supportive. At about the time Noel and I moved from Milwaukee *back* to New York, my younger son, Ben, who'd stayed with us in Milwaukee as he took his pre-med requirements, was accepted to medical school, so he left as well. Not long after that, my father died. Within two years, my mother also died.

My husband and I moved five times in the years we were married. This wasn't so unusual in the field of hospital administration. But after his job contract was done in Milwaukee, he did locum tenens, which is temp work for doctors, as he looked for another job.

Finally, a really good prospect came up for him back in New York, so I packed us up and we returned to New York, the place where we met. This time, I was lonely in New York, as my family and friends were in the Midwest. However, I loved Noel. Wasn't this what good wives did? Didn't we follow our husbands to where they could make the best living, so that we could all prosper and live a good life? Our husbands would be happy! The family would be more stable and happier because of it! Right?

Our New York apartment was in Queens. It was very different from the dwelling we'd shared in Milwaukee. I could actually look out the window of our second floor walk-up and see the lanes of the Long Island Expressway. Our rent-stabilized building was set just over Exit 19 of the Expressway. It wasn't a pretty place, but I did my best to make it cozy with second-hand furniture and rummage sale knick-knacks.

Noel was a hospital-based doctor. On one particular Saturday afternoon, my husband was not working. Usually, he worked seven days a week. This day, he was home with me. Well, not exactly fully present, but physically, he was there.

A few years earlier—I'm not exactly sure when this ended—my husband had delighted in being with me all the time—if I had a manicure, he'd surprise me at the shop. When we lived walking distance from my workplace in Rego Park, Queens, if I was working late and he wasn't, after I was done, he'd wait for me in the outer office to walk me home. He called me at least twice, sometimes three times a day. It was as if we were having a constant conversation. I'd felt a strong connection with him.

I didn't understand what was different now, though I sensed something was. Scenes from our past ran through my mind. In one flashback, we'd just returned to New York from Milwaukee. He was seeing a therapist at the time. Feeling as if something was off between us, I begged that he take me to one of his sessions.

After we parked the car near his therapist's office, we crossed the street and walked toward her Central Park West address. Midway, he dropped my hand and assumed a position further away from me. It was as if he'd become someone else, someone I didn't know, someone he wasn't during on our twenty-five minute laughing and talking car-ride from Queens into Manhattan.

Another recent scene came back to me. We were with Nick and Sandy, who were Noel's best friends from their med school days together. Over my years with Noel, I'd became their friend too. They were always wonderful to me. A couple of weeks earlier, however, Noel and I had gone to visit them at their majestic and beautifully appointed home. Noel was chatting with his oldest friends. Only this time, I felt as if I was no longer a part of our foursome. This was possibly because Noel seemed unusually distant. It was terrible to feel like a stranger there. *Weird,* I thought, *I love Nick and Sandy. And they love me. Am I imagining all of this? Am I losing my mind?*

Blinking my eyes and realizing where I was, back at the computer in our apartment, I looked over at Noel. Why was he home? I took a breath and then quietly asked, "Have you been talking to your therapist about leaving me?"

"It has come up," he said in a matter-of-fact way.

It-Has-Come-Up were only four words. But these four words told me that the subject had not only come up, but that it may very well have been one of the most discussed subjects of his weekly therapy sessions.

If this had been the first time I heard about or suspected Noel's doubts about our relationship, I would have done everything in my power to work on our marriage in couples' therapy. That wasn't the case. We'd already been to couples' therapy for two years. In therapy, Noel had never said anything that might have led me to believe that our marriage was unworkable and, despite his grueling hours, I'd never suspected an affair.

So I was devastated and shocked that he was talking about leaving me in his private therapy sessions. But after ten years of marriage, did I want a partner who was still ambivalent about being married to me?

Now the mysterious morning phone calls from work to his sister and his mother, the evenings he spent with his friend Nick alone— the times that he was free but didn't make room to spend any time with me—were beginning to make sense. It occurred to me that not only did my husband not love me anymore, but that I was, perhaps, the *only* person in his inner circle who didn't know it.

My dream of the orange shirts became an epiphany; it made total sense! In it, I'd packed two shirts that I didn't even like for wherever it was that I was going. I didn't know where that place was, but there was no question I was going *somewhere*.

I couldn't stay with a man who kissed me like you would kiss your mother. . . .Just like in the dream, I might not like the choices I had, but my choices were either to leave the life I knew for a completely unknown future or else stay in a marriage where my husband no longer loved me.

Noel suggested we separate for a time, date one another and go to a different therapist. But after I digested the whole thing, I realized that I wasn't so low on self-esteem that I wanted to hold his hand as he waited for "the right woman" to come along. If I did that, I would be only delaying the inevitable. A couple of years later, a couple of years older and with even fewer resources and less self-esteem.

At this fragile point in my life when I was no longer young, having lost my mother three months earlier and with both of my sons living far away, I realized that I would need to leave Noel. And at sixty-two, with a social worker's salary, just a few years from

Medicare, I wouldn't be able to afford pricey New York City at all, not even in Queens.

So where would I go? Who would want me? In my sixties, when many couples are smothered in grandchildren and comfortably settled in together, the hard years behind them, I had no idea where I would live, how I would support myself, whether I could find a connection to community or family. I was heartbroken, but I would need to set out on a quest for another life, unexpectedly on my own--and this is where my journey begins.

CHAPTER TWO

Backstory: *'That Girl'* and *This Girl*

This wasn't the first time I found myself in the middle of what felt like a dream and without much direction. For me, everything starts with a dream, either by day or by night. And back in the summer of 1968, I was a few months shy of twenty-two. Though *my* twenty-two was more like somebody else's sixteen. My dream was to move to New York.

The early part of my life was spent enveloped in the bosom of the safe little post-WWII suburb of Skokie, Illinois, a town adjacent to Chicago. My parents were of the Great Generation. They were grateful that their parents left Europe before the Holocaust, since as Jews they probably wouldn't have survived. My father was a soldier in the Pacific during The Second World War. He was relieved to have survived that, too. My parents were happy to be working and raising a family in our safe little house. Both sides of their families lived within a mile or two. Thanks to the GI Bill, they'd bought a small ranch home. My parents had dreams, but they never dreamt of living far from their families, far from Chicago, where their parents had settled when they first came to America, one generation earlier. For me, New York was the stuff of dreams; The Big Apple, with neon lights that announced its being the Capital of Everything. As Frank Sinatra sang, "If I can make it there, I'll make it anywhere! It's up to you, New York, New York."

Where did I get the idea that New York was calling my name? Wasn't that where all the free-thinking, interesting people lived? When I lived in Skokie, I was just outside of what was known back then as "The Second City," meaning second to New York in the world of big cities in 1968. I could take the "El" (Elevated) train into Chicago and be downtown in a half hour. But could I be a flower-child if I lived within driving distance of my conservative parents, with a slew of sweet, but judgmental aunts and uncles peering over my shoulder? Could I sleep with a boy? Date whomever I wanted—a gentile, a black man, a woman—without my family's killjoy moralistic fingers wagging in my face?

My New York vision was pretty much gleaned from the popular Sixties hit television series, *That Girl*, starring the perky Marlo Thomas as an adorable and scrappy aspiring actress, living in Manhattan and keeping a chaste engagement to her fiancé, Ted. Anne Marie, Marlo's *That Girl* character, was at once adventurous and virginal. But I was afraid of losing the values I'd been brought up to believe. *Would God hate me*, I thought, *if I slept around, just for the experience, or heaven-forbid, fun of it? Would I be hurt and shocked by people who were just using me?*

I wanted a New York life and I simultaneously didn't. I was a little envious, but also in awe of the girls who were braver than I, finding their own way, rather than following some rigid patriarchal idea we'd had drummed into our heads.

Back in the Sixties, I may have seemed brave, moving to New York and leaving the safety bubble, that, to me, in the years of Free Love and Women's Rights, had morphed into smothering shrink-wrap. I saw myself as Dorothy, leaving the dull black and white of Kansas for the Technicolor magic of Oz.

I'd saved up my summer waitressing money and had $772.50, which seemed like a fortune at the time. And I had two college friends who wanted to become my New York roommates.

But once I stepped off of the plane in New York, I felt way out of my league. I thought, *They'll eat me alive here, Little Virgin From Skokie, Illinois!*

I stayed with the families of my two college roommates; Debbie, then Alice, as we looked for jobs and apartments in "The City." Debby was from Long Island and Alice from New Jersey. Both towns were Manhattan suburbs, and, like me, my friends were itching to have a Downtown Girl experience.

When Debby's father found us a rent-controlled apartment to share at an amazing $175 per month, the three of us snapped up the deal and moved in the very next week. Somehow we managed to share one bedroom with three single beds, a tiny kitchenette, a small living-dining area and one bath.

Both of my friends got paid for working in their dads' offices while they looked for their dream jobs. Alice wanted to teach young children and Debby wanted to do something in the art world. I thought I wanted to be an actress. But I knew that in order to pay my rent, I'd have to get a day job.

I got hired as a receptionist at B'nai Brith, a Jewish social services organization just walking distance from our apartment. In my job, there were Jewish mothers everywhere, only none of them was mine. As if I had called home and spoken to my real mother, I would hear from my co-workers, "Have I got a (nice, Jewish) guy for you!" or "You have a college degree. Why aren't you getting a job as a teacher?"

Our apartment was not the glamorous one of Ann Marie, the Marlo character on *That Girl*. Out our window, I actually could have hailed the Second Avenue bus. That is, if my hand could fit through the bars that adorned our first-floor windows to keep burglars out. I'd never thought about burglars back in Skokie.

In a relatively short time, we three girls came to share our modest dwelling with some night-boarders, an indeterminate and rapidly growing number of cockroaches. It seemed we missed the "Exterminator Time Sheet" sign up. When all the refugee roaches from the other apartments took to the road, they ended up in our kitchenette, multiplying by the moment. They had plans to form their own city. It didn't help that we occasionally left dirty dishes in the sink. Eventually, we gave up. My roommates and I offered them the kitchen. One day, however, I found one of our unwelcome little guests hitching a ride to work with me on my favorite blue sweater.

The apartment was noisy too! The bus ran downtown throughout the night, the fire and police sirens wailed, and the garbage trucks clunked us awake at one in the morning, with their beep-beep noises and sanitation workers who probably figured if they had to be up all night, why shouldn't everyone?

There were never any bars on That Girl's windows or bugs in her apartment. I think she must have lived on the Upper East Side of high-rises and heftier incomes, rather than the more cost-effective Murray Hill area we called home.

One day, I had an insight. To get a part in a play or a film or a television commercial, you actually had to: 1. Read "the trades" to see when and where auditions were being held; 2. Audition; and 3. Take acting classes to hone your art and network with others "in the business." Since I wasn't doing any of these things, there was virtually no chance of my becoming an actress.

On Friday nights, my mom and dad called with weekly newscasts. "Hey, guess who's getting married?" my mother would say. "And tell her about cousin Renee's baby," my father would chime in. "How's New York?" they would ask in unison.

Given that I'd told everyone back home I was moving to New York to become an actress, turning around and going home would have been tantamount to admitting defeat. Had I just stuck with it, conquering my fears, auditioning and getting out there, maybe I would have had a chance. But I was facing my twenty-second birthday and, without consciously knowing it, I was hearing the faint ticking of my biological clock.

Did I make a big mistake in moving away without much of a plan for myself? I had images in my head of certain failure, should I risk an audition. Countering those images were the ones of my returning home, my tail between my legs.

Yes, actress or not, I think I was beginning the search for the part I was historically groomed for, following in the footsteps of my mother, my grandmother and the shtetl women who came before. Someday, I wanted to become a mother—and, in those days, in order to do that I would need to become a wife.

• • •

It was a chilly New York March. Friday night, St. Patrick's Day, actually. I felt like I was coming down with a cold, so I hadn't washed my hair in a couple of days. I had no plans for the weekend and my roommates were both away. Debby was visiting her parents and Alice was spending time with her fiancé. After work on Friday night, I took to my bathrobe. The phone rang. It was my friend from college, Donna, who lived uptown.

"Want to come to a party in my building?" she asked.

"I'd love to, but I'm coming down with a cold," I whined.

"That's too bad," said Donna, "Because some of the TWA Stewardesses are having an 'Open House' for St. Patrick's Day."

"Really?" I said, "Probably all married men and other predators there."

"Okay, if that's how you feel. But if you feel better or change your mind, the party's in my building, eleventh floor."

Back then, Flight Attendants were called "Stewardesses." They were all women and each possessed the essential qualification of being a major 'babe.' They were young, super cute, sexy.

In my insulated, middle-class neighborhood, being a "Stewardess" in the Sixties was thought of the way Victorian folks viewed being an actress, as if such adventuresses were clearly "loose women." In this decidedly unfeminist stereotype, the Stewardess's adventures were not only in travel but in sex, as in not-just-the-boyfriend-you-intend-to-marry, but (shocking to my shrink-wrap system) with other partners as well. I wanted their freedom. I had come to New York to get it, but it was too late; my inner-voice had already swallowed the doctrine of *girls must be virgins.*

My ambivalence created a kind of jealousy, yet awe, of the more experimental women. I wanted to stay a virgin and yet somehow be a New York Woman, too. Like Anne Marie did in *That Girl.* I wanted to experiment on my own terms, if I could figure out what my terms were.

I pooh-poohed the party as any self-respecting little "good-girl" might have. But the later it got, the more the ugly reality hit me: I could spend the evening picking cockroaches off my pajamas and out of my Chinese take-out, or I could go to the party.

That chilly gray dateless March evening rolled in, and it felt unbearable. I pulled my unwashed hair into a ponytail and hid it beneath a beret. I checked my clothes for hitchhikers and pulled on my coat to trudge to the Uptown bus. My chariot to party territory.

There were St. Paddy's Day revelers everywhere, wearing green hats and singing off-key, stumbling around the streets, several ales too many. The bus whizzed uptown, while from my window seat view, I observed unfamiliar goings-on and the changing scenery. We definitely weren't in Kansas anymore.

I shook, as much with fear as with the blustery March wind as I stepped off the Upper East Side bus into a world of tall steel-and-glass buildings, so unlike the place I lived with my friends.

Dodging enthusiastic party-goers coming from various bars and house parties, I found myself at Donna's glass-doored building. The white-gloved doorman barely looked up from his newspaper when I told him my destination. "Eleven," he said, pointing to a bay of shiny elevators. I waited briefly, then an elevator opened its steel doors and spit out a staggering, green-hatted couple.

The lift went up-up-up to the eleventh floor. I so very much wanted to push the down button and go back to my familiar unglamorous digs. But the thought of who would be keeping me company at home stopped me. I couldn't stay in that apartment forever. When the elevator finally reached eleven, I stepped off and followed the party-sounds to a homemade sign on a door: "TWA Stewardess Open House St. Paddy's Day Party."

The door was already a bit ajar. Pushing it open further, I was assaulted by the scents of alcohol and cigarettes.

Adjusting my eyes to the smoke, I saw, like a nerdy-girl's nightmare, a wall of Nordic blondes and exotic brunettes—all tall and sexy—to my five-foot-two chubby girl. And no Donna anywhere.

Suddenly, I was back in Mrs. Hubbard's fifth grade class on the first day of school, the year my family moved to Skokie—a short pudgy under-confident dork, surrounded by her already acclimated peers. It felt to me as if the whole class froze in horror as I entered the classroom, wearing an awful plaid coat that was so tight that its buttons threatened to pop across the room.

I blinked. I was back at the Stewardess party, a pygmy among giant, beautiful Amazon Warrior Princesses. Attempting to remain calm, I said to myself, *These women are not my rivals. I am more of a slightly short, slightly overweight, but dignified, Miss Congeniality in the Miss America Pageant, while they are the slutty, sexy Ursula Andresses of the Miss Universe variety.*

From behind the wall of not-me's, I heard a man's voice beckon, friendly, and almost familiar. "Hi, how've you been? How's the family?" I couldn't quite make out a face, but I did see a pair of horn-rimmed glasses.

I didn't know this young man, but I could tell he was joking. He had a friendly, Jewish-looking face. My first thought was, *He's not my type, but he's cute and he's funny, kind of like one of my male cousins.* I breathed a sigh of relief and stepped toward horn-rims.

On this St. Patrick's Day, little did this cute, funny guy know that he had not only been notified he'd passed the New Jersey Bar Exam, he'd also received a letter to report for active duty in New Jersey's National Guard. Not just that, but he'd also just met his wife-to-be and future mother of his children. I suppose that this meeting and its future events-to-be set an early precedent for me in finding a new direction in my life, one for which I hadn't planned, at least consciously.

CHAPTER THREE

Backstory: *I Believe in Miracles*

So, I married the guy in the horn-rimmed glasses within a year of the day we met. We didn't really know one another, other than superficially. We were both single and Jewish and professionals. Perhaps we assumed the rest would just fall into place. But over the next ten years, we seemed to grow further and further apart.

I don't think it was anyone's fault, but this was not how I was expecting my life to go. My parents weren't perfect, but they seemed to share everything and to love one another, whether pounds were gained or illness endured. I feared I would become stuck in a marriage in which I was not or no-longer loved, one in which a resentful husband and I might, in public, appear to be together, but secretly really be quite apart.

By the time I was twenty-eight, we had two children and a mortgage. I would sometimes take pictures of the boys and me reading stories or going to a movie together to preserve these moments together. But sometime after my thirty-second birthday, it occurred to me that I was not going to manifest some of my other dreams.

I comforted myself by bingeing on chocolate and gazing blankly out our Levitt-development, Jamestown-model, kitchen window. Yet, I felt isolated in the burbs and disconnected from my husband. It wasn't so much the long hours he worked. When he was at home, we didn't have much connection. Maybe it was my ADHD-style that turned him off to me or the ten to twenty pounds I was always fighting, but I just didn't feel loved. Had I expected too much? Perhaps this was normal for a ten-year marriage. I wasn't thinking about divorce as an option, but I didn't know how to fix my situation or whether it was even fixable.

I was reading voraciously, both as an escape and as an attempt to get a handle on my life. I was attracted to the short stories and novels of Isaac Bashevis Singer. This, because of our common ancestry: a long line of religious Polish Jews and because he was a bohemian and I guess I was always a bohemian wanna-be.

I threw my ennui into "Gimpel the Fool" and "Yentl" and all the Singer characters torn between love and lust, worldliness and tradition.

With the gift of his years and his words, I believed Mr. Singer understood human ambivalence. I read him in the hope that he would cast some reflected light upon my own ambivalence.

When he won the Nobel Prize in Literature, the first Yiddish writer to do so, I followed his publicity, reading all the articles and watched him on television. In a television interview on *The Dick Cavett Show*, Mr. Singer suggested that an author could be less interesting than his work. To me, reading about him in the Magazine Section of the *New York Times* and seeing him on television, he became *more* interesting. Here's how I remember him being interviewed by Dick Cavett:

Cavett: "Mr. Singer, you once said that you wouldn't go out of your way to meet Tolstoy."

Singer: "I might go across the street, but I wouldn't go to Queens."

Cavett: "I understand that you are a vegetarian. Is this for reasons of health?"

Singer: "It is for the health of the chicken."

Cavett: "Mr. Singer, many of your characters are religious Jews. Are you religious? How do you feel about the ten commandments?"

Singer: I think that with *nine* of God's commandments, I would still agree."

And that accent—that self-effacing sweet Yiddish lilt, the legacy of the Polish Jew—sounded just like my grandmother's. As crazy as it may seem, I felt a connection with this man, a mysterious and irresistible feeling that either I had known him somehow or that he had an important message for me. Either way, I felt the need to contact him.

So, I sat down at my kitchen table and typed the following letter on my Sears Manual typewriter:

Dear Mr. Singer,

I am not at all sure I believe in this, but I feel, from seeing you on television and from reading your stories, as if I've known you before.

My maternal grandparents were from Grydyk, a little town outside of Warsaw. Their family names were Pomerantz and Lieberman, and they were (and some still are) observant Jews. But I am 32 years old and have never been to Europe, or any place where we could have met.

I really am not a nut. Nor am I seeking contributions, interviews, photographs—anything, other than to explore this feeling and my accompanying compulsion to write to you.

Please write if it would be at all possible for me to meet with you.

Sincerely yours,

And just as I signed my name, I considered the futility of sending a message to a famous author and, in an impulse, scribbled my telephone number as a postscript. Not knowing his address, I sent my note to his publisher.

Then I forgot the letter and resumed my Hebrew school-to-soccer field suburban car-pool route and the preparations for Hanukkah.

$\bullet \quad \bullet \quad \bullet$

I've always loved it when Christians and Jews celebrate our holidays together. For me, it felt like everybody feels festive at the same time. On this first night of Hanukkah, it was also Christmas Eve. Our house smelled of cinnamon and vegetable oil. I was making applesauce for the potato latkes that my sister, visiting us from Chicago, was helping me make. We had a family party that would begin in a few hours.

Between applesauce stirrings, my sons and I danced around the table to a record made by my cousin David's balalaika group.

The telephone rang.

A ploy to buy a newspaper that I already subscribed to? A free estimate from a carpet cleaning company?

"Linda Benjamin?" said the unidentifiable, yet vaguely familiar voice. *A Polish-Yiddish accent. Perhaps a long lost relative, a Holocaust survivor, had somehow traced our family from Grydyk, Poland to Chicago to me, now living in Matawan, New Jersey.*

"Yes?" I responded with curiosity, motioning for one of the boys to turn down the music.

And then, "This is Isaac Singer."

A joke? No. The letter. He got my letter!

"Mr. Singer, Mr. Singer, you got my letter!"

"How *else* shall I be calling you?"

I don't remember the rest of the conversation, but the gist was that, if I wanted to meet him, I should come to his New York apartment. Now.

Strange how you wait for something you've dreamed about to happen, and when it does, you wish you had more time to get ready. Maybe I should prepare some questions? Look over his books? Lose some weight?

What to wear? And what to bring for Hanukkah?

Hadn't I told her, my sister reminded me, that Mr. Singer was a vegetarian, and so, why not bring him a plate of homemade latkes and applesauce.

When I told my husband I was leaving to go to New York and why, he felt abandoned and angry. I called my sister-in-law and she seemed to understand. Everything was ready and my sister was there to co-host and serve the food. But, my husband was still annoyed with me, as I went to meet this famous writer I admired.

The bag was warm in my hands as I left to drive to Mr. Singer's apartment on West 96th Street in New York. Back in those days, the drive was about an hour and half, without traffic.

Once in the city, I found a parking space near his building, and I went inside, climbing the four flights to his door. Then I knocked. He answered himself. Needing time to collect my thoughts, I stared at him and stammered my first words,

"M-m-may I use your bathroom?"

He smiled, gesturing for me to follow him. "Come," he said, "I'll make light."

In the high-ceilinged, unpretentious Old/New World living room, I sat on Mr. Singer's sofa, wordless. I saw this very room in the two-part New York Times Magazine Section interview I read, just a week or so ago, and, now, miraculously, I was inside that very picture.

When I managed to blurt out how nervous I felt, Mr. Singer said (and I am paraphrasing here), "Oftentimes, when I was a younger man, I would fancy a woman, desiring her from afar. I would dream about meeting her, and perhaps sometime later, we might actually meet. If she fancied me too, we might keep company. At that moment, I would ask myself, 'Am I really here? Is this a dream?' Afterwards, perhaps on the way home, it would hit me," he said as he slapped his cheek, "'I did *that?* That happened to *me?*'" The truth-teller of Eastern European Jewry captured with words just how I was feeling at that moment.

That sharing opened me up. And Mr. Singer spoke about himself very little that evening. He listened, really listened, and he asked many questions about me. I mostly talked about how lonely and frustrated I felt, knowing I had some artistic creativity inside of me, but I hadn't yet known how to tap it.

And he told me it was a good thing that I wrote down my telephone number, because he found it difficult answering all his mail. Also, he asked me to come to a Hanukkah party that he was giving the following Tuesday for a few friends.

Then, with a paternal peck on the cheek, Mr. Singer led me to the door.

I felt refreshed, lifted out of my ennui, as I glided home on heightened spirits and the powdered-sugar snow that now covered the New Jersey Turnpike.

· · ·

By Monday, my husband had heard from his business partner that it was a really big deal to meet Isaac Bashevis Singer, the Nobel Prize winner for Literature, and he wanted to drive me into the city. He said that he would drop me off at the party, while he went shopping for a Burberry coat.

Seven or eight people, all young artists, were gathered at the party; Mr. Singer's secretary, Devorah, an American Jew and aspiring writer, and her Israeli husband, Avram, a photographer and New York City cabdriver; one of Mr. Singer's editors; several dancers and a male model/actor, the boyfriend of one of the dancers.

The other guests worked in and around the kitchen. Avram stirred an aromatic vegetable soup, two dancers gracefully tossed a gigantic salad and I helped Devorah with the latkes.

Isaac, as everyone called Mr. Singer, was the proud host. His compact form looked scrubbed and his blue eyes twinkly, as he popped into and was shooed out of his own kitchen.

Surely, I thought, *Mr. Singer and I are the only ones here over 30.* I wondered at the arrogance of youth, as the others, none of whom had children, spoke so confidently about child-rearing.

The communal supper was appreciated with "mmm's" and "ahhh's" and the sharing of secret ingredients. There was wine. We ate and drank. And Isaac Singer told stories of the past, what he called, "my father's world," of how he couldn't say no to a shoe salesman and so owned a closetful of ill-fitting shoes. He told us the story of how at the Nobel ceremony, his napkin kept slipping from his lap, so he asked Sweden's Princess Christina, sitting next to him, how she managed to keep hers in place. She answered with a mischievous look, "'I sit on it.'"

Most often, Mr. Singer listened to or asked questions of his guests. Some of the young guests didn't understand how special this time was with the master storyteller, and they left the room from time to time. And from the scent that was coming from the bathroom, I knew they were smoking marijuana.

After he understood what it was the male model, a boyfriend of one of the dancers, did for a living, Mr. Singer said that the model had been supporting him for all these years.

When all around the table looked at him in shock, he explained that since the model displayed, and thus, sold products that sold the magazines, editors could afford to buy stories from writers like himself.

After supper, we lit the hand-carved menorah—a homemade Hanukkah gift from Avram and played the dreidel game, using raisins and nuts as our winnings.

The doorbell rang. It was my husband, crashing the party. And he joined us for the game.

When the dreidel game was over, we told jokes and ate our booty.

I never saw Mr. Singer again, although I did think about my meeting with him in the years since—and what, for me, it would come to symbolize. When I sent off my urgently-felt message to him, I followed an instinct in search of the answer to a not-as-yet-formed question, and I came away from my meeting satisfied. I had no material thing to take away with me that Hanukkah, only the tale and the experience itself. I think what I learned was something about miracles; that a suburban housewife, without connection or fame, could send a letter to a Nobel Laureate and have it answered—a perfect lesson about the Festival of Lights. That, even in modern times, it is possible for an ordinary person to manifest a miracle. Just as he promised when I first appeared at his door with my plate of still-warm latkes, Mr. Singer had indeed "made light."

CHAPTER FOUR

Backstory: *A Cardinal in Queens*

I'm no marriage slut. My first marriage lasted eighteen years and my second, twelve. For me, good things happen when I'm doing my life, going about my business and not looking for something or someone out there to make me happy. No prince on the white horse or perfect balance in my savings account can really do it for me. It's all an inside job.

Just so you won't get confused about husbands and because I told you about how I met, married and divorced my first, here's how I met Noel, my second husband, the one who dumped me in the first chapter.

Maybe three months pre-Noel, I dated a sociopath. Unbeknownst to me, as he was inching his lying ass into my life, I came home one Friday night, walking like a duck, with pedicure cotton between my toes, carrying grocery bags so I could make us a nice dinner. And, as I was putting the groceries away, I turned on my message machine (what we had in those days, instead of voice recording cell phone apps) to hear a woman's voice, "This is Aimee, Mark's girlfriend, and I want you to know that on the days he says he's going to choir practice and on the days he says he's playing basketball, he's with me. But we're not the only ones. He'll probably tell you I'm crazy and will do anything to get him back. But call me and we can talk."

Instinctually, I knew she was telling the truth. I had a gut feeling about Mark ever since I met him. He seemed almost like a textbook smoothie: he could sing and was a good dancer, clever with jokes and was always saying the kinds of things a girl wants to hear. He was a college professor and a friend of my friend. She hadn't said a negative word about him. In about five months, Mark had already finagled a key to my Greenwich Village apartment (a sublet I had for a year) and he was moving things in, little by little. After Aimee's call, I took his shirts and toiletries and threw them into big green garbage bags near the door.

Our building had a dignified white-gloved Albanian elevator man/doorman named Esad. So after Mark and his green garbage bags took the elevator down, Esad, ever the gentleman, came up to my floor to be sure I was okay. Esad said, in his gentle and tactful way, "I see you and Mr. Mark have had a tiff."

I said, "Esad, it's more than a tiff. I have already called a locksmith to change my door key and if you see him in this building again, I want you to call the police."

At this point, I came to the conclusion that I'd had enough dating in my life and I was determined to be satisfied with what I had: work I loved as a therapist; a number of good friends; my boys, grown and on their life paths; visits to my parents and sister in Illinois and to cousins and friends around the country.

When I was a girl, as many Sixties' girls did, I wanted an exciting life, but I also wanted to find the right mate as husband and father to my children. Later on, I realized that I didn't even know myself. How could I possibly have recognized the right man, even if he was in front of my face? And Mark was the proof of how totally bamboozled I could be.

Before Mark, men seemed like frosting on the cake. After Mark, I learned that frosting could have a moldy side.

Rego Park, Queens, where I then worked, was just a twenty-five minute subway ride away from my apartment on 10th Street in Manhattan, in the heart of Greenwich Village. The Rego Park neighborhood was friendly and unpretentious and it became a hub for Russian immigrants. In the outpatient clinic where I worked, I was one of two people who didn't speak Russian as a first language. I did learn to say, "Saditez pazhalasta," or "Please have a seat," and to callers who wanted one of my Russian-speaking colleagues, I learned to say in Russian, "If you give me your number in English, I'll have her call you back." My Russian would be met with peals of laughter. I asked one of my Russian-speaking friends what was so funny. Was it my American accent? And she answered, "No, you have a Polish accent and they probably weren't expecting it." (Most likely, when I spoke an Eastern European language, I took on my grandmother's Polish-Yiddish accent.)

One Saturday, I was at my office doing some research. I was the liaison for our drug and alcohol unit and I was supposed to be on a television taping that week, talking about drug prevention. This was about four months after I had sworn off men.

On the way back home, I stopped at Anna's Bagels for a coffee. Anna's was a deli and luncheonette on the main floor of my office building. Anna was an émigré from Russia who operated the place with the assistance of several newcomer-émigré employees. I always identified with immigrants. Like them, I felt a little like an outsider, even coming from the Midwest - trying to learn the language and the customs of this part of the country. I admired the bravery of the people who came to America for freedom and opportunity. I was only one and a half generations from being an immigrant myself. My father's parents came from Romania and Russia and my mother came from Poland with her family at eighteen months old. So it was always easy for me to be kind to Anna's employees, even if they got my order wrong.

Some folks, perhaps impatient with Anna's staff's accented English or angry that their orders sometimes got bungled, would bark out their orders and complain if the person behind the counter misunderstood. I felt that eating at Anna's was an adventure. If I didn't get the tuna salad on a raisin bagel that I'd asked for, I got the tuna salad on pumpernickel instead. Eventually, I could come to like pumpernickel better than raisin. My feeling was that it was better to eat the bagel I got, than to threaten my immigrant worker's first job. So I smiled and ordered. That Saturday, I only wanted coffee.

I noticed, a little behind me at the counter, a man dressed in black and resembling Boris from the "Rocky and Bullwinkle" comic cartoon show, which featured Boris, a Russian spy in a black trench coat and black fedora. This Boris-looking guy looked like a writer to me and he smiled at me rather sweetly. I smiled back. He didn't look like a sociopath or a spy. He didn't even look Russian. He looked young.

When I got my coffee (just as I'd ordered: with cream and no sugar), I took it over to a small table facing the wall mirror. I was looking at this man in my peripheral vision and I saw him looking at me too. I thought, *This guy must be as young as one of my sons.* Before I knew it, he came over to my table and said, "Mind if I sit down?" With the name of Noel, he seemed harmless, sweet, even innocent. I answered, "Not at all," thinking him brave to try to be cordial outside of a dating situation. New York is a city where people keep to themselves and for good reason. Generally, in smaller, less sophisticated towns, someone might talk to you at a bus stop or a lunch counter just to pass the time. In New York, if a stranger spoke to you and wasn't asking directions, you tended to be curt. Otherwise, you might find your wallet missing or you could end up at Reverend Moony or some other cult meeting.

This guy looked like a decent guy. He sat and told me he liked how respectfully I treated the deli people. Could I trust myself to be a good judge of character after my last guy fiasco? Noel didn't seem flirty, just friendly. And then I had a pleasant thought: *Maybe he's gay!* Even before *Sex and the City*'s girls had gay best friends, gay men had wonderful reputations for being great friends and interesting company. They talked about their feelings and they could generally dance. Often they had good taste and made terrific shopping buddies and relationship coaches.

Early in our conversation, so he wouldn't be embarrassed just in case he was *not* about to become my new gay best friend, I told him I had two sons who were twenty-two and twenty-six. That way, he would know my approximate age.

If he wasn't gay, I considered that he might think of my age or the age of my sons as daunting, but he told me later that my telling him this seemed to draw him toward rather than away from him. I wondered about this at the time. Later on I came to understand.

Anyway, he started by saying that we were probably the only two in the place who spoke English and he liked how I treated the deli employees. Passed the sociopath test on this round. And after an hour-long conversation, he walked me to the subway. We agreed we should meet up again for coffee. He didn't have a business card, he said, so he delved into his Levi's pockets and came up with a crumpled-up pink slip of paper. Then he found a pen in his shirt pocket. Pretty nerdy. How refreshing after The Markster.

He scribbled his name and number on the back of the paper. After saying goodbye, I descended the subway steps, stuffing the paper in my purse.

Once seated on the subway car, I became curious and took the wrinkled paper out of my purse to read it. It said, "Noel Sanders" with his cell number right next to his name. And when I turned the slip over to inspect what was on its face, I saw it was a cleaning ticket for some shirts from Cardinal Cleaners.

I tend to be a little kookie this way. I believe our spirit guides or angels or The Universe gives us symbols of hope. For me, the cardinal always seemed to signify good things to come. Its bright red looks so stark in the snow, and it's the bird of Illinois, the place I was born and grew up and my sister and parents still lived. So I thought, *This must be a sign!*

Later that night or maybe the next day, I called Noel's number and left a message, "This is Linda. We chatted at Anna's. This may seem weird to you, but I see that you wrote your cell number on the back of a Cardinal Cleaners ticket. The cardinal is the bird of Illinois, where I'm from. Since the cardinal is my lucky bird, I wondered if you had a message for me."

He called me back when I wasn't home and left this message, "This is Noel Sanders and I do have a message for you: "Never use Cardinal Cleaners, they ruin your shirts. The only reason I do is that the owner and his wife are both sick, and they're going out of business. So they need all the work they can get."

Somehow, when we finally connected by phone, we had a long easy conversation and decided to meet for coffee again the following Sunday.

I was a little late for our date at the Union Café, just walking distance from my apartment. The date was as relaxing as our last meeting and it turned from just coffee into brunch. We pretty much cleared the brunch crowd out without noticing the time.

It was a brisk day in March and after the brunch, we talked and walked around the Village, stopping for hot chocolate and then, once our toes felt like icicles, stopping for a glass of wine. Because I could see it was beginning to get dark, I said, "I should probably get back. Let me walk you to your train." We walked to the subway stop and, just remembering, he said, "I forgot! I brought my car. It's parked near here. We have to eat anyway, so why not have dinner before I leave?"

We picked a neighborhood Thai restaurant for dinner. Then, he paid the check and offered to drop me off at my apartment, which was only blocks away. When he pulled over to leave me off, he gave me a quick kiss on the cheek and said, "Let's do this again. How's this Saturday?" And I happily agreed.

After that, we became inseparable. He would pick me up from work to save me the subway fare home, and we would see one another every weekend. Eventually, one night the following September, in a closed Anna's, he got on one knee and proposed.

It turned out he was only seven years younger than me. And it didn't seem to matter to either one of us. Eventually, we met one another's families. He and my sons seemed to like each other. He was kind to people. That was important to me. I learned that he was not a writer. Artists always drew me, but, somehow, I never married one. Noel was a doctor and a hospital administrator, working and living in Queens, where I was also working. At just around that time, I was about to sublet an apartment in Rego Park, Queens, since my lease on the Greenwich place was almost up. Anyway, working in Queens, I'd have two bedrooms, so my sons could stay whenever they wanted. And also the Rego Park sublet was only a few blocks from my work.

In the conversations that followed, as we dated, Noel told me he had been married to a young widow, a single mom who had two sons, four years apart, like my sons.

Our marriage seemed good to me. Noel was always welcoming to my sons. It would have been a deal-breaker if he weren't. We went through some tough financial times together, emotional times too. But I never felt insecure about our relationship.

What was particularly fascinating about Noel was that his parents adopted him when he was only a tiny infant and he loved them dearly and considered them his only parents. Up until he was in his fifties, he had little interest in finding out about his biological parents, even out of medical curiosity.

When he finally found his birth family, he learned that his mother was an unwed mother from the Bronx. Back in the 50's having a baby without being married was considered shameful. Noel's grandmother threatened to ostracize his mother if she kept him. So, brokenheartedly, she went to have her baby and then adopted him out through a Jewish agency in Staten Island. (Only the Jewish agencies wanted Jewish babies.) Noel learned later that his aunt, his mother's older sister, was supportive of his birth mother.

His birth mother never told anyone who his father was and very likely his biological father never even knew about Noel at all. Noel's mother married about a year or two after his birth. She did tell her husband about Noel. Two years later, Noel's biological mother and her husband had the first of their two sons, then four years later, the second.

Noel started to research his family after we were married eight or nine years. In retrospect, I wonder if while we were still in New York, he was already feeling restless and separate from me. Possibly, even then, he might have been considering making that separation formal.

Just after my own father's death, we met his aunt, a cousin, his brothers and their families. When we did meet his brothers, it was amazing how much Noel and his brothers resembled one another. But, to me, even more astonishing was Noel's adult history, marrying two single moms who each had two sons, four years apart. Noel's two brothers were four years apart. On some deeper level, perhaps he was always, somehow, searching for these younger brothers?

Maybe there really is some type of memory in our genetic codes. Noel marrying *one* woman with two sons four years apart might have been coincidence. But two women with two sons four years apart, I don't think so.

CHAPTER FIVE

*What Do You Do When You Know You Are F**ked?*

So, here I was, alone in Queens, getting divorced for the second time. I'd love to tell you that I dried my eyes and then pulled myself together, calmly considering my options. But it wouldn't be true. I was a wreck! I couldn't work or write, and my mind was a muddle. I was frantic with experiencing the grief that goes with ending a marriage.

I wasn't jumping off of any bridges, but I was in agony. And nothing but time was going to make this go away. Rejection is never any fun, but at sixty-two, I felt as if my life was over. My parents were dead, my sons Sam and Ben lived far away, and I was being dissed, approaching old age and alone on the drab block in the now especially depressing apartment Noel and I once shared.

It was painful to put the pieces together: the mysterious early morning phone calls to Noel's mother and sister that showed up on our phone bill. (We used to call them together.) Also, that he was sharing his feelings about ending our marriage with people I came to love and regard as family over the years I knew them.

Much as they might have cared about me, they couldn't have warned me. And I was furious with myself for not seeing the signs that I was about to become the stereotypical doctor's wife—there in the tough times and then an albatross weighing him down when the hardship and hard work we put in together finally looked as if it could become the life we dreamt of.

I lost my appetite (no small matter for a compulsive eater) and my self-confidence. I was terrified and nothing seemed to comfort me. I was sad that I wasn't a better example of what a good marriage might look like; a role model of a strong woman, rather than the whiny weakling I became.

My sons were beside themselves with trying to help me from afar. Ben would call from his apartment in upstate New York, where he was studying for his medical school boards and Sam from where he lived and worked, at the time, in Spain.

I felt awful for them, too. I thought I found them a stepdad they could count on. And now he was dumping me, which would likely mean he was dumping them too. An eligible doctor would surely not be on the dating market for long. Now, in all likelihood, Noel would marry some bitch who would be jealous of his relationship with my sons and any close contact with Sam and Ben would not be likely to continue. It happened all the time.

And I was disappointed in myself as well. Here I was at sixty-two and I had to somehow find a way to sufficiently support myself and live with the fact that I chose him and believed in him without question.

In between bouts of weeping, I began to think, *I have to make a plan or else I'll end up dying in some deteriorating tenement where, eventually, the smell of my decomposing body will alert my neighbors and the police of my presence.*

Though to be fair, Noel was wonderful to my sons. He welcomed them to stay with us whenever they needed to, as they were getting launched in their twenties. He helped my son Sam by being there for him after 9/11. Sam was working only a block and a half away from Ground Zero and he lost his job, but, at least, not his life. However, Noel was working locum tenens, temp jobs for docs, which he took when his Milwaukee contract was not renewed. And Noel took a temp position in New York, so he could stay with Sam in our former Queens apartment (which we kept when we moved to Milwaukee) post 9/11, probably the most difficult time of Sam's life.

Noel encouraged Ben in his mid-twenties to return to school for pre-med classes to prepare him for med school. Then, when Ben completed his applications, Noel took a full day off of work to drive from New York to Trenton, New Jersey, at least two to three hours each way, where Noel sat all day on a bench to wait for Ben's Official

Apostate Seal, the last document required to complete Ben's application to his preferred medical school.

Here, the man I believed in, the man I trusted, the man I thought was my best friend, turned into someone I didn't know, and now I'd have to go to court to request the return of my last name and to plead that my parents' investment in "our" future be returned to me. My father used to say, "Your ship will come in." And he was right, our ship finally did come in. But what neither my father nor I could have known at that time was that this ship would be leaving the dock without *me*!

When I married Noel, I was fifty-one, he forty-four and he didn't have children. And though I was post-menopausal, I seriously considered the option or having an egg-implant or finding a surrogate to carry his child. I loved Noel and I didn't want him to feel that marrying me would deprive him of having a child. My sister, my closest friends and my sons felt that my having a baby at fifty-one, when I already had two healthy grown sons, would be a disaster for me. In following Noel for the best life he could have, I lost my own moorings. And in retrospect, it was a good thing Noel and I got poor, or I might have been a single mom at sixty-two, stuck living near Noel, as the law would require that a child have access to both of his or her parents.

Noel's initial separation plan was that we live separately, have a weekly date and go to counseling. But since he and I already spent enough time in couples' counseling, I thought, *What will the difference be this time? I'll just be holding his hand, till he finds the right girl.* In our counseling sessions, Noel acted committed to restoring whatever he thought was missing from our marriage (which, as it turns out, was him. If he had issues with me, I never heard about them from him in therapy.)

Only after the dream of the orange shirts did I realize that there was a whole other side to Noel. Though, even as early as when I first moved back from Milwaukee to Queens with him, I had suspicions that something was wrong, I was completely clueless that it was something we couldn't fix.

Now the guy who called me throughout the day, who dragged me all over the country, trying to find the right position, now seemed to see me as a potential liability that he had no time for. Maybe he thought a fresh start would be that much fresher if it didn't include someone who knew him when things weren't going so well.

I spent so much of my energy on behalf of Noel's work and his happiness, uprooting myself and packing and unpacking us, and finding a life for myself wherever we lived, that I stopped taking my own dreams seriously, completely lost a sense of myself. Okay, I could work part time. (As, once back in New York, I tried, but I couldn't get a fulltime job) or I could take a night course in NYU's Continuing Ed Department, but it was his work I took seriously, his work I was counting on to sustain us in old age. I felt betrayed and terrified and paralyzed about my future, given that I was getting close to the age of retirement.

But never for a New York minute did I feel so frightened that I would consider living with a man who didn't love me, a man who knew it and didn't let me know it until he was practically out the door.

It was like that joke, where the seventy-something husband says to his wife, "Sylvia, I'm leaving you."

Sylvia: "But, Harold, I cared for your alcoholic brother till he finally went into recovery. I nursed both of your parents, in our home, till the day they died. And I tended you throughout your prostate cancer, through chemo and radiation. . . .How could you leave me?"

Harold: "I know, and I finally figured it all out. . . .Sylvia, you're a jinx!"

But, between the kindness of friends and my own resilience, I realized I would need to have some way to earn a living, build a support-system, and find a way to get health insurance. And if I didn't work quickly, I would be dodging bullets in some hovel, while begging now-successful Noel for money he conveniently forgot my parents had lent him and I was entitled to.

It especially broke my heart, remembering the tears of my beloved elderly father, whose multiple strokes left him in a wheelchair—cry because I had to go from living just an hour away from him in Milwaukee to be the "good wife" and join Noel in New York, just when he and my mother needed me most.

But screw the past! What was I going to do *now*? I needed to look for a place to live, a way to go on. I needed to be near people who cared about me.

I remembered Andrea, who worked with me when we did newscasts for a small radio station. At a staff meeting our cocky boss, Scott Pratt, gave her the worst broadcast hours a newscaster could have, midnight to early mornings on the weekends, with early mornings during the week.

After the meeting where the boss delivered the message to Andrea, the two of us walked out together. Andrea whispered in my ear, "Scott should have kissed me."

I said, "Andrea, are you delusional? You hate Scott. We all hate Scott!"

Andrea replied, "He should have kissed me. I always like to get kissed before I get f**ked!"

CHAPTER SIX

There's No Place Like Home

I was in fifth grade when my family moved to the little house on East Prairie Road in Skokie, Illinois. My parents continued to live in that same house for over fifty years. If I was broke or lonely or needed a place to go, I knew they would always have a place for me, help me, even welcome me. It was home. And at this time of my life, I felt a little like ET, from the Steven Spielberg film, I wanted to *go home*. I felt so alone and "over," I just wanted to be in a place where people knew and loved me, if such a place still existed.

But now my parents were gone and the house on East Prairie Road belonged to somebody else.

I couldn't have known back in my youth that someday, I would be alone, worrying about being a bag lady without enough earnings or savings to live on my own. It's what happens to many older women with the kind of priorities I had back then.

I felt like the little lost bird in that children's story I used to read my sons when they were small, "Are You My Mother?" In the story, a little bird who falls from his nest, keeps running around to cows and tractors and others who were not his mother, asking, "Are you my mother?" Like the little bird, I felt as if I didn't belong, didn't fit anywhere. My childhood life, full of extended family and friends, people coming and going in my house, were times now long gone. And my circumstances left me in the role of a vagabond. Okay, I did not yet need public assistance, but I certainly didn't have the opportunities or the energy I did when I was younger.

And though Ruth and Irv and Lee and Dave, my two good couple friends from Jersey, would pick me up from Queens to spare me the lonely weekends, and my sons, my sister, and my Milwaukee friend Mary called every day, no partner or adult child or roommates could help me recapture the more resilient me. Now, I was on my own, and for what felt like might be forever.

It was as if I was superfluous; almost as if should I simply disappear, no one would *really* miss me. What was I going to do? Move to Europe where my older son lived? Move to where my younger son was establishing his work-life and might not stay? I couldn't be following them around, cramping their style, glomming a life off of them. I would feel as much of a burden as I had when I fully understood that Noel and I were done.

It was as if the alien craft from the film "Cocoon" landed and took away everyone I knew and loved. The life I knew, the one that was always so filled with friends and possibilities, the one in which I felt *so loved*, now seemed to be forever over.

What do you do when you don't have a home anymore? When you might be welcome a weekend with family or friends, but you certainly couldn't be setting up house there.

After investing in Noel's career, I wasn't sure how long the money my parents left me, the only pension I had, would last. Plus, starting over at sixty-two? Although I had an excellent attorney, in the then male-dominated courts, the formula for women my age was pretty much the same as the one used for women far younger: This is how much you can have for this many years to start again. (Hear gavel's knock on the judge's bench, sealing my fate.)

Start again? Seriously? Compete with women or men half my age? I was a clinical social worker with over twenty years of experience, but even social work agencies and private practice groups might think an investment in a younger person would be smarter than an investment in me. I was approaching what has been called "The Youth of Old Age." At sixty-two, nobody seemed to need me, there was no home in Skokie or New Jersey or Queens or New York City. No place, really, where I felt comfortable taking refuge.

Because I was worrying, I would often still be up at 1 AM or later. It was too late to call my friend Mary in Milwaukee or anybody locally, but in LA, it was three hours earlier than in New York, and I knew my cousin Laura would still be awake.

I called Laura one sleepless night. "Laur, I'm lonely and scared and just lost right now."

"Why don't you come out here and hang with me and the rest of the family," she suggested.

Going to LA seemed like a welcome escape from being in my now trauma-inducing apartment. The only thing that made the place bearable was Noel and now Noel was gone.

I thought, *Where have I always felt happiest?* And what kept coming up for me, next to my old family home, was L.A. Los Angeles was a place where most of my closest Midwestern cousins and my niece moved. It was sunny and there were movie star sightings all around. In the past, every time I went there, even if it was for a funeral, our family from all over the country gathered and I felt so much a part of it all and so loved. And, feeling like an Alien in New York, the name of an old Sting song, I needed to feel that love and connection.

What better to pick up my spirits than a trip to the beach, to a place where the people lived who shared my history as I did theirs.

I found a cheap flight and arranged to stay with Laura. A widow in her forties, after her sweet husband John died, Laura was always a role model for me. I'm sure his illness and his loss were excruciating. Yet now, over ten years later, Laura seemed content with her lot. I wanted to learn how to be content with mine. Feeling like a woman who screwed up her life, I wanted to study someone who seemed full of joy in the-little-things-that-aren't-so-little.

I found it relaxing to be around Laura. She was flexible; and, together, we could enjoy her children and grandchildren, our mutual relatives, meals, shopping, and binge-watching cable TV series while eating dark chocolate bark until we were either nauseous or in a sugar-induced coma.

By pre-arrangement, I texted Laura as soon as my plane landed at LAX, "Just landed!" and she texted back, "'Leaving in five." And by the time I gathered my bag from the terminal and stepped outdoors into the warm sunny air of Southern California, I saw Laura smiling and waving from her car. She seemed so genuinely glad to see me, such a comforting sight, that I ran into her arms for a huge welcoming hug.

Usually when I visited L.A., Laura would take it upon herself to notify the rest of the family—our cousins Stu and Sandy and Judy, Laura's brother David and his young family—and my niece, Hadar, to let them know to check their schedules for times to meet for dinner or to arrange gatherings during my stay. Then Laura and I would commence our plan of having-no-plan. This meant we'd do whatever we felt like doing around the commitments Laura had in place in her life; her work as a family and school psychologist, occasionally babysitting her grandchildren, and helping a friend whose husband had Alzheimer's. Outside of this, Laura and I took in the little pleasures of life, cable television series and "screeners," movies she could get early from friends whose kids worked in the movie business, good food, afternoon naps and hot baths. She was as Zen as our somewhat neurotic, accomplishment-oriented family got. Plus, she'd lived in L.A. for most of her life, where the weather was a little warmer and the living seemed a bit more chill.

It happened that one of Laura's grandkids was having a birthday party only a day after I arrived, so there was already an excuse for a family get-together.

I went to LA because it was associated with happy times for me, family times. But on the heels of Noel's rejection, the feeling I had on this trip was different. I felt more like a pitiable loser and it was almost embarrassing for me to present myself to my family in this way. Not that they were rejecting me, but there was something about being de-wifed at sixty-two that felt hopeless and humiliating.

My cousin Stu even offered to call Noel, because, like the rest of us, he couldn't believe this turn of events. Maybe, too, I think he wanted to make sure I was not misinterpreting Noel and making a big mistake. After all, for many years, Noel and I seemed such a loving couple. Because I, too, was concerned and confused about the way things went down, I was anxious to either do what I could to save the relationship or at least gain some insight on why it was ending. So, I gave Stu the go-ahead to reach out to Noel.

Stu removed himself to the next room to have his telephone talk with Noel. But I wasn't so far away that I could not pick up at least Stu's side of the conversation. I thought I heard Stu say, "Noel, do you love Linda?" After a few minutes, Stu returned, but he was not smiling. While I could not hear Noel's answer, I could see from Stu's face that the answer Stu got was probably not what I hoped to hear.

"What did he say?" I pleaded. Looking puzzled, Stu said, "He said, 'Everybody loves Linda.'" It was as if Stu had asked Noel if he liked ice cream, and Noel had answered, *Well, of course, who doesn't?* Noel knew that he was being asked if he still loved *me*. And his non-answer told me everything I wanted to know. So, there it was. There was no misinterpreting that Noel couldn't even say he loved me.

I wondered aloud about living in L.A. and my cousins brainstormed together on who they might know who could find me a job. While they had some good ideas, there was nothing concrete. Also, in order to practice therapy in California, I would have to pass the state licensing exam. The exam had the reputation of being very difficult and it seemed daunting for me to when I had so little confidence.

I could see that, though they loved me, my cousins had well-developed lives of their own that they built over the last ten to fifty-some years. Laura moved there with her parents when she was four, the rest of the family moved to L.A. when most of us were in our twenties. They had established communities and families and long-term friendships, with work or retirement plans in place.

And living in L.A. was at least as expensive as living in New York. I knew if I moved there, I could go through my savings rapidly with no real likelihood of replacing them.

So Los Angeles, the home of Disneyland, the place my cousins moved before they had kids, where Midwestern girls went in hopes of getting discovered at soda fountains or while waiting tables, was not looking like a promising home for a sixty-two year old marriage-loser.

My cousins could welcome me into their open arms and include me in their gatherings, invite me to their tables. But unless I could take care of myself, I realized that every one of them already had enough on their plates. Surviving widowhood, divorce, financial crisis, health and caretaking concerns and dealing with the needs of their own children and grandchildren, they could be cheerleaders, but they couldn't really take me on.

How had my life turned out this way? What had I done so terribly wrong? I felt as if I was being punished, but I wasn't sure for what crime.

After the week was over, Laura dropped me off at LAX. And I walked into the terminal, given that L.A. was out, wondering what I would do next.

As I cleared security and got to my gate, my cell phone rang. I pulled it out of my purse and saw it was my friend Karen who worked at Milwaukee Family Services. Karen visited me in New York just before Noel and I split up, and we'd stayed in touch.

"Good news," Karen said happily. "Someone just retired and there's a job with your name on it. Should I talk to the director of the agency about you?"

"You betcha," I said. And then, I thought, *Maybe my angels are watching out for me after all.*

CHAPTER SEVEN

The Itsy Bitsy Spider

After one interview where I flew to Milwaukee, I was living alone in the Queens apartment, waiting to hear about the outcome of the job, occasionally wondering whether I was moving too quickly to resolve my relationship with Noel. He did want to see another marriage counselor, after all, and live separately, but date once a week.

I know other women who'd waited out his kind of mid-marriage doubt, even when their husband was been having an affair. And then, these patient gals had been rewarded with coupledom's Chapter Two. And, then, as I was thinking and re-thinking all of this, I got a spider bite on my foot.

I had been in the Denial stage of Termination, as far as my marriage went, as in, *Once he thinks it over, he'll change his mind.* But, then, I got a spider bite.

It was, at first, just itchy. I was saying to myself, *Just what I need when I'm scared enough to break out on my own at sixty two—a spider bite!* Usually I could take care of such things with over-the-counter staples, like Bacitracin. But, not long after I noticed the red, swollen bite, it contorted into an ugly-yellow-and-greenish mess and I knew I had to go to a doctor to treat it. I found a nearby doctor. Then, I called and drove myself there.

The doctor confirmed that I had a nasty infection. He gave me some topical prescription medication, but with a warning, "Be sure to call me or get to an emergency room if it looks as if the infection seems to be moving up from your foot. That could mean you have a blood infection, and a blood infection is serious, even life-threatening." *Gulp!*

It is horrible enough to feel terrified, but to feel terrified alone, on the heels of ending a marriage doubles the fear, and being an anxious person to begin with triples it. The night passed, with me all by myself in the apartment, and as I awakened during the night, I kept looking at the spider-bite, and it did look to me as if the redness was moving up my leg.

During the more loving days of my marriage, Noel was extremely supportive. Although he was a hospital administrator, he was an MD himself. And many times, he would even accompany me to doctor's appointments or, at the very least, talk to the doctor on the phone, doc to doc, to find out what was going on. To know that he cared in those ways made me feel loved and safe.

And I tried to be supportive to him and his family too. Noel couldn't get away from work when his father, a severe diabetic, had a foot infection that turned into a leg amputation. His parents lived in Florida. So, because Noel couldn't get away, I flew to Florida to be with Noel's mother while his dad had the surgery. The good side of this experience was that I felt I was doing my part to be supportive to Noel and his family. The bad side was that his father's amputation, which started with a small infection in his foot, stuck in my mind, now making me even more fearful that I could very well suffer the fate of having to live my life with one leg.

I probably should have just gone to the emergency room—and maybe this was some unconscious way of seeing if Noel still cared. But, much as I had to sit on my pride to do it, I had nobody else nearby to count on, so I called Noel. He was staying at our friend's apartment, but he picked up the call on his mobile phone. I could tell he was in his car.

"Noel," I said, "I have a nasty infection on my foot and the doctor told me if the redness looked as if it moved up my leg, it could become a blood infection, which is an emergency. It has moved up my foot and I'm terrified!"

A long pause and then some Noel-replicant replied in a cold, robotic voice, "I'm on my way to work. Go to the ER."

And there it was. His words and his tone said, "We. Are. Done. Here."

Because I was almost as afraid of the emergency room as I was of losing my foot, I first called the doctor to see if he could squeeze me in and determine if I really needed to go to the ER. And, due to the pain in my foot, I couldn't drive myself there. The doctor said he would see me if I could come right then and, that way, he could send me to the hospital if my infection had gotten worse. So next, I called Becky, an organizer-friend who lived nearby in Queens, had a car and often helped me with attention-deficit challenges. I felt like such a sad case to have to hire someone to be with me in a time of need. But I knew I needed support and, for me, Noel could no longer be counted on. Now, I really got it, firsthand, how older people must feel humiliated and discarded having a paid assistant, instead of close family or friends when they needed help. I never would have thought I would end up in those circumstances. But here I was.

The doctor saw me and said he was glad I came in. He gave me a stronger antibiotic salve and said I should return in two days to see if I needed a shot as well. I was so relieved to see that, at least so far, it looked like I would get to keep my foot.

When we first married, Noel told me about his first wife. He described her as a terrible person who was mean to him and to her children and awful to live with. Then, back when he was trying to impress me, he told me he'd hired a lawyer and rented his own apartment before he let her know he wanted out of the marriage. Maybe, at the time, I empathized with him as the victim of some horrible harridan. Now, I could see him, not so much as smart, but as calculating, figuring things out the way they would work best for him. This was a side of him I hadn't seen until once he must have felt pretty set up on his own—new job, better prospects—-he was ready to be a bachelor again, or at least ready to be rid of me.

I find anger way more empowering than victimhood. Now I knew I needed to buck-up, man-or-no-man, and find a way to support myself. I spent enough of my time, my energy, my resources on Noel's life. Now it was crystal clear that I would have to fully focus on myself.

There is a braver voice inside of me (I call her My Cowgirl) who kept saying , "Girl, you got to know when to hold 'em and know when to fold 'em.'" And given recent circumstances, there was no doubt that Milwaukee looked pretty good to me.

In my ambivalence about doing the right thing for myself, concerned about whether I was being hasty in making another plan for myself, I might have risked the social work job in Milwaukee. Who would have thought that an infected spider bite, which looked like a terrible thing happening at a terrible time, actually would catapult me into action. But, now, I realized that it would be foolish to wait for Noel any longer. And for this, I can thank an itsy bitsy spider.

CHAPTER EIGHT

Waiting in the Hall

"It's in the in-between that the real magic happens. The seeds are planted. The roots take hold. . . .and we blossom into who we were meant to be."

–Kristen Jongen

I love this quote, but somehow, it still never gets me through the in-between. That's the place where I feel lost and as if I'll never be found again. Ever been there? Once, I quoted to my friend whose boyfriend just broke up with her, that old adage about God closing a small door and opening a big one. Her response? "Sure, but what do you do while you're waiting in the hall?"

My spider bite turned into a kick-in-the-pants—and Milwaukee looked like my brightest prospect. I suppose these in-betweens are times I should remember other seeming disasters-in-my-life-which-became-turning-points. But frozen in a negative moment, I can't even entertain the thought that anything will turn out in a better way than I've imagined, because I feel so paralyzed. At these times, I feel like there are no other alternatives than the negative ones I construct in my head.

This is when the message I've absorbed, *Nobody wants an older woman,* feels like a death sentence that will never be revoked. I believe it's one of the only prejudices I'm aware of that is still politically correct and can even be said aloud. Hillary Clinton, in her 60's was once openly called "Hideous." Carrie Fisher was once said not to have "aged well," simply because she hadn't had the procedures that women in Hollywood tend to have to make them look younger than their years.

What are the choices for older women? It's no wonder Greta Garbo, once one of Hollywood's most glamorous stars, isolated herself in her older years from the public eye, and is quoted to have said, "I want to be alone." Maybe she was misquoted, but the sentiment of shame at growing older for a woman remains real. It's just that the Hollywood phenomenon has now reached the rest of our culture, so we actually *expect* to look a good deal younger than our biological ages.

So not only did I feel fear at the natural process of ageing, and depressed about being rejected, I felt guilty about caring about it all. Worse than just a rejectee, I was a failed feminist.

I grew up at a time when society was in flux, women's and men's roles were evolving. Betty Friedan in *The Feminine Mystique* and, later, Gayle Sheehy in *Passages* were predicting that both genders were on the cusp of gigantic changes in our lives. In my growing up years, men were scripted to work hard and provide for the family— and this was the measure of a man's success as a husband, a father and a man. Even now, when families may choose to have the man stay home and be the househusband, many men feel themselves "less than"—and are called "lazy" or, worse, "girls," if they aren't behaving in traditional hunter-gatherer ways.

Women have traditionally held the roles of helpmates and nurturers of husbands and children and parents. If a woman worked *and* had a family, she was still the one held responsible if the house wasn't clean enough or meals weren't nutritious. She was the one blamed if the kids weren't clean and well-behaved and doing well in school, if her parents weren't visited regularly and then cared for when they grew frail (often her husband's parents were her domain, as well). Men were considered too busy, as either the only, or the most lucrative, breadwinners in the family, the tasks of home and family fell to the women.

Work became something that was now also allowed to women, but the important, yet unpaid and unrecognized work of negotiating family relationships, keeping family traditions, educating and advocating for the children and doing or, at least, delegating the cleaning and cooking and social networking—all the tasks that generally go unnoticed unless they are left un-done, almost always are still "women's work."

But, from the time I was a kid to the time I grew up, the rules changed. The economy changed. Women needed and wanted to work. Even so, we were as responsible for the family as if we were stay-at-home moms. And dads who shared the housework and the chores were revered. It wasn't expected of a man to do more, especially if he made a good living. I mean, who can do everything, let alone do everything well? The same rules did not apply to women.

I remember my first divorce and how I wasn't sure how I could do life on my own at forty-two, with two teenaged boys. Of course, this second time, being twenty years older, I felt really in shock and discouraged about my future.

So, I cried and blamed myself, and I kept wondering why I didn't fully see this coming. I thought, *I'm an intelligent woman. How did I do the PhT or "Putting Him Through," as Gail Sheehy's The New Passages called it, instead of getting myself a PhD?*

• • •

Occasionally, Noel called. I cringe to recall his quivering voice on the phone, telling me his dog, who he took with him when he left, was dying. "Minnie has to be put down," he said sadly. And I responded, "I'm so sorry. I loved Minnie, too."

Then a beat later, I humiliated myself, saying, "Does this call mean you still care for me?" He recoiled in disgust that I might be thinking so selfishly at a time so traumatic for him.

Or, once we were formally divorced, he called to tell me not to forget about putting alimony as income on the tax-return, and I'd interpret the call as an excuse to talk to me, an *I'm sorry. I miss you.*

Thankfully, my prospects in Milwaukee were looking brighter and brighter. Milwaukee was a place Noel and I lived for one year together when he was working at a hospital there. Then, I continued to live there while Noel did temp jobs, waiting for the right career opportunity to come along.

I flew to Milwaukee for a second interview at Milwaukee Family Services and I got the job. I was elated!

As soon as they hired me, I found an apartment in the complex not far from Mary's home. I'd be regularly seeing Karen, who worked at MFS and recommended me for my new job. There were plenty of friendly women who worked there and I felt pretty confident I'd make some new friends. Now, with the promise of some good friends, a job and a potential work community, the pieces of what seemed my fragmented life were beginning to fall into place.

CHAPTER NINE

On Milwaukee/Finding My Inner Cowgirl

Once I got the call from my friend about the Milwaukee job, my life looked as if it was showing promise, at least for the moment. Noel and I had lived in Milwaukee for four years, before we returned to New York. Milwaukee is about an hour and change from the suburbs of Chicago, where I grew up and where my parents, then alive, lived in a lovely retirement village, and where my sister and my college roommate lived. At that time, I answered an ad in a social work magazine, only to find myself invited into a therapy practice in the suburbs of Milwaukee. Since I closed that practice to move East with Noel, I was needing to find a job. And this Milwaukee Family Counseling job was just the thing for me; I could work in a pleasant environment and, perhaps, make a community of friends through my agency colleagues.

After I flew to Milwaukee and I got hired, I found an apartment right near Mary's place. Then, I flew back to Queens to give notice on my part-time hospital job there and start packing.

I needed to move back to Milwaukee and be ready for work in September. I always associated airports with reunions, where I was greeted like a soldier returning home by my parents. Mom would be waiting in the car while Dad came into baggage to find me and my kids. I thought it would be too upsetting to brave my transition from New York to Milwaukee alone.

So, I asked Mary and my sister Susan to meet me at Milwaukee's General Mitchell Airport. Mary had plans for us for the day I arrived, and Susan agreed to join us. Mary's priest, Father Tim, was letting go of his condominium to move back into the church rectory and selling his possessions at low cost in a rummage sale.

Mary, a rummage sale expert and a genius about saving money, thought I could find some necessary household items from Father Tim to start my new single-woman life in Milwaukee. Because I did not know Father Tim, I imagined that the items a priest would own would be some worn-through, dark, second-hand furniture. But when Mary and Susan and I arrived at his condominium, we were surprised to find a lovely mix of modern furniture and antiques.

I bought Father Tim's nineteenth century English Barrister bookcase, as well as a hand-knotted antique Persian area rug, both at reasonable prices. My sister saw Tim's Crate and Barrel candelabra wall hanging and bought it. Father Tim sold us these things at low cost and then threw in his microwave, his dishes, pots and pans and his silverware for free. It was as if Target had the best rummage sale ever!

Afterwards, Mary and Sue and I stopped for lunch. And that evening, Mary's group of friends held a spiritual film evening. I don't recall the film, but I remember that the point of the gathering was to use the film's themes as springboards for discussion about our own values. I left feeling hopeful that Milwaukee had a lot to offer me. Though I'd lived there as a part of a middle-aged couple, I felt hopeful that I'd be able, in time, to build a community even as a singleton approaching old age.

Susan went back to Illinois. And I put away my dishes and pots and pans. I carefully laid out Tim's Persian rug and placed the bookcase in a suitable corner. I'd stuffed a blowup bed in one of my suitcases, but there were echoes and a sense of loneliness in my scantily furnished apartment. So, just for the night, I camped out at Mary's.

Night One in my new city: Accomplished.

• • •

When I began work, I was fine during the day, but when I got home in the evening, without a partner or roommate or a pet there to welcome me, I felt lost. Long weekends were the worst. I still had a few items to pick up from Queens and I needed to drive my car, which I'd left in New York, back to Milwaukee.

In my haste to start my new job and to leave Queens, I hadn't really thought out all the details of moving, and if you've moved as much as I have, leaving one place for another is all about taking care of details. As an ADHD person, with a lot of anxiety, I wanted to simplify my life as much as I could. And for an anxious-ADHD-er, I was not yet thinking coolly ahead about things like saving money for the future. I was just doggie-paddling, doing my best to simplify wherever I could, thinking a minute at a time about doing things in the simplest ways and making myself feel better in the hurt places.

I'd been renting a car by the week and it was getting expensive. I had no one I knew anymore in New York who could retrieve my stuff and my car and get them back to me. I left my grandmother's wedding ring, my dad's World War II dog tags, some pearls my parents gave me for my sixteenth birthday and a locket with my sons' baby pictures inside in a safety deposit box in Queens. My move to Milwaukee would not be entirely finished until I had these family heirlooms and my own car with me in my new home.

My plan was to find a long holiday weekend and drop the Enterprise rental car I was using by the week at the car-rental franchise in Queens. Then I would pick up my ten-year-old Ford Focus, parked near my former apartment, gather my precious heirlooms, and close the safety deposit box. I'd bring my car to a gas station to check the tires, fluids, and fill up with gas. After that, I'd head straight back to Milwaukee.

Mary couldn't join me for my road trip to New York. And there was no one else available, so I would be going on this little adventure by myself. *As a singleton, I'd better get used to it*, I thought.

Because this was a time before people had directional phone apps or GPS systems in their cars, a traveler like me would go to a Triple A office and get a Triptik, a step by step booklet, which was bound in a wired notebook, each page containing a map of one leg of the journey.

So, I visited the Triple-A office near where I now lived, to route me from Milwaukee to Queens and back again, and to book Triple A approved motels along the way. My three requirements for overnight places to stay were that they be: 1. Safe. 2. Clean and 3. Cheap. Once I got my Triptik and my motel reservations, I hit the local used bookstore to stock up on audio books to keep my mind occupied on the road.

I knew it would take about sixteen hours or so to drive from Milwaukee to Queens. And, if I had to do it alone, I would need some inspirational company. I liked the fictional heroines from the past, like Jane Austen's characters or biographies of courageous women like Eleanor Roosevelt and Helen Keller.

Whenever I go through a crisis, I find strong role-model women an antidote for self-involvement and temporary despair. I needed books, CDs and films that smacked me in the head, as if to say, *Your husband dumped you and at sixty-two, you have to go it on your own? Big f**king deal! Your so-called "crisis" is* nothing *compared to the crises of other women all over the world. Be brave! Woman-up, woman!*

I used my cell phone to call Mary. It felt as if she had an ethereal hand and she was holding mine, just keeping me going along the way. Still, even with Mary's telephone encouragement, I found myself feeling very rattled, alone on the road.

Driving, whether in the cities or for long distances, never bothered me in the past. I used to lose my way a lot, but I still loved taking a spin on the city streets of Manhattan, making my way through cabbies and citizens, too busy conducting their important mobile phone lives to be bothered with oncoming traffic or stoplights as they crossed the streets.

But now, I found making this long journey on my own uncharacteristically frightening. I guess when my confidence weakens in one area, it tends to have a downer-domino effect on the other areas of my life.

Scared as I was, once I got on the highway, I was doing pretty well following my Triptik routing plan. The weather was decent for a Midwest October, and despite being a person who tends to be afraid of just about everything (except, oddly, driving in New York City) I was not as perturbed as I might have expected by the eighteen wheelers whizzing by or by aggressive drivers tailgating my little rented Malibu.

Wanting to take the drive slowly and carefully, I planned two overnight stays from Milwaukee to New York and two on the way back. That way, I could drive four hours, stop for lunch and gas, drive another four hours and stop for dinner and some sleep. Around sundown, my energy was waning. So, I began getting ready to find the motel that Triple A reserved for me that was supposed to be close to the highway.

I was somewhere in Ohio, when I pulled into what I thought was the address of the designated place. What I saw next made me shudder. *This can't be right,* I thought. This rundown shack of a place was in dire need of a paint job, had missing window shutters, and the "L" on the word motel was just about hanging off its hinges. *I must have the wrong address,* I said to myself. But when I checked and double-checked my Triple A Triptik, I confirmed that this *was* it, my overnight "home-away-from-home." While I could have continued driving, I was tired, and I worried that I wouldn't be able to find anything else along the way and might have to drive all night or pull into one of those stops where all the truck drivers (usually guys) were. So, I felt stuck.

Apparently, either the owner let this place go since his last motel-rating or maybe my Triple-A guy didn't hear the first two of my three qualifications for a place to stay, "safe" and "clean" and went directly to "cheap," unless he was trying to help out some motel owner brother-in-law.

Since it was already getting dark, I resigned myself to the idea that it was better to stay here than be a woman alone on strange roads at night and risk not finding a place to stay overnight at all.

So, though there was only one parking spot taken in the lot (I assumed it was the manager's), I took the spot closest to the motel office and brought my one bag to the desk.

My room was, as were all the rooms in this seedy place, on the first floor. It looked like the kind of place that might charge by the hour, where seamy hookers brought their johns and drug deals were made. Feeling a little wary, I paid the disheveled-looking guy sitting behind the desk with the sign, Manager, and I wondered if he would be the last person to see me alive.

Then, seeing the number on the key, I went around the corner to my overnight stop-over, Room Two.

Room Two distinguished itself by sporting a long crack in its ground floor window. The room was giving me flashbacks from the Hitchcock film "Psycho," where the female traveler, played by actress Janet Leigh, gets stabbed to a gory death in the shower. I actually started to shiver with fear.

But, oddly, as I opened the door to Room Two, I thought I heard the faint sound of singing. Somehow, I could hear the words, "I kin do anything better than you kin, I kin do anything better than you." And, thinking that maybe I'd fully lost my mind, there, by imagination or manifesting her from the Beyond, I saw Annie Oakley, my tomboy Cowgirl alter-ego, who was rough and tough and could handle anything as well as, or, as she might say, *better* than any man.

"I don't git it, girl. Why are ya shakin' in yer boots?"

"Annie, I'm alone, without a man, and I have to stay at this scary motel overnight."

'Well, butter my buns and call me a biscuit, you got me and my Remington, right here with you. And anybody knows Annie Oakley kin shoot any perp plumb inta next week! Now, you be fixing to settle down and git yourself a good night's sleep."

"Annie, I don't think I'm being paranoid to say it wouldn't surprise me to find Jimmy Hoffa's body in the abandoned gas station behind this building."

Annie chuckled at my tendency to get a bit dramatic. But, just to calm my nerves, she reassured me, "Yer as nervous as a fly in a teapot! Why, I beat the heck outta Mr. Sharpshooter himself, Frank E. Butler—Used to shoot cigarettes right out of his mouth--before he proposed. I'll stay up all night and keep guard. You'll be fine and yer leavin' first thing in the mornin'."

Oddly, I didn't even question where Annie came from or whether a drug had been slipped into my roadside coffee, I just accepted that somehow, Annie's tough-gal energy was with me. I felt stronger. Now, in case anything, dead or alive, jumped out of the closet, I wouldn't have to go it alone.

Checking under the bed, I found a decaying and half-eaten Mars bar. Then, Annie watched as I turned back the covers on the bed and we were both completely sickened when a stray grayish pubic hair was revealed beneath the sheets. Undaunted, Annie said, "Don't you worry 'bout a thing, baby girl." And pointing to her gun, she said, "Nobody'd dare try to get by Lil' Sure Shot if he values his life! It's a dern fact that I kin hit a dime tossed in the air from ninety feet away!"

I didn't change into pajamas. I just slept in my clothes, and every time I even thought about taking a shower, the bloody shower scene from "Psycho" would be all I could see, only this time, I'd *be* the one dying a terrifying death at the hands of the wacky Norman Bates motel proprietor. I said to Annie, "Cleanliness may be next to godliness, but I think, given the circumstances, God will forgive me if I shower in Pennsylvania. The rest of Ohio's gonna have to take me au naturale."

Annie said, "Do you think I never went a day without a shower? That's sissy stuff. Don't you worry 'bout that! Now, put on yer big girl panties, and let's get through this night!"

Even with Annie at the door, I slept fitfully through the night, lying on top of the covers, with my coat covering my body and my sweatshirt hood covering my hair. After the light of morning seemed safer and my nausea from this place subsided, I could stop at a roadside inn for a coffee and maybe an egg-sandwich to go. I figured that, by that time, I could head to the nearest town for an open hardware store that carried pepper spray.

When I woke up in the morning, Annie was gone. Of course, I was curious. Did I channel her? Was she a dream? Where did she go and would she be back if I needed her? But all those concerns were washed away with the gratitude that it was morning and I was alive. Vision or reality, my confidence was buoyed up. Surely if I could make it through the night here, in this horror show of a place, I could make it to New York and back.

Pennsylvania turned out to be an improvement. The second motel I stayed at wasn't fancy, but it was clean and seemed safe. All the way,

I was saying to myself, *You can do this. It's not so hard. You can do this. It will make you strong. You may be sixty-two, but you can drive and you want your stuff and your car and there's nobody to do it for you or with you. And if you need her, maybe Annie will appear again. So, yes, you can do this. You must do it.*

Finally, I got to New York. I'd lived in New York and New Jersey for the better part of my adult life, but the East Coast never looked so bleak to me as it did then. Everything I'd formerly associated with Manhattan and Queens and the little towns in New Jersey where I'd brought up my sons seemed to be crying out, *You don't belong here anymore. Nobody who loves you lives here anymore. Go home.* Only I didn't quite know where home was. At least, for now, it was Milwaukee.

Because I'd stayed in touch with Becky, the organizer who helped me with the spider bite and who lived in Queens, I asked if I could stay on her fold-out living room couch for the night. On the plus side, *At least*, I thought, *I will have it done. I will have got my stuff and my car.* I would be proud of myself. Even if I was lost and lonely, at least I was—with a little help from Annie—brave.

And so, the following morning, I hugged Becky goodbye and returned my rental car to the LaGuardia Airport franchise. The Enterprise guy gave me a ride to my parked car, near my former Queens apartment. Then I drove off to retrieve my few possessions from the Queens bank and close the safety deposit box. Afterwards, I checked out my car at a gas station and headed back to Milwaukee.

Never was I so glad to cross the state line into Wisconsin as I was this time. I felt as though, having handled this round-trip drive, the scary motel, and driven my car and my valuables home, whatever challenges I might face next, I could trust that someone or something would show up for me, even under the most harrowing of circumstances.

CHAPTER TEN

You Are Getting Sleepy: The Hypnotherapy People

Once I got back to Milwaukee, car and possessions in tow, my work kept me feeling connected and full of purpose during the day. However, returning from work in the evenings, especially on Friday nights, without a husband or partner, a roommate, or a dog to greet me made me feel like the loneliest person on earth. Growing up, there was always a cousin or a buddy or a guy I was dating dropping by. The phone was always ringing with friends and invitations. In short, I felt connected to others; *loved.* In Milwaukee, my friend Mary was working and dating, involved in her church and had old friends with whom she hung out. I found myself alone most weekends, serial-watching cable series on television.

I am not one who can tolerate depression for long. Weekend after weekend with Netflix series and On Demand films as my sole company, caused me to quickly realize that I was the only one who could do something about my isolation.

I tried a local mindfulness meditation group, but what I needed even more than the practice of meditation itself were people with whom to connect. It seemed to me that most of the meditators had partners or friends in Milwaukee who they brought with them.

I looked into, then attended, a local all-faiths worship house, but I found myself feeling uncomfortable there, too. I guess I was expecting a welcoming committee to greet me, but there wasn't one. I took a screenwriting class. But when the class ended, despite a lot of exchanged phone numbers and plans to meet after the class ended, eventually the group connectedness dwindled down to a Facebook friend or two.

It's not that people weren't nice to me in Milwaukee; they were. But I needed a close friend or two who were available to make plans with me for the weekend, maybe someone to check in with me in the evenings. That was the thing I missed most about being a singleton. Someone who would ask me about my day, someone who would care about my worries and concerns, maybe want to meet for a movie or dinner, grab a cup of coffee or a glass of wine.

The closest I got to anything where I connected with others was my twelve-step program for people with eating disorders. Even there, however, none of my sponsors seemed available outside of the program. It looked to me as if people in Milwaukee already had their families and old friends and busy lives without room where they could fit somebody new.

Then, I registered for a Kabbalah class in the closest center I could find, in Highland Park, Illinois. The drive took me an hour and twenty minutes. In order not to drive back and forth at night after working all day and driving there in rush hour, I stayed overnight with my sister.

I was hoping Kabbalah would help me feel the comfortable connectedness which I yearned for. But the classes could be expensive and tithing was encouraged, which meant donating ten percent of one's salary to the organization. The thing was, I was already tithing in my own way, in that there were clients I would continue to see if they lost their jobs and thus their health insurance. I had a strong ethic about not discontinuing therapy at a time when my client/s might need it the most.

Though Kabbalah teachings were quite positive and well-intentioned, I was finding it was not my path. I did get something important from Kabbalah, however. I met a man at one of the gatherings who gave me his writing coach's contact information.

Thus, I started doing writing assignments for an online class and by telephone with his writing teacher. This class was something I looked forward to each week and I did my assignments enthusiastically. This connection got me back into writing again.

• • •

At the same time, I happened upon an ad for Holistic Hypnotherapy training. I was always attracted to this therapeutic tool to help my clients and to meet like-minded people. The ads featured a lovely woman, her salt and pepper hair blowing in the wind and her face the picture of contentment. She was the director of this hypnotherapy school.

Turns out these holistic healers had a center in the Chicago area and this seemed like the perfect time to try hypnotherapy. First, I went to a training introduction in the suburbs of Chicago. Next, I decided to commit to an internship of four weekend retreats per year for two years and held only forty-five minutes from where I lived in Milwaukee.

When I arrived at the first retreat, I was a little apprehensive. I didn't know most of the others, but they seemed to know one another. Later, I found that they'd bonded at their earlier introductory session. Even in my sixties, I find when I don't know people but they know and seem to like one another, I can feel a bit insecure.

We were each assigned a roommate and were supposed to turn off our cell phones and iPads and just focus on being together, in order to practice hypnotherapy on one another.

The trainers, all therapists, seemed warm, welcoming and gentle. None of the interns knew exactly what was going to happen. The first night, we were asked to sit in a circle for meditation and to introduce ourselves. There was a shrine near the circle, where people placed spiritual symbols of personal meaning to them; Gaia, Eastern Asian Gurus, pictures of Jesus Christ or Mary or St. Francis of Assisi, statues of Buddha and photos of other mentors and teachers were placed there. (I guess I missed the part about bringing something spiritually significant—but then what would I have thought to bring? Maybe something Jewish, plus something Buddhist, but I'm not a follower of anything in particular.)

When I got to my room, I met my roommate, a beautiful therapist and mother of two from the Chicago suburbs. It was a terrific surprise, given the age difference between us, when we found out we had a lot in common. Even though I had sons her age, the pulls of motherhood and career were feelings I remembered well, so I could commiserate with her own concerns. Also, she was hilarious! We giggled well into the night. Since we'd both once had show-biz aspirations and tried the beauty contest route to get there in our younger days, we joked:

Toni said, "I think I'm going to be named Miss Codependency for this weekend's retreat."

"No, you can't be more codependent than I am!" I argued.

"Did you set up your lonely college roommate with your boyfriend?" she countered.

"I'm capable of it," I retorted.

"Capable doesn't count," she giggled. Then we broke into hysterics, quieting down only when someone in the next room began knocking on the wall.

At the beginning of each day, if you wanted to rise at six in the morning, a fellow hypnotherapy student and yoga teacher in his early forties led a series of gentle stretches. After the yoga, chairs were set up for chanting, an East Asian meditative group-sing. I think I made it to a yoga or two. I'd never experienced chanting before, so I tried to make it to that every day. Fellow chanters would don prayer shawl-looking garments, which were usually cotton fabrics with Hindu symbols on them; Ganesha, the Indian elephant-headed deity, mandalas or the Om Aum symbol. Considered spiritually Divine sounds, the chants were transliterated from Sanskrit on a large white board in front of the room, so that we could all chant along. This group-sing gave us a nice ritual for starting our day.

After chanting, all the participants quietly helped put the chairs away and headed down to the first floor dining room for buffet breakfast. After breakfast, we gathered again in the main room, where the yoga and then chanting had been, and the folding chairs, arranged in church pew style, were converted into a circle for our morning intention meditation and group share.

One participant said, "My intention for today is to process an old trauma that I think has been blocking me."

Another said, "I'd like to be able to share more with others and be less self-conscious and shy."

In my first share, I said, "I came to be trained, but I hadn't fully realized that we would be practicing on ourselves and one another, with teachers nearby. And I'm scared that something awful that I don't consciously know will come out. And you'll have to call the straight-jacket guys to take me away." Other than the introduction, where we each got a practice-chance to be the hypnotherapist and another to be the client, all I knew about hypnosis was where some guy, often in a cape, would say, "You are getting sleepy..." and then he'd dangle a watch in front of a subject, who would subsequently follow the hypnotist's suggestions. *Perhaps,* I thought, *just like in these Las Vegas-type shows, I might start acting ridiculous or, worse, lose all free will. Maybe I'd cluck like a chicken; or maybe, like in the movies, I could do something evil, entirely out of my conscious awareness.* This thought terrified me, but I was just as scared to be working on my own issues, as I shared in the group intention gathering, when I pictured myself freaking out. But that's always been my modus operandi: I am at once afraid of doing something new, and at the same time, drawn to it. Most of the time, my curiosity attracts me towards these challenges, at least to test them, more than my fear keeps me from at least trying them out.

Each retreat had a theme and the theme of this one was Codependency. This hypnotherapy retreat was for training mental health professionals to help their clients and for helping us, if we felt stuck in some area of our lives. Had we internalized messages from our childhoods? Could we recapture now obsolete beliefs from the past and revise them to become positive messages that would be more effective today? My fear was that there might be secrets about my life or my family that I might not even want to know. Were there messages about myself that I wasn't even aware of holding me back? I was lonely, that I knew, but I felt that if I could solve that problem, one I believed to be a problem of circumstances, I thought I would be content with my lot.

To me, the other participants seemed to have more settled lives with partners or children, communities and families. In my self-conscious eyes, most of my fellow trainees looked to be so much younger than I was, possibly in their forties or fifties.

Especially among the teachers, I noticed a lot of self-care and self-confidence. Several brought or ordered special foods from the kitchen, macrobiotic, vegan, or with extra protein for their particular diet. Some brought coolers with smoothie ingredients and their own smoothie makers and others brought yummy-looking organic goodies made out of recipes they prepared at home.

The teachers and their assistants, the women in particular, seemed to have a kind of body confidence, having very little to do with the slimmer image to which I aspired. Some wore what looked to be carefully chosen, colorful clothing and jewelry, tie-dyes or funky garments, the kind people wear when they appreciate their bodies or, at least, don't give a damn about what anybody else thinks. (And, of course, most of us are drawn to those who feel good about themselves and are doing the best they can with whatever physiques or facial features they were born with.)

Due to my own fat-kid childhood, I had a very self-critical body image, no matter what others saw. But I longed to be someone who loved her body just as it was and who treated that body with care. I didn't want to hide just because I didn't have the fashion magazine body of a fifteen-year-old anorexic boy or the voluptuous curves of a Sophia Loren or a Marilyn Monroe. At this retreat, I loved being inspired by women with healthier and more realistic body images than mine.

Most of my retreat-mates seemed to have a deep appreciation for the rural surroundings—the animals, like the goats and horses, in this farm-like setting. The retreat site sported a small pond, a labyrinth path for meditative walks, and massage therapy. Also, many of my fellow trainees were excited about the part of the retreat that took us to a nearby Wisconsin Native American Sweat Lodge, featuring a shaman who gathered herbs for healing and his wife, who told wonderful, mystical stories about the Grandmothers and Grandfathers.

Sweat lodge? Me? All I could think of was, *I don't fit in here either. I must be the oldest person in the retreat and I don't know if I can survive in a ninety-something degree outdoor steam bath for four hours. I don't want to commune with the spirits of the Grandfathers and the Grandmothers! I want to go back to my room!*

In the end, I attended the sweat lodge in my own skittish way, as so many of my fellow students were looking forward to it. To forever-cautious me, putting on a special muu-muu, sitting around a roaring fire and conjuring up spirits in a teepee that was about ninety degrees hot seemed like a death sentence. Few others seemed to fear it.

I stayed as long as I could tolerate the heat, but I left the teepee when it became uncomfortable.

Each day, as we practiced hypnotherapy, the other students would let loose, screaming and wailing and pounding the ground, I would think, *What's* wrong *with me? Am I numb? Or repressed? Or am I just plain boring?*

All of the practice sessions were held in the rooms of the retreat house, the rooms in which we were staying. In one early practice session, I hypnotized this very lovely woman. I found out later that she and I were the same age. The instructors walked around and checked us as we were first learning to do hypnosis. Anyway, this woman who was my practice subject, Martha, went right into hypnosis. But then, when she wasn't talking much, I asked her, "Where are you now?" She sounded a little confused and answered, "I'm not sure, but it's dark." Fortunately, one of our instructors came into our session at just that time. She saw that I was not quite sure what to do. When she understood what was going on for Martha, she whispered a question to me, "Have you ever worked with past lives?" I shook my head, and the instructor gently took over the session. The instructor asked Martha, "Are you in a body?" And whether this was fact or metaphor, it was fascinating that our hypno-subject saw herself in a man's body, and she said that she, as this man, made a contract with her former self's wife in a past life. Martha gleaned from this that her current difficulty in setting limits with others came from a past life contract and that it was no longer useful to her. Whew! The hypnotherapy instructor did a process to cut those cords and release her.

Little by little, I found myself feeling a part of the circle when we were sharing. I found out that some people can release old memories by shouting or pounding on the ground, but that when I was uncomfortable or frightened, I tended to detach as a coping technique. Like many trauma-survivors report, I would drift off and not be present in the moment (disassociate), which is another way of coping. As I became part of the sharing, I felt really, really heard.

One of our teachers, commenting on my share in the circle, named what I just said: "Random Thoughts From An Open Heart."

I began to feel as if my thoughts were actually interesting to others. As I looked around me more closely, I realized that there were others there who were my age or possibly older. In these retreats, people from many different backgrounds became a community. After a while, we came to share a sense of being our authentic selves whenever we were together, whatever that meant at the moment. There was none of the "putting on a pretty face" for others in this setting.

These gatherings were different from anything I'd ever experienced before, where I could feel comfortable being authentic, even if how I was at that moment wasn't all delightful and happy.

After several of our weekends, I began to feel so good about being with my hypnotherapy friends that I shared my fantasy of taking all these amazing people with me when I went back home. It was the closest I'd come to having a family-like setting since my kids grew up and left home.

Most of the other participants lived around Chicago. Even if they got together, I would need to stay over at someone's house. I'd become close with a couple from the trainings, Lisle and Ian, and they generously gave me a key to their house and welcomed me to stay over in their spare room whenever I liked.

After get-togethers of what was starting to feel like my soul-family, I actually began considering moving to Illinois, since most of the hypnotherapy people lived there, as did my sister. Perhaps it was because I was raised in the suburbs of Chicago, but I felt more at home in Illinois than in Wisconsin.

I also looked forward to weekends in Chicago, meeting with my friends and my sister. I was feeling less lonely. We arranged a Mastermind meeting, which was a weekly phone meeting of several of us, to help one another visualize our goals. At first, I thought it was a little crazy to believe that a few people could visualize with you and that this was going to help you in some way. And yet, one member of our group moved from Atlanta to Chicago and was able to complete his therapy studies and build a life there. And Marina, another member of our group, became more assertive and braver, asking for what she needed. Marina and I became very good friends. She was a Registered Nurse with a very caring heart. She encouraged me to move back home to Illinois. I'd be near her and her husband Mischa and others from the hypnotherapy group.

I did have a couple of strong connections in Milwaukee, my good friend Mary, and my therapist. Maybe it's sad for a therapist like me to say, but at times, the highlight of my week was seeing my therapist. It might have been the interesting insights he had that helped me become a better therapist or the eclectic nature of his knowledge of dreams and archetypes, neuroscience, and Attention Deficit Hyperactivity Disorder. Or it might have been that he had a male energy that I missed. That father-husband-son piece of the puzzle was absent in my present life. He seemed to agree with the Hypnotherapy people, that I could be a good therapist and write, too. Something about that, believing I could write, that I had something of value to say, something worth listening to, especially at that time, was important to me.

CHAPTER ELEVEN

Healing by Magic or Meditation?

As I entered the world of hypnotherapy, I was intrigued by healing methods I'd never heard of before. It seemed to me that there was more to life than what we already knew or thought we understood. Some of my new friends called themselves "light workers," though I wasn't quite sure what a "light worker" was. Some of the hypnotherapy people said they were "energy healers"; some used pendulums to see where someone might be "stuck" in their chakras, which I now understood as an ancient way of naming the body's energy centers; and others said they could read or even see auras in color around a person, kind of like mood-rings, revealing one's energy field.

Who was I to say they were flakes or fakes? Wasn't Germ Theory considered kind of wacky before microscopes actually saw these little guys inside of us and antibiotics were discovered as cures for infections?

When I was a girl, my mother used to read "Prevention" magazine, which back in the Sixties and Seventies, outside of California, was thought to be a little "out there." Mom strongly believed in supplements and environmental toxins well before doctors were prescribing Vitamin D or C or Calcium and telling us to eat organically. Back then, when my mother would share what she thought of as her most revelatory readings about the powers of Vitamin C or the dangers in food additives, I would roll my eyes and wonder if she wasn't being a tad extreme.

Certainly, ways of thinking about the not-yet-accepted were familiar to Harry Houdini and The Amazing Randi. Both were magicians and both believed that many unexplained phenomena existed in the world. But each was determined to debunk charlatans and frauds. I wondered, were some of today's reported healings real, but cutting-edge or as-yet-not-accepted, treatments? And maybe there were truly gifted individuals with special healing powers, even connections to the Divine, which most of us knew little about. On the other hand, I also considered whether some of these "miracles" involved placebos or charismatic personalities using their popularity or authority to make them believable, kind of like celebrities who act their way into politics.

I was suspicious that some of the people who claimed mystical knowledge might actually be delusional or sociopaths who made their livings taking advantage of the desperate, frightened and naïve. Although I was curious, even somewhat open to alternative healing, I was also wary.

Since my initial foray into the world of alternative medicine, I'd made some friends, most notably Lisle and Ian, who long believed in the power of alternative healing over traditional medicines. They made convincing arguments for their thinking and they became trusted friends. When they referred me to someone or were doing something interesting, I took notice and wondered about it for myself.

When Lisle told me that Ian was going to participate in a shamanic healing, I found myself fascinated and asked her to tell me more.

She explained that this shaman, who worked out of Germany, had achieved great results in the past with Lisle's son's anxiety and panic attacks. Because of this, I thought the shaman might remove whatever was keeping me in a funk. I was making progress, but I felt my life still needed a re-start.

These "psychic surgeries" were said to be as real in results as traditional surgeries, where something concrete was repaired or healed in your body.

Yet in Lisle's son's case, the procedure affected him psychologically. And, hey, I don't understand legalese, but I trust that some things can be handled by those who do, like lawyers. So, I figured, even if I didn't get how this worked, it could still possibly benefit me. After all, who was I, a brain surgeon, or an online-know-it-all? So, while I had no physical pain to remove, I thought if the shaman could help Lisle's son, maybe he could catapult me out of my Debbie-downer mental state.

Lisle told me that thousands of people flocked to see this shaman from all over the world. It was rumored that Oprah sought him out. Dr. Wayne Dyer was said to have had a complete remission from leukemia at the time. He eventually died of the disease, but perhaps the shamanic healing gave him a few more months or years or a better quality of life.

At first, I wondered if Ian was going to Germany for his healing, but Lisle told me that one didn't have to go there at all for this to work. She said that Faith Jonas, a healer friend of hers and Ian's, would be in Germany as she was several times a year, to assist the shaman in his work. Faith would act as a surrogate for friends who couldn't get there in-person.

Ian was going to have what the shaman's followers called "psychic surgery" to deal with a sensitive stomach, In order to have this surgery, the would-be patient had to send a check for $200, and a photograph of themselves dressed in white, which Faith would take to the shaman's headquarters outside of Berlin. Also, one was required to follow certain instructions, which seemed fairly harmless to me. You stayed quietly in the positive energy of friends, ate lightly, drank lots of water and no alcoholic beverages, read spiritual and uplifting books, slept and meditated for a week. Then, after the surgery, Faith would bring back all-natural herb capsules specially made for you and blessed by the shaman. You were to take these as directed to complete the healing process.

My inner-skeptic thought, *Hey, why are people bald if the shaman can heal anything? Wouldn't bald men be anxious to be healed? If the shaman can really heal anything, why are the morbidly obese going through stomach stapling and gastric sleeves? Couldn't they just avoid all the complications and see him instead?* But I calmed my inner voice with, *Well, what's the harm of trying something new?*

The shaman was said to work by going into a trance state and, in this state, he was supposed to be able to channel ancient healers to do the psychic surgery through him. If the patient could not come to Germany, Faith or one of his other assistants would be stand-ins during the psychic surgery. Then, the patient had to rest, just as you would for traditional surgery.

I thought, except for a week away from work and the $200, if the shaman didn't work for me, at least I tried. But it would be worth it, placebo effect or not, if the work of the shaman catapulted me out of my rather stuck state.

Lisle and Ian, more experienced than I was at this kind of alternate-stuff, kindly offered that I could stay with them for the week of my surgery and they'd guide me through the process. I was glad not to be alone and to spend time with my good friends instead, as an additional draw for me to do the shamanic healing.

Lisle told me our surgeries would take place that Saturday at midnight our time. So I stayed awake, waiting to see if I felt anything. Would an alien come tearing out of me, like in the movie with Sigourney Weaver?

At midnight, lying on a blow-up bed in Lisle's and Ian's guestroom, I was a little apprehensive. Would it hurt? Would I feel something weird happening in my body? I waited till 2AM, but I didn't feel a thing. Finally, bored with waiting, and relieved not to see anything terrifying or feel any pain, I fell asleep.

Resting a few days after the surgery, I got a text message from my sister. I texted back that I was at Lisle's and Ian's. She knew their home was near where she lived.

She texted, "Wow, you're right in my neighborhood! Want to meet at Starbucks?"

I texted back, "Absolutely!" and I started getting dressed to go. As I was about to go out the door, I called out goodbye to Lisle and Ian, who were on the sun porch, reading and drinking herbal tea. Lisle got up and came inside, staring at me with alarm.

"Where are you going?" she asked.

I replied, "To meet my sister at Starbucks."

Lisle implored, "Your chakras are all open right now. And—I mean it's totally up to you, but exposing yourself to others' energy fields just after psychic surgery might not be a good idea. You have to think of psychic surgery the way you think of physical surgery. You need to rest and keep yourself away from other people's energy. You don't know the people you'll be exposed to. After spending the time and the money to do this healing, do you really want to take the chance that anything might interfere with its success?"

I loved my sister and I was really craving a cappuccino, but I thought Lisle had a point.

I texted my sister, "Can't meet you at Starbucks. I'm told my chakras are open and being in a public place might not be optimum for my healing right now."

She texted back, "Are you in a cult? Where are you exactly? I'm coming to get you!"

I called to reassure her that I was just experimenting with shamanic healing and I figured since I'd already invested time and money, why not at least listen to the people who had been through the healings before?

After our phone conversation, she texted me, "Good luck with whatever it is you're doing." She left out the "weird sister" part, but I could almost read it there anyway.

I changed back into my white meditating clothes, found my copy of Louise Hay's *Heal Your Life*, helped myself to some herbal tea, and went out to join my friends on their porch.

Later that night, my sister texted, "I am at a Kabbalah class on Reincarnation."

I returned her text with, "Woo woo sisters, huh?"

And, yes, I did get out of my funk and eventually I moved from Milwaukee to the suburbs of Chicago, commuting for my work in Milwaukee a few days per week, while looking for a workplace in Illinois, as well.

Did I feel better due to the shaman's psychic healing? Ian said he saw positive results with his stomach. Lisle and Ian thought my shamanic healing was what lifted me out of my personal quicksand. I wasn't as sure. I thought it might have been the week of unstructured activity, rest, and meditation.

Oh, and about two weeks after the surgery week, the specially-made and personally blessed by the shaman herbal capsules arrived in the mail. But, just between you and me, I am a little skittish about taking anything when I don't know what's inside it. To this day, though I never breathed a word to Lisle or Ian, the shaman's capsules remain tucked behind the cinnamon and cardamom in the spice rack of my kitchen cabinet, their seal unbroken.

CHAPTER TWELVE

Interview with the Green Juice Guy

I'd moved and focused on my work and building my friendships. Since Noel turned out to be such a surprising disappointment, I thought, *Guys? At my age? I'm done with all that!* Through my friend Marina, I was renting a place in Illinois, but commuting to my therapy practice in Milwaukee. I had my Illinois social work license to practice, and I was ready to supplement my Milwaukee practice and start looking for work in Illinois. The day before my sixty-eighth birthday, I got an interview with a psychotherapy practice connected with the prestigious Northwestern University in Evanston.

To me, growing up in Skokie, Evanston was the place where Northwestern students and their professors hung out. It was all hip jazz bars, Ethiopian and Vietnamese restaurants and cool people I might want to meet. Evanston was the Berkeley or Greenwich Village of the Midwest (Well, next to Madison, Wisconsin and Ann Arbor, Michigan), while I believed Skokie, where I came from, was a dull and conservative bedroom community for Chicago, where working class families like mine lived. My inner-snob was drawn to this job.

The day of the interview, I drove to Evanston and parked my car not far from the interview building. My destination was in an old art-deco building, with a security guard and a gold-plated elevator, reminding me of my old New York apartment.

When we did the interview, the owner seemed very into the business end of therapy. Now, I'm no businesswoman, but I get that we all have to make a living. The feeling I picked up was like, *Book as many clients as you can, and if you drop dead, we'll replace you in no time.* Not a good fit for me. Somehow, after the interview, the owner of the practice thought I could bring in the clients and keep them, so she asked when I could start work. She had a therapist leaving, which would mean there were already clients to refer. Otherwise, if I were establishing a therapy practice in a new setting, it would take a few months, a year, or even more to build up a client-base.

I left the interview, partly feeling that, working there, I could not only do what I loved, but I could earn a really decent living. Of course, there was also another thought at the back of my head: *Would I like working with this director and in this businesslike and thus somewhat pressured environment?* Not that there aren't excellent Clinical Social Workers who earn a great living, but they are often very focused and businesslike. And anyone who knows me knows I am neither focused, nor businesslike. If that was the style of the social workers here at this Evanston practice, how would I feel and how well would I fit in?

I do have positive attributes. I am intuitive and flexible and I like people and they often like me. That's what I'm good at. And because I know my strengths and my weaknesses, I'd always rather work in a practice where people "get" me and where there are people who are good at business to do the things like billing and referrals.

This practice had a Whole Foods Market nearby, which I noticed on my way in. After the interview, not yet entirely convinced that this would be a terrible match for me and envisioning myself as not only an excellent therapist, but a highly successful wage-earner, I thought I'd do my food shopping at what Seinfeld once called "Whole Paycheck." I entered the pricey but colorful world of Whole Foods.

Let's see, I said to myself, *I'll get myself flowers for my birthday tomorrow, and iced teas, the kind in the glass bottles, and hmm, fruit.* Then I saw a man at a display table with a green energy drink. *EWW*, I thought, as I passed him holding out his Dixie cups of green juice. I smiled, but declined his samples, and disappeared down the vitamin aisle. Halfway down to the calcium pills, I remembered: *I actually have tasted some green juice that was delicious. And, furthermore, the guy selling the juice looked about my age.* So, I said to myself, with the confidence of a soon-to-be comfortable therapist/entrepreneur, *Stop avoiding men and go back there.*

Despite my new resolve to just focus on work, my family, my writing and building a social network nearby and my intention to put the matter of men aside, I went back up the aisle to taste the guy's juice samples.

The Green Juice Guy told me, "I developed this juice as a way to keep my blood-sugar stable after I was diagnosed with type II diabetes—and at seventy years old, I'm still doing marathons."

To which I responded, "I'm sixty-eight." (I was definitely not Evanston-cool!)

Green Juice Guy asked, "What do you do?"

And I answered, "I'm a clinical social worker."

Then he asked, "Do you have a card?"

"Not with me," I answered, dreading wading into my A.D.D. style purse.

And he asked, "What kind of therapist doesn't carry a card?"

I answered, "A therapist who's not such a hot businesswoman."

He then asked, "You married?"

I answered, "No." Then I paused before asking, "You?"

The Green Juice Guy said, "No. My name is Don. And you are. . . ."

"Linda."

Then, he went on, "I live in Missouri, but I'm around every few weeks. If you give me your number, I'll call you when I'm here and maybe we can have dinner."

So much for my I-don't-need-men resolve. I was a little buzzed at the prospect of a date with an interesting guy.

He said, "Here's my card. You should consider carrying one. How about you write your phone number on the back of mine."

Ms. Who-Needs-Dating bought a dozen Green Juices.

Done with my shopping, I left Whole Foods, dragging my heavy eco-friendly paper shopping bags along and grateful that I parked across the street. I went out the door, walked a block to where I thought I left my car. Uh-oh, no car!

So I walked further. And further. My shopping bag bottoms were starting to wear and I was starting to tear up. Where was my car? Who would I even call if I couldn't find it? At this point, my bags were dribbling blueberries behind me. I muttered to myself that this whole eco-friendly thing was not very friendly for a woman who hadn't brought her own bags and, furthermore, just lost her car.

I came back to the interview building and tried another direction. I was worried that both of my bags would succumb to the occasional rubbing along the ground that the bags' weight caused when my arms could no longer hold them further up, and then they'd tear even further, so I walked back to Whole Foods and bought two of their repurposed bags for the rest of my car search. *Hey,* I thought, *look on the bright side. At least, if I'm hopelessly lost and without a car, I will still have something organic to eat.*

Finally exhausted, I found the first place I could see to sit, the steps of a church, and feeling like a bag lady, I watched well-dressed Evanstonians ignore me as they passed. I contemplated what to do. *If I called my prospective employer,* I thought, *she might consider me, as an older woman, a possible victim of cognitive decline. Not a good idea.* I then tried to flag down a cab, just to drive around with me as I looked for my car. Even with repurposed bags, I must have had a bag lady look. No cabs stopped.

Next, I called the Evanston Police, who referred me to the towing folks. The guy who answered at towing asked for my plate ID (my car still had Wisconsin plates). He put me on hold, saying, "Today, we towed a lot of out of state cars." Apparently, he was looking to see if they had my car. Then, he got back on the line and cheerily reassured me, "Good news. We don't have your car. Maybe it was stolen."

So, I figured, *I can't get a cab, the police aren't helping, I can't drag these bags around much longer without collapsing.* And then, I remembered the Green Juice Guy. I fished through my purse and found his card. Thinking that this could be a Hollywood "Meet-Cute," a story we told our friends down the road about our meeting, I texted him. "Help! I'm the social worker who met you at Whole Foods, but I lost my car, and I don't know anyone around here. I wonder if you would be willing to help a damsel in distress? Thanks, Linda."

I waited. Nothing. Waited some more. Nada. Had I told him my name? I thought so, but even if I hadn't, it was on the back of his card, where I wrote my cell number.

Ah-ha, I had an epiphany! I could go back to the job interview building, near where I parked my car, and re-trace my steps. So I found my way back, taking short breaks to sit down wherever I could find a place to sit, and then gathering and rearranging the items in my bags again. I kept walking. Finally, I was back at the building and hoping the lady who interviewed me was not going out for lunch, so she wouldn't see me and find out I lost my car. I didn't want her to assume that I was not-so-competent. Once inside, I realized I hadn't left the building by the same door as the one I entered, which explained how I might have gotten confused about where I parked my car. I have many "learning differences," but one of them is directional. I have many times wept, inside an indoor parking lot, thinking I was going crazy or that I'd never find my car inside—and that's while still holding a ticket indicating the floor number where I parked.

All of this was making me crankier and crankier. And Green Juice Guy was not even answering my text with a "Sorry-Busy-Right-Now", Probably, he would decide I was some crazy lady or else he had a collection of Whole Foods ladies' numbers, potential Green Juice customers he was flirting with for the sake of sales.

I went out this different door and as soon as I stepped outdoors, there it was, my little blue Honda. No tow, no ticket, not stolen, just parked where I left it and waiting for me!

When I got home, I put my flowers in a vase to restore them from our ordeal and put the remaining groceries in the fridge or the cabinet.

I thought about the job. Could I work from 9AM to 9PM two to three days per week, plus see my clients in Milwaukee a couple of days per week, as well? Would I have to ask permission for vacation time when, for years, my work allowed me a lot of freedom from that kind of control? I knew that this job would mean money vs. autonomy. I thought, *I want to see my sons, be there for the clients I already have in Milwaukee, and I need some down time.* And *at sixty-eight, I don't have forever.* So, I wrote the psychologist with the Evanston practice an e-mail, thanking her and telling her that, after further consideration, I didn't think the job would be a good fit for me.

And, never being one to "leave well enough alone," I wanted to know about Green Juice Guy. Did he not get my text? Was he a technophobe, who didn't text? Or perhaps he had a girlfriend back in Missouri and a dinner buddy in every port. Maybe he was selling his energy juice by flirting with vulnerable Whole Foods shoppers like me. So, I found his card and e-mailed him:

Hi Don,

Shortly after our conversation at Whole Foods (the one where you wrote down my number and said could you call me when you came back to town and we'd have dinner), I finished my shopping and spent hours looking for my car.

After calling the police, the tow people, and trying to hail a cab, I texted you, asking if you could possibly help a damsel in distress. I wasn't sure whether you got my text and ignored it, thinking I was a possible weirdo, whether you don't text, or whether you were a guy who was just trying to sell juice by flirting with various Whole Foods singletons of the feminine persuasion.

Curiously yours,
Linda

Shortly after, I got a return text:

Hi Linda,

I did get a text from a number I did not recognize, saying, "Found it! Must have walked out the wrong entrance." I had no clue who it was, nor did I understand what you found.

I'm not the kind of person that just stands there and flirts with people. I try to understand their needs. It sounded like you were having some health issues and could possibly use my product. I found you very interesting and would very much like to see you next time I come to town, which will probably be in January, based on Whole Foods' needs. Just wanted to clear up any issues you might have about me and what I do. Thanks for your text, sDon

I realized that I didn't know this guy and I must have been lonely and needy, or maybe he didn't get my first text at all. Plus, January? He'll call me in January? It was October! I could be married or six feet under by January!

Sometimes, it's just so embarrassing being me.

After a short funk over my me-ness, I began to think, *Maybe I do need some male energy, the kind that is not married or boyfriended and likes to go to movies and dinner and to cuddle and doesn't live in Missouri.*

The next day was my birthday and I celebrated the coming year with the revived flowers and by taking my re-found car out for a spin. Men? Hmph! Maybe my response to Mr. Green Juice indicated more interest in dating than I was admitting.

After a little drive in my car, I went to my fridge and toasted the year I'd just survived. I also toasted Green Juice Don, for awakening my subconscious to thoughts about men. But the very next thought that came to me was, *Now, what should I, could I, do about it?*

CHAPTER THIRTEEN

Serialkillers.com: The Over-Sixty Dating Site

Feeling lonely—and guilty of being a failed feminist for wanting *a man* to fill the void, I went to a dating website, which I prefer, here, to call serialkillers.com. This was not its real name, of course, but most of the guys looked a little bit Anthony Wieneresque. As if they could probably function in the daytime world, maybe even become the next Mayor of New York City, but as if they had a secret, compartmentalized part inside just waiting to come out, very likely right after they met me.

In the world of internet dating, as an older woman, when you tell your real age—and I refuse to lie about anything other than my weight or my pants size (Okay, I'm a "Large"!)—you can get some strange responses from much much younger men—or else no responses at all. And friends my age who dated warned me about the men who might be "looking for a nurse or a purse."

I am pleased to tell you, though, that there was one exception to the lack of choices on *serialkillers*. There was this one kind of attractive, but not movie star material guy, who I'll call Arnie.

Arnie exchanged e-mails with me. He was single. He had a job. All good signs, so far. We spoke on the phone. He sounded pleasant enough to talk to and I could decipher his texts and his e-mails. Not always the case. I agreed to meet him. In broad daylight. At a mall. In a restaurant where there would be plenty of people. And just in case I was wrong about Arnie, I had my pepper spray in my coat pocket.

On the day we arranged to meet, I was waiting at the restaurant's bar, when a guy who vaguely resembled Arnie's profile picture walked in. And while I didn't get that I-Must-Have-You-Now feeling, he was not unattractive in his sports jacket and chinos. Although, maybe at this point in my life, sexual chemistry was something I could forget about.

Arnie and I had a lovely conversation about work and kids and singleness in our sixties. He paid for our dinner. (I like that in a guy. It may be old-fashioned of me, but to me, it seems gallant and I assume the guy has a generosity of spirit, even if he's not wealthy. Especially if he's not wealthy.) He walked me to my car and we arranged for another date. And I forgot all about the pepper spray in my pocket.

Arnie was a totally nice guy, but there was simply no boy-girl attraction for me. Now, attraction, I'd found in the past, can get you in trouble and lead to bad choices, but it can also self-correct when you get to know someone. With Arnie, it just never did. I went out with him for five, maybe six months. And he just got nicer and nicer.

On one date, my son was flying in from New York for a visit and, after Arnie drove out to see me from Indiana, he generously volunteered to drive with me in his car to pick Ben up at the airport, full knowing he'd have to drive all the way back later that night.

Another time, Arnie even went shoe shopping with me at the mall, a true test of any man's endurance.

I kept trying to talk myself into him. But my self just wasn't having it. So, I had an idea. I said to myself, *Remember how you got yourself to go to the nude beach at Club Med back when you were in your thirties? Here is the way to force yourself to have sex with Arnie.* My thinking was that perhaps if I drank a little too much—and for me, three glasses of wine should do it—I could see if Arnie and I had a chance. After all, even in your sixties, you can't have a boyfriend you aren't attracted to at all, can you? I mean, sex isn't everything, but even in my sixties, I wasn't entirely ready to give it up.

So, one night when Arnie and I went out to dinner, I had my three glasses. The amount was just enough for me to be really tipsy, yet not nauseous. I brought Arnie home with me and, though I don't remember the progression, I somehow got naked.

Once naked himself, Arnie revealed that he had the thing we girls fear the second-most in a guy (the first being HIV). He said, "I have type two diabetes-related erectile dysfunction." *Oh, well,* I thought, *women have sex together without anybody's dick, why can't Arnie and I? There are other ways to make love,* it's just that none of them appealed to me with Arnie because, even though I was rather wobbly, Arnie *still* didn't appeal to me. In short, I just couldn't force myself to be with somebody just because he was nice. We kissed a little. I didn't want him to think it was his diabetes, though I knew we were through. *It will be hard to tell him though,* I thought. And then after a very short time, the alcohol got to both of us. I fell asleep and he did too.

The next morning was awkward with this kind-of strange man in the house, but I composed myself, put up some coffee, toasted some bagels and scrambled some eggs. After all, he was my guest. Grabbing a bagel, Arnie kissed me perfunctorily, and said his goodbyes, and made his way back to Indiana. For myself, I had a class I was taking that day which would start in an hour, so I showered and got ready. I was so relieved he didn't stick around, as I hadn't yet thought of how I was going to tell him the it's-not-you-it's-me story I was preparing in my head.

The class was an all-day continuing education class for social workers. At the lunch break, I checked my cell phone, expecting that Arnie would have left me a message, something like, "Nice evening. Let's get together next Saturday night, if you're free." In the past, like a boyfriend, he'd called me daily. But I found no message.

After the class, I re-checked my phone. Nothing. I checked my texts. No Arnie. I called him and left an annoyed message, "I'm surprised you didn't call," because in the world I came from, the last time I had an experience of the nakedness kind, a guy always called, at least if he ever hoped to see you again.

Now, at the time, even though I was still not attracted to Arnie, which our previous night's experience had confirmed, *I* wanted to tell *him.* And I was, somehow, furious. It never occurred to me to give him the benefit of the doubt; to say, *Poor guy, he's embarrassed about his type two diabetes* or *I didn't like him anyway and this saves me from hurting his feelings.* But *I* wanted to tell *him,* not the other way around!

Instead, I thought, *Anyone who is not an alien to this planet* knows *that you have to call a girl after seeing her buck naked, especially if she's in her sixties, with her share of body image hang-ups!*

After a full day passed, and then another, I wanted to call him and scream into the phone, "You asshole! Why didn't you call?" Of course, I knew this would be dopey. I mean, why did I even care?

The way I saw it, there were only three explanations for his lack of semi-bedside manners. One, he had been injured in a car accident and was now quadriplegic and, thus, unable to pick up the phone next to his hospital bed. Two, he and his ex-wife, twenty years divorced, decided to reconcile. Or, three, he was an asshole, making his way through the internet, hoping to find someone to help him with the side effects of his type-two diabetes.

I was taking that on-line writing course I found through a Kabbalah friend then, so I wrote down my feelings about my last date with Arnie. I snickered aloud as I wrote my mean little essay. But even the snickering and writing wasn't enough to totally eradicate my anger. So, I called my friend, who was also a writer, and I read it to her over the phone.

She laughed her way through it with me and, being a younger woman who dates, she totally understood. Carrie once read her essay on a popular Milwaukee radio morning talk show; so she suggested I query the producer about my story. Her reaction surprised me because so many younger people think people over sixty either don't have sex or are adorable anomalies if they do.

Of course, I changed any of Arnie's identifying features, so that anyone who might know him in Milwaukee (though he was from Indiana) could not possibly recognize him and I e-mailed my query letter. I was shocked when the producer gave me the go-ahead, scheduling me for the following Friday morning, to come in to record my story.

In retrospect, I do think Arnie had some self-consciousness that kept him from calling me after our sleepover. And, how I got so angry about it when I didn't want him anyway - that was just my ego having a tantrum. I very much doubt that he was a sociopath, sleeping his way through the internet. As it turned out, I learned that you can't force chemistry—or, at least, I sure couldn't.

Here's the happy part of the story. The whole unpleasant episode turned into an essay and then a series of essays on Milwaukee radio which eventually became my own segment, "Psychobabble."

Looking back, I don't recommend trying to force yourself to be attracted to someone you just plain aren't attracted to. I think the way it should go is that you should feel attracted to someone first. _Then,_ should they share your interest, you should do it. It doesn't seem to work in reverse.

Making fun of the whole experience, my faulty thinking, followed by embarrassing behavior, had its perks. Without _serialkillers.com_ and Arnie, I might never have gotten my essays on the air, which validated me as a writer. Somebody liked my writing enough to put it on the radio. This on-air gig was what led to my gaining confidence and actually taking myself seriously as a writer. I now believe that dating Arnie, my ridiculous behavior and even dumber reaction, and the way I dealt with it, may have, one baby step at a time, even led to my writing this book.

You know that dopey, trite, even maddening quote that people say to you when you are going through something: "Things happen for a reason." It used to drive me absolutely bat-shit crazy when people who were _not_ going through what I was going through said that phrase to me. But, in retrospect, after my _serialkillers_/Arnie/radio experience, I now think, _What if this stupid saying is actually true?_

And, as for Arnie, I never heard from him again. It was as if he fell off the face of the earth. But I do wish him well with his diabetes and its unfortunate side effects.

CHAPTER FOURTEEN

"Psychobabble: The Simple Secret of Being Attractive"

At first, as I began living alone, I railed at the thought of it: How unfair! Me with no husband or boyfriend with whom to exchange Valentine's Day cards or New Year's Eve kisses.

I probably get as many offers to go to dinner or for coffee or a glass of wine as any "Woman of a Certain Age," not living in Boca Raton, can be expected to get. But here's the problem: either I don't "click" with them or they don't "click" with me. Have things really changed very much since our early dating years?

For me, "The Click" is an indescribable quality. It's not looks, really. It's who a person is. It's certain qualities, like kindness and generosity of spirit and a certain kind of confidence that's not the narcissistic kind. Rather, it's more like, "I like you, but I'll be fine if you don't like me."

Here's the secret I learned at an Overeaters Anonymous meeting I've been going to for the past skeighty-eight years. My friend's husband, who goes there as well, heard about a recent dating experience I'd had, and he asked about it. I said, with disappointment, "No, that's over." And I wondered aloud if all the good men were now taken.

He thought for a moment and then he said what, at first, seemed like a non sequitur. "We businessmen know this one rule about bankers. If you want to borrow money from a banker, the one thing you have to do is...."

And I (as I have a tendency to do) finished his sentence, "You have to *look like* you don't need it, right?"

"No," said my friend's husband. "You have to *not need* it."

So, here's the thing. Following this advice, which makes more sense once you make yourself into the businessman and the object of your interest into the banker, you can't lose. If you don't *need* someone else to give you a life, you have a good life, whether there's a special someone with you or not.

And if you attract someone because you are whole within yourself, then you have a good life *and* a good partner; the kind of a partner who isn't threatened by, but attracted to, a woman with a life of her own. I think it works for men this way, too.

CHAPTER FIFTEEN

Psychobabble: It Is What It Is: The Kreplach Story

Did you ever hear anyone say, "It is what it is," and say to yourself, *What the f*** does that mean? Everyone knows you can't define a word with the same word! 'It is what it is,' indeed!*

I never understood this seemingly redundant saying until I heard The Kreplach Story. For those who don't know what kreplach are, kreplach (pron: krehp-lacccch) are like Chinese wontons. They, like matzo balls, can be featured in chicken soup, the kind typically made by Jewish mothers.

So, here's The Kreplach Story:

There was a young boy named Izzy who was terrified of kreplach. And his mother made them every Friday night with chicken soup for their Sabbath meal. Every time he saw the little meat-filled dumplings floating in his soup, he screamed, "Eek, kreplach!" and he'd run out of the room.

His mother was beside herself, trying to change this irrational fear. Finally, she came up with a plan to help him overcome his strange behavior around the harmless little meat pies.

So, she brought him into the kitchen with her one Friday afternoon and took out her kreplach ingredients. Together, she and Izzy mixed the flour and egg, salt and oil and rolled the mixture into a round doughy ball. "It's like a big ball," said his mother.

"Like a ball," mimicked Izzy, smiling.

Then, mother and son kneaded the ball of dough and sprinkled some flour on the cutting board. Using the rolling pin, Izzy and his mother rolled out the dough ball into a flat cookie dough shape. Izzy's mother said, pointing to their creation, "It looks just like a big pancake!"

Izzy repeated, "Just like a pancake."

Next, Mother enlisted Izzy to help her cut the dough into little squares and place a spoonful of filling inside. "It's like making rugelach," said Mother.

"Like rugelach," Izzy replied happily.

And Mom boiled a big soup pot of water, sprinkling in salt, and she and Izzy plopped each little Jewish ravioli into the pot, covering it with a lid. "Just like donuts," said Mother.

"Donuts." Izzy repeated, as he helped.

Twenty minutes later, which is about how long it takes to prepare kreplach in boiling water, Mother called Izzy back into the kitchen. And together, they put on their oven mitts and expectantly lifted the pot-lid. "Eek!" shrieked Izzy, running out of the room. "Kreplach!"

I guess the meaning of what seemed like a dopey saying to me is a lot like The Kreplach Story. It's the idea we hear in twelve-step meetings, "God grant me the serenity to accept what I cannot change, the courage to change what I can, and the wisdom to know the difference." It's about accepting what you cannot change: thus, "It is what it is." And sometimes life just gives you kreplach.

CHAPTER SIXTEEN

Psychobabble: "You Talk Too Much"

Wouldn't it be nice if there was a computer chip we could all wear that would tell us where we're going wrong, like, "You have broccoli between your teeth." Or, "You could use a breath mint," or "Stop talking and give others a chance. Although you mean to look smart, you actually look insecure and self-involved."

My friend Andrew becomes irritated because he's always full of what the texters might call TMI, Too Much Information. Andrew will take a complete detour from the point (and I plead guilty to the same flaw) and say something like, "There's Bob, he's an old friend of mine and he's *famous!*"

I guess most of us assume what interests us also interests the people around us. Or maybe we just haven't given it much thought. It's only when we point out these details to someone else, instead of seeming like we know important people, we appear as if we want to impress others or are insensitive to those around us. Instead of finding us fascinating, they begin wondering about their grocery list.

When someone has a glaring flaw, I think, *Everybody knows but the person herself.* Perhaps we could do a personality improvement intervention, like with drug or alcohol interventions. The afflicted person would be gently and lovingly confronted about their behaviors. Our friends and family, if they are pretty well-balanced themselves, can see behaviors in us which we may not see. Why don't they tell us?

Why? Because people are afraid we will become defensive or "unfriend" us, as they say in Facebook-speak. Or, perhaps others have tried to tell them, but they don't seem to hear or else they go stiff with defensiveness.

Yet, don't we all want to know if we have bad breath? I'd like to know if I don't let anybody talk without following up with an I-can-top-that story. Are we so sensitive that we'd prefer not to know what's tripping us up, rather than be told something that is not pleasant to hear, but which will ultimately help us?

I mean, we could say, as one does in an intervention, "Sally, we all love you. But when you talk without giving anyone else a chance to respond, we begin to feel as if you aren't interested in anybody but yourself."

Of course, if Sally feels picked on and embarrassed in front of everybody, rather than seeing that we just want to help her, she may not be receptive to what we have to say.

As for my chicken-hearted self, I like the computer chip idea. That way, nobody gets hurt. Or, if they do, the computer chip can easily be removed. Of course, when I think of the ways the chip could be misused…Maybe it's better to let people talk too much and wear their tooth-broccoli like gold caps. Those of us who are irritated by these "flaws" can just learn how to live with them. Maybe all of us, including me, could stand to learn some flaw-tolerance.

CHAPTER SEVENTEEN

Psychobabble: Flexibility

I was trying to think of the most important qualities people could have in life. And I thought about how I'd survived the many changes that life always provides. I sometimes thought of myself as the punch-clown toy I remember from my kids' growing up years. You could punch it down, but it would always pop right back up again.

I think of myself as a survivor. However, being a survivor didn't spare me the human emotions we all endure from time to time: anger, disappointment, sadness, confusion. Like most people, I wasn't so positive I could survive during the challenging moments in my life. I realized that I've moved twenty times since I left home after college, I've been married and divorced and I've brought up children. Sometimes, I wasn't sure how I would get through being a single-parent or moving to different apartments for one reason or another, or helping my kids get through their own life-crises.

But, like it or not, life is always changing. Often it changes so gradually, we don't even notice. I realized, recently, at a high school class reunion, if we hadn't worn ID-badges with our high school pictures and names on them, many of us wouldn't have recognized one another. But the people who saw one another frequently felt as if their friends hadn't changed much at all.

All of us, now in our sixties, had come through certain losses. Some dealt with caregiving or health issues; most lost parents, siblings, even children; and many had sustained unexpected financial losses. Never easy, but especially challenging in our older years.

Attitude is important, but attitude is about how we think. Support systems of partners and family and friends are keys to adjustment as well. But I think it's having flexibility that matters most, particularly in one's sager years.

And the only way to develop flexibility is to practice. Because I had to practice this skill as a single mom, as a woman who needed to move rather often, I had to make changes, be able to bend without breaking. Yes, I could move from a big house to a tiny apartment, move from one state to another, change my job if need be.

It was only in my sixties that I profited from all that flexibility practice. It's not that I wasn't afraid, but my earlier experiences taught me that something unexpected and good seemed to come my way, just to show me that if I could be flexible, life would do its part — an apartment opening in a friend's building, a new job when I needed to move, old friends and new ones showing up when I most needed them. All of these came just in time, as if I placed a specific order with The Divine.

One example of Flexibility was Frances who surprised her family when Phil, her husband, of many years, died. Both of them were in their late-sixties then. But Frances began to find she could do many things she never believed she could, as Phil always did them. Of course she missed Phil, but she found new ways to enjoy her life— and she seemed happy right up to her death at ninety-something.

What are our choices? We may not like the adjustments we have to make in life and they may not be decisions we would have chosen if we had the choice. Problems: Everybody's got 'em. As the saying goes: "Let go or be dragged." I might add "Be patient with yourself." Even if you are flexible, integrating change takes time.

CHAPTER EIGHTEEN

Psychobabble: Chickflicks: My Go-To for Tough Times

I approve of anything that gets you through the night. Possible exceptions are alcohol, if you are an alcoholic or a problem drinker; Ben and Jerry's or the like, if you are a compulsive eater; sex with a toxic person or a stranger; drugs, unless they are prescribed by a doctor and taken as directed; or buying things as an impulsive mood moderator. The Ben & Jerry and the buying things options are my usual impulse-fallbacks.

But when I've got my head on straight, I have a much more effective technique for dealing with pain. My secret formula for staying alive during perceived life crises or miserable mood-swings are strong women stories. I usually find these role models in films, television series, and recorded books.

For me, these are the moments—in my first divorce and again in my second, when I could have been adding another fifteen pounds to the twenty I never lost after my baby weight.

Many a night in the separation and divorce evenings, I felt pretty unlovable (even worse than unfuckable). At these times, I would take basketsful of ironing, along with my ironing board and steam iron, over to my video player (back before dvds) and keep company with the likes of Meryl Streep, Susan Sarandon, Diane Keaton and Jane Fonda.

One Friday night at the beginning of my first divorce, my teenaged sons were out with their friends. I put in the video of *Married to the Mob* with Michelle Pfeiffer and Alec Baldwin and took my basket of ironing and ironed away as I lost myself in the film and its theme (brave single mom wants to get away from the Mob life her dead hit man husband was involved in and moves from the safety of the suburbs into New York City). Angie (Pfeiffer's character) attempts to start over, even getting wired by the FBI in order to trap the leader of the Mob who killed her husband.

The movie inspired me, and the ironing, which I mindlessly did in order to not stuff my face, led to my shopping in my own closet, so to speak, which afforded me forgotten-about wardrobe choices.

Another time my Chickflicks came in handy was when I was dating a man for a couple of years after my first marriage, and we briefly decided to try living together in his small New York City apartment.

He had bouts with his temper, where he yelled and even threw things, sometimes stomping out of the apartment, saying he was going to his mother's. Out came my Chickflicks.

One night after one of these incidents, I watched a double feature to stoke up my courage; *Stanley and Iris*, followed by *Passion Fish*. *Stanley and Iris* starred Jane Fonda as a widowed working class widow, trying to cope with raising her kids on her own and working in a factory, where she meets Stanley (Robert DeNiro), a brilliant and inventive, but illiterate guy, who she helps to learn to read. *Passion Fish* features Mary McDonnell and Alfre Woodard, as two strong and determined southern women from very different backgrounds, one white and one black, who meet at a place in their lives where each really needs the other. McDonnell plays a former soap opera star, who becomes paraplegic after a taxicab accident and Woodard is her caregiver, who needs to stay off drugs and away from her drug-pusher boyfriend and keep her caregiver's job to regain custody of her young daughter.

Spending time with these gutsy women is far superior to compulsive overeating or spending money on an impulse. First off, I get to see a movie with a strong woman role model; usually a woman whose crisis dwarfs my little mood swing, negative rumination, or anxiety attack. Then, I am reminded that there are wars and clitorectomies and holocausts women all over the world are dealing with and bringing their children through. Seeing these women through the brilliant gifts of actresses who are most often, like myself, no longer young, is particularly meaningful. And the women whose stories I take in do not have the first world luxury of sitting around, feeling sorry for themselves. They are too busy trying to survive.

Actually, it isn't only heroines in dire circumstances that help me in near-nervous-breakdown mode. It's also heroines that are Little Mary Sunshine's, having to deal with difficult lives that would certainly turn my brown eyes blue. (Actually, my eyes are hazel, but you know what I mean.) Somehow, these women have the trust in the universe to help them, while I can easily forget all about the many times amazing synchronicities have saved my sorry ass.

Of course, let it be noted that these women often look at their crises as challenges, opportunities, walking sticks on their paths to enlightenment. While I, under the same circumstances, might be found weeping in my room, binge-eating anything chocolate or charging something well over budget in my catalogue du jour, even though my credit cards may be close to maxing out.

Amazing as it might seem, in that moment of need, I actually believe that the boots or the dress in some catalogue will change my life. And they do for about twenty minutes, though they also come with a heavy buyer's remorse hangover when the bill arrives. My mood *really* plummets when I try the ordered item on my slightly pudgy older woman's body and wonder what I was thinking when I saw it on a teenaged anorexic model.

If I grab my old steam-iron and ironing board as I watch Chickflicks, I find I can spend only the few bucks it takes to rent the film I want. (Now, the monthly rate for Netflix, Amazon Prime or cable television costs a bit more.) And the library generally carries a lot of these films for the price of a library card.

Sometimes cable series or television shows comfort me in times of need. I love "Grace and Frankie," and I can cuddle up under my comforter on the couch or in bed, watching episode after episode, until I can no longer stay awake.

I also find listening to what we used to call books-on-tape, either in CD form or on a telephone app, gets me back in a better place when I'm feeling down. One favorite is *The Help* by Kathryn Stockett. I've read the book, seen the film, but my favorite way to enjoy it is by listening to it on CD or on a recorded book app. During a time in my life when I was feeling particularly lonely and sorry for myself, I found the ways Black American women back in the 60's bravely dealt with racism in the South infused me with courage.

When crises paralyze me, I watch movies, binge on series, and read or listen to books!

And popcorn, thankfully, is filled with healthy fiber and is low in calories. I've included a list of some of my favorite inspirational movies, television series, and books (recorded or read-it-yourself).

Films, television series, book suggestions:

Films/Documentaries:

A Man Called Ove
Antonia's Line
The African Queen
Baby Boom
Baghdad Café
The Best Most Exotic Marigold Hotel
The Big Sick
The Book Club
Bread and Tulips
The Driving Lesson
Embrace
The English Teacher
Fargo
Fences
Finding Your Feet
Five Flights Up
The Fundamentals of Caring
The Guernsey Literary and Potato Peel Pie Society
Heartburn
Hidden Figures
How Stella Got Her Groove Back
Hysteria

The Intouchables
It's Complicated
Jenny's Wedding
Mama Mia
Mama Mia, Here We Go Again
Maggie's Plan
Mask
Moonstruck
Out of Africa
Passion Fish
Ricky and the Flash
The Second Best Most Exotic Marigold Hotel
Shirley Valentine
Silkwood
Silver Linings Playbook
Stanley & Iris
The Tango Lesson
Tea with Mussolini
Transamerica
Turtle Diary
Unconditional Love
An Unmarried Woman
Waiting to Exhale

BBC Series:

Agatha Raisin
The Bletchley Circle
Call the Midwife
Doc Martin
Downton Abbey
Mum

Netflix Series/Specials:

Atypical

Grace and Frankie
The Kominsky Method
Special

Amazon Prime Movies and Series:

Don't Worry, He Won't Get Far on Foot
The Marvelous Mrs. Maisel
Love Sarah
New in Town
Transparent

Hulu:

The Handmaid's Tale
Shrill

Cable TV:

Big Little Lies-HBO
Episodes-Showtime
Game of Thrones-HBO (not for the faint of heart)
Gentleman Jack-HBO
Insecure-HBO

Broadcast Television:

Madam Secretary
Mom
Scandal

Books for Reading or Listening To:

The Alice Network by Kate Quinn

The Artist's Way: A Spiritual Path to Higher Creativity by Julia Cameron

The Bette Davis Club by Jane Lotter

Bird by Bird by Anne Lamott

The Bookish Life of Nina Hill by Abbi Waxman

The Cactus by Sarah Haywood

Conviction by Denise Mina

Daisy Jones and the Six: A Novel by Taylor Jenkins Reid

Escaping the Whale by Ruth Rotkowitz

Evvie Drake Starts Over by Linda Holmes

The Giver of Stars by Jojo Meyers

Heartburn by Nora Ephron

Homework by Julie Andrews

The Help by Kathryn Stockett

How to Walk Away by Katherine Center

I Almost Forgot About You by Terry McMillan

In Grace's Time by Kathie Giorgio

It's Not All Downhill from Here by Terry McMillan

Ladies Always Shoot First by Summer Hanford

The Love Song of Miss Queenie Hennessy by Rachel Joyce

Maybe You Should Talk to Someone by Lori Gottlieb

Mrs. Saint and the Defectives by Julie Lawson Timm

My Life So Far by Jane Fonda

The Nightingale by Kristen Hannah

One Day in December by Josie Silver

The Overdue Life of Amy Byers by Kelly Harms

The Rosie Result by Graeme Simsion

The Sage's Tao Te Ching: A New Interpretation by William Martin

She Wants It by Jill Soloway

Something in the Water by Catherine Steadman

Still Life with Breadcrumbs by Anna Quindlen

Where'd You Go, Bernadette? by Maria Semple

When Life Gives You Lululemons by Lauren Weisberger

The Wife by Meg Wolitzer

The Thursday Murder Club by Richard Osman

What You Wish For by Katherine Center

Where the Crawdads Sing by Delia Owens

Whisper Network by Chandler Baker

CHAPTER NINETEEN

Stuck in the Snow

Some of us say that there are four seasons of winter in the Midwest: 1.Almost Winter, 2. Winter, 3. Still Winter, and 4. Road Construction. On one very snowy Midwestern inside-by-will-to-live day, all I could do was thank God I lived on the first floor.

Serial days of isolation can make a person who might otherwise be cuddling with a partner or cooking with a buddy feel pretty blue. For myself, I go toward my negative thinking on such days. The if-onlies on a succession of days left alone in my head, without enough stimulation, can lend themselves to self-involvement.

But this day, I prepared. I know my tendency toward negative rumination when left on my own for several days during blizzards when it's not possible to open my front door. In advance of this particular snowstorm, I looked up ingredients for a few soup recipes and stashed them away in the cabinet for just this kind of weather. Because of my shopping preparations in advance of the snow, I was ready for comfort-food making. And, just at that time, I was making a new recipe for split pea soup.

But then, I thought, *If it snows for the next few weeks, how many soup recipes do I have? And I actually own the bible. "The Soup Recipe Bible," that is. Will I need to stay in solitary forever?*

I wasn't cut off from communication altogether. Thanks to the magic of my iPhone, I did get a hilarious text about dating from a favorite cousin, "I would rather have a colonoscopy, than meet another dating app guy at a Starbucks!"

Not only did Jude's e-mail give me a giggle, it reminded me of a man I dated once. After I'd sworn off dating, I had a weak moment and went back to the dating sites. And I saw a nice- looking man. I thought, *Hey, maybe I should give dating another chance. This guy is attractive and he's a learning disabilities teacher. Usually pretty decent people choose professions like teaching Special Needs kids.*

I notified him on the site and he said he was interested in meeting. So we found a cozy Starbucks where we could meet.

When I got there, he was already sitting. And he looked remarkably like his picture, maybe better.

It was a warm day and he was wearing his khaki "Semper Fi" green tee shirt.

Semper Fi is a motto for the Marines. He was in his early- to mid-sixties and muscular, and as rugged and handsome as he looked in his picture.

When I met Dick, I joked with him, "Okay, admit you were planted on this sixties-plus dating site just to give us girls hope; to offset the less-than-interesting potential matches."

We talked for a while and then I said, "Dick, I've got to get going." (His name really was Dick.)

I should have been excited about meeting Dick, but I'd been burned before and I said to myself, *There must be something wrong with this guy that he's, one, so attractive, and, two, still available.*

He texted me not long after, "Linda, I'd like to see you again." And I was astonished.

So we dated for a while. I'd drive out to meet him in one or another of his favorite bars.

Over time, he would call me at night, in a series of drink-and-dials, and it became clear that Dick drank too much for me. I broke up with him, saying, "It's me, not you."

This happened a few months back, but, just as I was thinking about Dick, on this snow- bound day, he texted me. His text said, "I feel misunderstood and I think we should talk."

Well, hating to hurt a person's feelings, I texted him a long-winded emotional-sounding apology in response. Something about how my not wanting to continue our relationship was no reflection on him. Actually, it was a reflection on him, but hadn't I retired from the business of changing a potential mate? If I wanted fixer-uppers, I'd be getting my real estate license.

The fun part came a moment or two later, when he texted me again. "Louise, I think you are a really lovely woman and, if your relationship with Bob doesn't work out, I'd like to see you again."

Well! Louise? So, he has a *list* of potential women companions! Semper fi, this! I blushed at my serious long-winded No-Reflection-On-You text that he and the guys at whatever bar he was at were probably now howling over. I lowered the heat on my soup and sent his text back to him, with a curt, "I think you meant this for someone else."

In no time, I got a defensive, "Louise is just a friend of mine. I was watching the game (read: having a drink or ten) with my buddy George in her neighborhood, and I thought I'd ask her to join us!"

I shot back, "Well, if she joins you, what's she gonna do with Bob?" I could just see D. on a barstool, doing shots with his buddies, as they watched the game. At least, now, they could chuckle, not at my unsuspecting nature, but at him. "Busted, you *** hole! You're buying!" I could hear them laughing and could LOL, as some texters might say, thinking about it.

And so, I poured myself a glass of sparkling organic pear juice and started my marathon viewing of Allie MacBeal, the old TV show, now on Netflix. I find that sometimes being alone can mean being in pretty good company, especially when I treat myself well. I mean, I love Chickflicks, but what guy is going to put up with a full afternoon (and possible evening) of them? And my split pea soup with chicken sausage made a delicious dinner.

CHAPTER TWENTY

Soul-Dating in My Sixties:
I Finally Meet My Better Half

After my experiences with Mr. Diabetes and Dick the Drinker, here I was, getting my "senior" movie discounts without a partner. Having to figure it out all on my own. I guess I came to the conclusion that my relationship journey might actually be over; that internet marketing and advertising made me, at my age, obsolete.

And, lo and behold, who should turn up? (And, no, it wasn't my high school sweetheart, trying to find me on Facebook!) It was My Soul. As it turned out, My Ego had been making all the decisions for me love-wise and My Soul had been trying to get a word in edgewise for most of my life, but I never listened at all! In the past, if she whispered in my ear, "Beeee careful, bee very careful," I simply ignored her, and hoped she would stop pestering me and go away. I *knew* what I wanted, so why listen to a frumpy old soul?

But, this time, maybe because it seemed I had no other options, I was ready to at least hear her out.

"You and I can make it together," she said, "I know we can."

Before long, I was stretching my comfort muscles, trying things I felt drawn to, things which I might not have made time for, if a man-in-my-life was there. I am embarrassed to admit it, but the guy always became my first priority—before friends, and before myself, even when I wasn't his priority. Maybe *especially* when I wasn't. My soul said she suspected I was in some kind of trance. Then she marched my sorry ass off to a hypnotherapy training, and she came along to be sure that I didn't bail or my Ego didn't find me some guy there.

She and I spent lots of time, learning about my pattern of abandoning myself (and Her!) for a man; how this script was practically imprinted on my brain. It's important to know about your habits. Though later on, I became aware that *having insights* about self-defeating patterns is much easier than the painful work of *actually changing those patterns.* I kept asking myself, *How can I be there for us—me and My Soul,* things I found easy to do for a guy.

My Soul suggested, "Maybe it's your Ego that makes you feel like you aren't a whole person without a man! What if we tried new things, even if they were hard for us? Maybe *especially* if they were hard for us? What if we stretched our comfort zones, having small adventures, even if we have to force ourselves? Might be a great way to have fun experiences and learn new things. This may be a couples' world, but we're *people*, too!"

"You're right!" I said. Then, after a pause, I questioned, "Er, like what adventures? Sky-diving in our sixties?"

"No, silly," she laughed, aware of my fear of heights. "Just enjoying the simple things in life. Listening to our Inner Knowing. You know, doing things, not just because they are a means to some end, but doing them because we are drawn to them; kind of enjoying the process itself, instead of using up our energy, making ourselves loveable for some not-so-loving guy. After all, we went to hypnotherapy retreats. Would you have committed to all those weekends to the trainings, if you had a husband or boyfriend?"

I had to admit it was true. I'd always been drawn to learning hypnosis, but would I have done it if I had a guy in my life? Probably not if I could be cuddling with my guy, enjoying a heavy dose of compliments.

When My Soul and I returned from the trainings, she found new projects for us to explore. One day, she'd bring home pastels just to fool around with. Then another day, a recipe book to inspire us to cook yummy foods for ourselves.

One night, My Soul caught My Ego encouraging me to check out some old e-mails from dating sites. I knew that My Soul would not approve, so I snuck over to my computer to write back to Mr. "Dinner in Paris?"

My Soul pushed me aside, commandeering my laptop. She answered my potential online suitor with, "'Considered the jet lag, buddy?'"

Turns out, while I was not consciously aware of it, Ms. E. was influencing my decisions about love all along, believing the superficial stuff a guy said he was, rather than what his behaviors proved him to be. "I'm generous, but I forgot my wallet." "I'm loving, but I want you to go out partying with me, when I know you have work to do." Hmm.

My Soul sat me down and gave me a talking to. "If we just do things that bring us joy and flow and inspiration, won't that enrich us more than trying to win or keep some guy's love? And then not *needing* somebody to tell us we're okay, if we do find someone special, he'll be a guy who isn't all about himself. He won't be threatened by you being your best self and you won't be afraid to be your best, fearing you'll displease him. He'll have his own Soul to answer to."

I thought it made sense, but I wasn't sure if I could withstand not going for the instant gratification that a man in my life could bring.

Knowing what a bad influence Ms. E. could be for me, one night, My Soul and I snuck up on her, while she was wrapped up (in my favorite afghan) in a deep sleep on the couch. We dragged her by the corners of the blanket to the second bedroom of my place, bolted the door, and put up a sign, "Grounded Indefinitely!"

And My Soul and I felt free to take on projects in the house that I might not have cared about before she began encouraging me. She planted an organic vegetable garden and I made a wall montage of our adventures together. I helped her with weeding and watering and she helped me with hanging the pictures for our wall.

We were getting along so well. . . .It was so different than the highs and the lows I would feel, listening to My Ego, and falling in and out of love. It was more like contentment.

My life began to change, now that I was attending to My Soul. I was enjoying our alone-time so much. But, you know what happens when you make a commitment. It often turns out that we make different choices and have different habits. But, if you want it to work, you have to be flexible.

Often, with a man, when I stood my ground about what I wanted, if it was different than what he wanted, I feared I would lose him or, worse, that I would find out he didn't even care about what I wanted. Could I show it, when I felt low? Could I expect him to tolerate the bad with the good? And if he didn't care enough to respect my needs, I would end up feeling resentful. In contrast, My Soul and I were always able to resolve our differences.

Sometimes we didn't agree, but we cared about one another enough, so that whether the living room was painted taupe or ecru wasn't as important as the bigger picture of our relationship. And one of us didn't need to give in all the time. We were just mindful of whether this or that was more important to her or to me. Sometimes, one or the other of us was able to live with her less favorite choice, knowing that she was making the other one happy. It wasn't always her and it wasn't always me, the way it can be in some relationships, where often one person seems to get their way about everything.

Occasionally, I relapsed and snuck a peek online, intrigued by a flirty dating site message, but My Soul was always right there, reading over my shoulder and reminding me that people are not so much what they say, but what they do over time.

She reminded me of a time, just a year or so back, when I found myself fascinated by the attentions of Mr. Music Man. My Ego egged me on, "Why, he's clever and good-looking and he's so talented. Any girl would want him," she cooed in my ear.

And, yes, when I met Mr. Music Man, My Ego was totally taken by his intensity and his charm and his crazy-about-you behaviors. For weeks, I was high, being Mr. M.'s favorite groupie; he seemed to love me so much more than I loved myself.

Then, very suddenly, he began to distance himself, calling and seeing me less. Not long after, came his e-mail to me: "I have become close to a woman I've known for a long time and we both want to see where this will go romantically." Ouch! I was devastated.

"How could I not have seen that coming? And why didn't you warn me?" I asked My Soul, casting a blaming look in her direction.

"I *lost my voice* trying to warn you, but you were so high on so-called love, you couldn't hear me at all." She shook her head mournfully and continued, "Would anyone real, someone who could be in a working relationship, have rushed you like that? Wouldn't he have taken your talents and interests into consideration? Would it have been 'all about him'? Wouldn't he want to work out conflicts, not just leave abruptly, picking some lame excuse, saying he was seeing someone he knew all the time he was courting you? I mean, didn't he care a whit about how you might feel? I just couldn't get through to you; it was like trying to have a conversation with an addict!"

What she advised was being able to hold the tension of the process; to let a dating situation unfold as a relationship in its own time, like a friendship. She recommended I work on not being so afraid to be alone or unloved that I twist myself into a pretzel to make myself right for his mustard.

Memorial Day weekend, the "kickoff" of summer, the time when families and couples often drive to their vacation cottages, I can find myself feeling down without a special someone. My Soul and I decided to do something special for ourselves; we took a long, lovely walk at the Botanic Gardens.

Seeing the waterfalls and the ponds, admiring the plants of all different varieties, we couldn't have been happier, just taking in nature and people-watching. The Japanese Garden and a Salad Niçoise on the terrace overlooking the fountain was just perfect. Instead of making up a story in my head about others' lives and finding my own life lacking, I truly enjoyed seeing all kinds of connection around me; couples and families, friends and lovers—and I felt connected too.

Lately, My Soul is not just the default mode for a guy. She's important to me—and she's helped make me important to myself. Not in a narcissistic way, but at least as important as anyone else in my life. I don't miss the manicky highs of a new man blinding My Ego with hot promises of love. My Soul is teaching me to prefer the quiet "being" of something more real. I find that I'm not as needy anymore and I don't have to be dragged into the Dungeon of Depression for Her to get my attention. I'd like to have a man in my life, but only if he has a good relationship with his Soul, a man who would give My Soul the respect I am finally giving her. Of course, we all have an Ego, but with My Soul at my side, now I can see that short-term pleasure is not worth finding the "keeper" kind of joy. With or without a man, My Soul is showing me the bigger picture.

CHAPTER TWENTY-ONE

Perhaps You Can Go Home Again

At this point, I was living in the northern suburbs of Chicago, but renting a house that was too expensive for just one person. I grew up in Skokie, Illinois, and my sister lived in a town just minutes away from there.

Maybe it was the geographical energy pull of the past which contained so many memories. But I actually believed that literally "going home," as in back to where I grew up, Skokie, would get me the moorings I so longed for.

Even so, I realized the advantages of Milwaukee; it was cheaper, people were less guarded, you could usually find parking right in front of wherever you went. These are no small matters to people who once lived in New York City, possibly the Stress Capital of the country. Well, for people like me.

I had fond memories of my Illinois childhood. Harmless pranks like toilet-papering the high school the night before Homecoming came to mind; uncles and aunts dropping by unannounced, as my dad started the coffee percolator and my mom warmed up the Entenmann's coffee cake she always kept stocked for these occasions. Our house was Grand Central Station for family and friends. And I loved that.

I felt grounded in that house with those people, as I took my adolescent leave—a friend or a date at the door. Whatever was happening in my life at the time, that place seemed like a mooring to which I could always return.

I guess, like the Spielberg movie alien, ET, I wanted to go home; and though the coffeecake-eaters were no longer around, I had the idea that moving back to the old home ground would relieve my feeling of somehow being "lost".

Olivia, my realtor, was not lazy. I was only a renter, but she was tireless in the pursuit of finding me a place to live.

When I told her I wanted to rent something close to my friends, Marina and Mischa, who lived in a "very desirable" (as the realtors say) condominium in Skokie, Olivia was doubtful I could find an available rental in that building complex.

I knew that living in a building so close to Chicago would have its disadvantages: Too close to The Second City to be as friendly as Milwaukee. It was an elevator building, which seemed, to me, a little assisted living-ish. Still, Marina and Mischa were living there and their apartment came with indoor parking and a washer and dryer, which sounded like paradise to a former New Yorker, whether one lived in Manhattan or in the less expensive borough of Queens. And I had done both.

Then Olivia called. "Linda, you have to see this rental! It's in that same building as your friends—I think it may even be on the same floor—and it's not going to be on the market for long." I agreed to meet Olivia in front of the Skokie condos the very next day.

When she first took me up the condo's elevator, I wondered, *Can I really live in an elevator building?* Though, I could see how an elevator might make life easier—coming up from the heated/air-conditioned parking garage with grocery bags when it was Chicago-freezing and not having to dig out your car in the snow.

When the elevator stopped at the third floor and Olivia and I stepped out and walked down the hall, I could see that the rental we were looking at was only two doors down from my friends.

An attractive and polite businessman was showing the place. It looked like a bachelor pad where the knick-knacks, wall-hangings and plants of a woman's touch might be just the things to turn spare into comfy. The appliances inside had names like Whirlpool or Kenmore. It was an apartment, but this apartment was so much lovelier than the one I'd lived in on the Long Island Expressway.

I guess I would not make much of a poker-player, as in front of the owner I could barely keep from jumping up and down, screaming, "I want it! This is IT!"

I didn't want to try bargaining and take the chance that another offer would grab the condo before I could. Olivia knew as soon as she saw my face. And, once the door to the apartment was completely shut behind us, she looked at me, and asked, "Draw up the contract?"

I made a deposit on the apartment. I am often blind to detail, but when Olivia sent me the rental agreement to sign, oddly for me, I noticed that in the document's right hand corner, beneath the owner's name, Daniel Wong, there was the name M. Wei. *Who is this M. Wei?* I said to myself. *Nobody mentioned that Mr. Wong had a co-owner for his condo. Am I just being paranoid or does this seem fishy?*

I called Olivia. "Who is this M. Wei on the contract you sent me?" I asked.

"I'll call Mr. Wong's realtor and find out."

Olivia called me back not long after. "Linda, it seems that M. Wei is Mr. Wong's ex-wife, Mye. They are going through a divorce, but according to their realtor, they have a good relationship. Since Mr. Wong is moving back to California, Mye will be handling the apartment—you know, the rent and if anything comes up. I guess they decided it would be simpler than trying to track down Mr. Wong for repairs or questions."

I said, "Liv, I have a funny feeling about this. I think I need to meet her before I sign the rental agreement." And Olivia, probably thinking I was overreacting, but in no mood to argue, arranged a meeting.

The following day, Mye and her realtor, Louis Chen, met Olivia and me in the lobby of the condo building. The moment I saw Mye, I was reassured; she seemed lovely and had a sweet smile.

I was reassured, so I signed the one-year lease, explaining that I would move in as soon as I could pack and find a mover.

One thing that is torturous when you're single and older and without a roommate or a gaggle of Seinfeld buddies is *moving*. And at this point, I would be moving for the umpteenth time since I moved from my parents' Skokie house, that beacon of stability for me for over fifty years. In my twenties I couldn't get away from the place fast enough, but in these times it took on new meaning for me.

Despite the time constraints, somehow, I did it. I found an inexpensive mover and an organized friend helped me to pack. *Okay, I thought, with a sigh of relief, Now I'm set: A lovely condo rental with an indoor garage. And, oh, the value of being able to throw in a wash. No running up and down the stairs to see if a neighbor is done or having to babysit the washer and dryer, prepared with pocketsful of quarters—which never seemed to be enough. Then to scramble to the nearest all-night-bodega, whatever time it was, trying to find enough change to finish my laundry.*

On the day of my scheduled move, the moving guys picked up my boxes and furniture and put them in the truck. I followed that truck to the Skokie condos, parked my car in my new parking spot underneath the building and went to greet the movers at the front door when they arrived. On the elevator up, I saw a woman who looked to be around my age and I introduced myself. "I'm Linda and I'm moving in today," I said.

She said, "I'm Sandra and my husband is the head of the condo board. I see that the elevators are not padded. Your condo owner is supposed to notify the building superintendent, so that he can pad the elevators and supervise the movers."

Hmm, I thought, Mye never said anything about reserving a time with the super. Then, I remembered how stressful it was to be divorcing, like Mye, and I scurried around, finding the building superintendent to get the elevator padded and move in as planned.

After the movers placed the furniture, Marina dropped by to visit me, now her new neighbor, on her way to work. She gave me a congratulatory hug, then over her shoulder, she looked around. She slowly walked around my apartment, her brow furrowed, as she inspected every corner. She took a close look at the walls in each room. Then she went to check out the kitchen. Hovering over the oven, she ran her index finger against the stovetop, and brought her hand back up for me to see. Eww, her finger was covered with oily grime.

"Lindotchka, the owner's responsibility is to have your apartment clean and freshly painted when you move in," said Marina with concern. She pointed to stains on the ceilings and the outlines of pictures that had been removed, evidence that the walls were the same as the day Daniel Wong moved out. "You need to call the owner," she said.

I always dread confrontations, probably because I think I'll just aggravate myself for nothing and then lose anyway. And, at this time, I thought, *I hate to be The Annoying Tenant Whose Contract You Don't Want to Renew.* Still, I knew Marina was right. Had I ever left any living quarters without being certain it was at least as clean as the day I moved in? But, before calling my realtor, I snapped some pictures on my cell phone of the stains on the walls and the grease on the stovetop.

Then I called my realtor, but my call went directly to voicemail. I knew Olivia would call back, but I realized with no husband, no parent, no advocate to argue my case, I would be on my own. In all these years, had I ever been entirely on my own? Not when my parents were alive or when I was married or had a man in my life. But right now, at this time of upheaval, I had only my own strengths to fall back on, and I wasn't feeling much confidence in my ability to get what I needed done.

When Olivia called back, she said she talked to Louis Chen, who spoke to Mye. Though Olivia would not be able to be there, she said, "Louis and Mye will be at your condo at ten o'clock tomorrow morning."

The two appeared at my door promptly at ten. But I could see by the expression on her face that Mye Wei, the delicate smiling woman I had met earlier was not at all pleased that I would bother her with these petty details.

Mye glared at me, then mumbled something I couldn't understand in Chinese to Louis Chen. I imagined she was saying, *WHAT! This fussy bitch must be out of her mind if she thinks I'm going to paint and clean!*

Louis took me into the dining room and he said in the tone of someone speaking to a mental patient, "I don't see a problem here and neither does Mye."

I thought for a minute. And then, as if channeling some strong source within me, I heard myself say, "No problem, Louis. I took photos on my cell phone of all the areas I have concerns about. I'll attach them in an e-mail to Daniel Wong, my real estate broker and to the condo board. You and Mye can leave now."

Louis became very quiet. He went over to Mye and said something in Chinese and she whispered something back.

Louis' unctuous smile transformed into his Big Bad Wolf smile, the one that says why-be-unpleasant-when-ultimately-I'll-be-having-your-grandmother-for-lunch. "Hey, why all the fuss?" he said. "Mye says she'll have someone in to clean and paint by next week."

Then Louis and Mye took their leave.

Sure enough, the next week, the walls were painted and the oven and sink were polished to a high shine. When Marina did her final walk-through, she was fully satisfied. And I felt like I was home at last.

CHAPTER TWENTY-TWO

Invited with My "And Guest" to A Wedding

Soon I was settled in my new place in the very town where I grew up. I thought that might have its advantages, in terms of re-discovering some old friends. Around this time, I got an invitation from my Milwaukee friend, Karen, who had helped me find my job.

One thing I dread as a singleton in my sageing years, is receiving a wedding invitation that reads "(my name) and Guest"! What if I don't have an "And Guest" in my life at the moment? Will I be punished by being seated at the *losers* table, next to my fellow dateless folks who won't be dancing the night away?

It seems to me, it doesn't matter if a woman is divorced, unmarried or widowed or without girlfriends to dance with, a woman without a partner at a wedding—or, at least, *I*, tend to feel like a "loser."

I can hide at the ceremony, as everybody is focusing on the bride and groom. But a wedding reception tends to celebrate coupledom, so even if I am beautifully coiffed and manicured and dressed in my best basic black, I feel I should be given a neon sign to hang around my neck that reads, "I FUCKED UP AND NOW I'M ALONE."

Yeah, sure, we gals can dance with each other, but unless I have a girlfriend there who I know well enough, or I see some woman bopping up and down seated nearby, it's tough to ask a stranger to dance. So, though I love dancing, I know it'll be a long night, wishing I was out on the floor with a date who wanted to fill my dance card.

When I was first invited to Rachel and Ryan's wedding, I thought I'd ask my son, Ben, to be my date. But, alas, when I mentioned it, it seemed that he was already busy that night. In retrospect, I don't recall telling him on *which night* the wedding was being held!

How would I get through the wedding alone? But then I remembered how Annie Oakley helped me survive the Psycho Motel, and I knew conjuring up that cowgirl-brave side of me was just what I had to do now. And just as I asked myself, "What would Annie do?" I began to hum her song, "I kin do anything better than you kin, I kin do anything better than you!" And, poof! I felt her presence, as if she was standing before me, toting her pistol and twirling her lariat.

"Annie," I said, "I love Karen and Marty. And I'm so honored to be invited to their children's wedding. I want to share this pivotal moment with them and I feel privileged to be asked. But, for me, it's so embarrassing to be a woman alone at a wedding."

Annie said, " Honey, you have two choices: Stay home like a pussy-footed coward or ignore the dumb-as-a-rock folks that think a woman without a man ought to be horsewhipped." And then, just to get me riled, she added, "A-course, a woman without a man ought to be ashamed to be seen at a weddin' or anywhere, donchathink?" She continued, "After all, what do you have to be ashamed of? I mean, you didn't murder your husbands. This wedding thing'll be a piece of cake. We'll go together and I do love me some cake!"

Even the cowardly side of me began to think, *There will be women there with husbands or partners, not because they are having a wonderful life together, but because it seemed too late to change things or because they had fears of poverty or loneliness*—I'd had those feelings myself when my couplings were no longer working. Though I couldn't have gone that route, I could truly understand.

I couldn't stay with a man who didn't treat me well or who no longer loved me or whom I no longer loved. And, thanks to my parents' support and good friends who showed up just when I needed them most, I was fortunate not to have to.

Annie, said, "Hey, Cowgirl, I'll be your 'And Guest" at this hoedown. We can do this thang!"

Her words buoyed me up, so I decided to go to the wedding.

I can get lost in a two-bedroom apartment, but the app on my phone can usually be counted on to take me anywhere. The ceremony was about an hour and a half away, on unfamiliar country roads, without counting the time I need to factor in for getting lost.

On the day of the wedding, I got my phone app all set to go. "Rockville, Illinois, wherever you are, here I come," I said, imagining Annie fussing about in the passenger seat, trying to get her seat belt snapped around her gun holster, which she never removes.

When I got there, the weather was perfect for an outdoor wedding. Not uncomfortably hot or too chilly or rainy and the sky was clear. The ceremony was simple and sweet. It was held on the grounds of a bed and breakfast. And because Karen and Marty are members of a religious Jewish community, many of the men sat on one side and the women on the other, in the Orthodox Jewish tradition. If some partners wanted to sit together, as they do in the Conservative or Reform Jewish traditions, they did. It seemed that the bride and groom and their parents carefully planned this occasion to be a comfortable blend of different cultural persuasions.

The seating was a godsend for the loners. Because many women sat alone or with women friends, I was spared sitting amongst all the hand-holding couples. I didn't have to hear as they reminisced about their own or their children's weddings, expressing amazement at how time had flown, while I stared down at my hands, biting back tears.

After the ceremony, the couples who sat separately, along with the ones who sat together, connected to take the short walk to the reception hall. I find these types of moments a particular challenge as a singleton. Picking up on my self-consciousness, Annie encouraged me to hold my head high. Was this happy occasion of the marriage of two like-minded souls going to be a time for me to be in my head, sorry for myself for not having a partner? And, Annie's face seemed to say, "No way, cowgirl!"

So, as we started down the hill, not shrinking behind other guests, but being among the first to be walking toward the reception, I marched down with Annie reminding me, "You got nothin' to be ashamed of, girl, bein' an independent woman. You walked, when you didn't like how you were treated, 'stead of hangin' onta' a man's coat-tails! Yer brave and yer strong and yer better off alone than bein' with a guy who ain't treatin' you right!"

Wisely, my friends had not set up the table where I was seated as the *Unchosen* table, but instead, with a great group of people. It seemed to me that, often, the strays at a wedding can be seated with other strays, but this time, one woman was the mother of the bride's best friend. She and her beau were in my age-range. There was a very attractive and personable married couple, and another guy, and, I think, someone he was either married to or dating. I couldn't hear his introduction over the band's rendition of "Celebration!" and the bustle of the reception, so I never really found out. Also at the table was a wonderfully Diane Keaton-as-Annie Hall dressed woman, in a white tuxedo, with her very straight black hair cut in a dramatic, angular bob.

I remembered the tuxedo-gal as the woman who gave the bridal shower at her home. I was told she was a widow and good friend of the bridal family.

I was relieved that my table seemed to be carefully thought out, or so it felt. I wasn't stuck next to some boring guy just because he was my age and single. I knew the woman with the boyfriend. The couple sitting next to me were from Peru and were friendly and interesting. I talked mainly to the husband who was sitting right next to me.

The woman from Peru told me she was acting in a film and her husband, who was a good conversationalist, was comfortable to talk to. He was enjoying talking to me, too. He was probably in his forties, about my sons' age.

Age has its advantages, among them, the feeling that nobody's mate would consider me a threat, almost as if attraction-wise, I was a total non-contender.

The woman I knew, whose name was Renee, was there with her fiancé, and she said, "Would you like to dance? I'll have Harv ask you." Which was nice, but, in my self-conscious state, her kind offer called attention to my awkwardness. I did dance with her fiancé, but I didn't want to take advantage of Renee's generosity, and I could see Harv was anxious to get back to his date.

I noticed the tuxedoed friend knew a lot of the people there and always seemed to have a dance partner. It occurred to me, I had my Annie and I could dance with her, if I could keep her away from raiding the sweets table.

I found a few things at the sweets table myself, and brought them back to my seat.

In her travels to greet the guests, the mother of the bride, my friend Karen, came around to my table. Leaning over me, she whispered, "You see that guy over there?" and she gestured with her eyes to a table to my left. "He's extremely shy, but he's a dear friend of Marty's and he is such a good person. Shall I introduce you?"

I said, "Won't it seem embarrassing to just walk over and introduce me?" I wasn't sure whether I meant embarrassing to him or embarrassing to me. But, Annie, popping a chocolate-covered strawberry in her mouth, prevailed, with a resounding (except the only person who could hear her was me), "Who cares, cowgirl?"

Karen and I walked over to this friend's table and Karen said, "Linda, this is Marty's oldest and dearest friend, Lenny, one of the best people I know." This was quite a recommendation, since Karen and Marty alone and together have the biggest kindest hearts around.

Lenny asked me to dance and then I sat with him for the rest of the evening, only returning to my table to get my handbag.

After a while of dancing and talking with Lenny, as Annie was scarfing down every sweet on the dessert-table, I glanced at my cellphone and realized it was nearly eleven. And it would take me quite a while on the dark country roads to drive back home.

I told Lenny, "Thanks for your company, but it's a long drive ahead for me, so I probably should leave." Then, I went back to retrieve my jacket and a hug from my Peruvian table-mates. I said my goodbyes to the bride and the groom and my friends, their parents, and I started to make my way out.

And Lenny, as sweet as Karen had said, called, "Wait!" and he accompanied me to my car and chivalrously offered, "I'll lead you to the highway, so you won't have to drive the one-lane roads in the dark alone."

Before I got in my car, I took a post-it note from my bag and wrote down my cellphone number. I said, "Call if you're in my neighborhood or want to get together again." I knew he lived way up in Northern Wisconsin, far from me, and Karen had earlier told me he was kind of a loner. I really just wanted him to know I appreciated his chivalry.

Unfortunately, I didn't think to ask for his number too, as I totally lost Lenny on the dark winding roads. But with my GPS and a number of wrong turns, eventually, I got back onto the highway.

Once on the highway, I realized my gas gauge was nearly on "empty." My fear kicked in. I thought, *Should I take the chance I could get home on the gas I have left? Wasn't there some kind of a reserve tank or something?* But, then, I countered that with, *Won't it be way worse if I run out of gas on the road?* I got off at the next exit's highway oasis.

I thought about getting myself "a little something to keep me awake" on the drive home, as a reward for showing up and even enjoying the wedding. Usually, my "reward" consists of a pint of Ben and Jerry's "Cherries Garcia," which I then scarf down (coincidentally, I keep a spoon in my car, just in case), only to suffer regret along with overwhelming nausea for the next twenty-four hours. I felt a little vulnerable, stopping at a rest stop or convenience store so late at night—a woman alone.

Then, Annie, who'd been dozing in the car, said, "Gimme a break! Let's jest git what we need n' hit the road, Cowgirl!" So, I filled up my tank, took a deep breath and checked to be sure my GPS was set for home.

Imagine me, I thought, *braving a wedding alone!* But, truth be told, with my inner cowgirl to count on, I wasn't alone at all. I peered over at the passenger seat at Annie, her face hidden by her Stetson, belted in, hunkered down, and snoring away for our journey home.

A week or so later, I did get a call from Lenny. We talked a couple of times after that, but he lived far away, so we'd have to feel connected enough to make the long drive to get together. And though he was a nice person and a very good dancer, and we'd both made the wedding a more enjoyable time for one another, our calls became fewer and eventually faded out altogether.

CHAPTER TWENTY-THREE

'Tis My Class Reunion

Shortly after my move to Skokie, I realized my high school class reunion was coming up. I'd attended a few when I could, but now, living in my hometown, I wouldn't have any reason to miss this one. Of course, going to my class reunion, as a two-time loser at marriage, not having achieved my stated Meryl Streepdom and having relocated more times than if I were in the FBI's Witness-Protection Program, might be challenging as well. But then who of us hadn't had our challenges in our lifetimes?

I felt as if going to my class reunion would make me feel blue about being alone and that I would envy those couples who'd made it through all the years, thick and thin, and were now sharing retirement and pensions and grandkids. *Life is so unfair*, I thought. And being a person of sensitive moods, once given a pity-pot trigger, I can, at times, get mired in an unrelenting (if temporary) funk-quicksand (not to mix my metaphors).

I wasn't a cheerleader or an athlete or a brain in high school, but since I'd gone to one or two reunions earlier on, some of the people who came to these things probably remembered me.

Ah, well, I thought. As Mark Twain once said, "Humor is tragedy plus time." Writing always cheers me up, so I wrote a not-so-great poem and then called my little group of friends (none of whom would be at the class reunion) to share a laugh over it:

My high school class of '64 will gather to imbibe
the merriment of reminiscence on the morrow.
When last we gathered, I was married; and now
I am alone.

A class reunion, without a lad, even one of advanced age,
yawning at our table, looking to make a run for it or standing
at the open bar all night,
Whilst I shared memories he had no knowledge of with my
classmates.

Every one of the Class of 64, would be now relatively
unrecognizable, were it not for the senior photo name badges
that would leave permanent holes in our lapels.
Unless, perhaps the badges were the brainstorm of our clever
Reunion Committee,

Sparing us the embarrassment of diminishing brain cells,
thinking we might not recall our own names, we could look at
our name tags to read them.

Seated at the jesters' table, I felt like a lobster, laid bare of her
shell; an oyster, bereft of her pearls. . . .or, at the very least,
some type of bottom-dwelling and undesirable sea creature.

Apparently, someone on the Reunion Committee fore chose a
seating plan, where the uncoupled women were seated with
men who were not devoid of wives,
but hadn't brought them to yet another festivity of olde,
especially the guys who had married much younger women
and were loathe to remind then of their own advanced years.

Had ever I dreamt of a life without a mate in my elder years?
I thinkst not.

Nevertheless, I have got it. . . . However, on the sunny side,
At least I am not on the list of classmates in attendance at the
Big Reunion in the Sky;
Though the food was probably better.

So, the weeks before the reunion, I fussed about what I would wear and how I would look and whether I should plan to go with a classmate who was herself a singleton.

I called my old high school BFF, Julie, who was divorced, so I'd have a friend of similar experience to hang out with. I even made a plan to rent a room at the reunion hotel, where we could have a post-reunion slumber party, sharing our friendship and memories, and feeling less lonely than if we'd each gone home alone. Though I lived in the area, Julie did not. So, I thought I'd book a night at the hotel and invite Julie to be my guest.

A slumber party as a reward for taking part in the class reunion—with the side benefit of sharing a room.

But, surprise, surprise! I got lost on the way to the hotel and Julie had to talk me in by cell phone.

Once my cell phone Waze-device said, "You have reached your destination," I saw Julie in front of the hotel, waving my car down like a taxicab. What a relief! As soon as she saw me, she pointed to valet parking.

After tipping the parking guy, I grabbed my overnight bag and Julie and I hugged. Next, since she'd already checked in, she directed me to our room, where I dropped off my bag and checked my lipstick and hair in the bathroom mirror. Then, the two of us set off to find the reunion room.

Passing the events at the Marriott that evening, there was the Posner-Chang wedding, the Midwest Toastmasters Association and the "Niles East High School Class of '64 Reunion."

Maybe it was me, but as I passed younger guests on my way to our meeting hall in The Sunshine Room, which ironically had no windows, I felt as if the younger hotel guests were staring at Julie and me, mumbling, *Look at those oldsters!*

I don't think Julie noticed anything at all. I know, I know, I've got to get over my self-absorption and the imaginary negative stories I make up in my head about what I think people are thinking, when they probably aren't thinking of me at all!

And then we rounded the corner, Julie and I, and I began to see older faces with nametags and senior pictures on their lapels, too.

Why, there was John Bergman (I could read his nametag with my peripheral vision while seemingly looking at his face). And over there, in a group of people chatting, was Susie Delaney, our former prom queen. She looked pretty much the same, slim and athletic. What I noticed was that people who might have snubbed or even bullied others in high school were so much more humble and friendly than the younger version of themselves.

On our tenth reunion and even our twentieth, people seemed to still be sharing their "wins," as they perceived them: "Look at me! Didn't I do well? I'm rich and successful, and my son is in a PhD/MD program at Harvard. Have you met my wife, Tiffany?" (Clearly Tiffany had not graduated with our class, though she might, possibly, be the classmate of the son at Harvard.)

Back then, some of my cohorts practically drove their Mercedes into the reunion lobby. Success, whatever that meant to us Baby Boomers at the time, was about status. But that was back in our thirties to our fifties. Now in our late-sixties, the game had completely changed. Now the conversations were about lost parents and siblings, even children, and how classmates, themselves, may have dealt with serious illness or death. The classmates who were left spoke about the subtler and deeper joys of happiness and health, longevity and the decency of our offspring.

Then, one of my female classmates warned me about our mutual classmate, Myron Robbins, telling me that he posted on the reunion website that he was looking for a wife and that he expected to find her at this reunion.

Sure enough, Myron found me in a group of reunion people and took me aside, saying he wanted to talk with me. He said, "You know in high school, all the guys had a crush on you."

I told him, "You must be thinking of somebody else. I was the chubby geeky girl who nobody even noticed!"

"Nope," he said. "I came here looking for you and I have something to give you." *Oh no,* I thought, *this could be embarrassing...* Yes, I'd been lonely, but I had already been lonely with men who didn't love me or whom I didn't love enough. If I ever reconnected again—it would have to be with someone who loved me and I loved him back. No offense to him, but Myron was not that someone.

Myron left for a few moments and returned with a pink rose, "For you," he said. Then, he spent far too long trying to convince me of his vast wealth. I must have been blushing, as there were people around, but I nearly fell off my seat when he said, "Will you marry me?"

It seemed to me that something was odd about a guy who was willing to propose marriage at a class reunion to a woman he hadn't seen for fifty years and had never really known at all. "Myron, I'm flattered, but you don't even know me. And if I ever do get married again, it will be to someone I know and am in love with and someone who knows and is in love with me. I'm talking about real love, not like when you have an illusion about who somebody is, with no evidence to go on. Then you meet their shadow side—and we all have one. I think that's what you are doing now. You are probably an amazing catch for some lucky girl back in Seattle (where he lived), but that's where I think you'll get to know someone who is a really good bet for you." Then I arranged the rose carefully in a half-finished glass of water someone must have left on the table, and, pointing to the rose, I said, "Thanks for thinking of me, but I'll pick this up later." And I went to rejoin the rest of the reunion crowd.

I am fascinated by stories, telling them, hearing them and am always interested in seeing how other people are living their real lives. However, much like posts on Facebook, people rarely share what they have been truly been going through, except with their closest friends and their therapists. And by this time in our lives, most of us had been through quite a lot.

We survived the 60's and made the transition from Free Love to Expensive Everything. A few of us were really, really wealthy. But most of us knew the health and financial and adult-child issues that tend to plague older people as our family constellations change and our relations don't necessarily feel the responsibility to help us, if we are their needier members.

I am always interested in the honest people, the ones who do share their story. Especially if it involves challenges and reinvention at a time we feel invented-out.

One member of my class, Lois, shared over a couple of drinks that her son suicided, having to do with untreated bi-polar disorder. And I shared that I was feeling exceptionally lonely.

She saw me with Myron and, looking over at him, said that, for all his supposed money, the word was that he and his ex-wife had a contentious divorce. Then, Lois had a brainstorm, "Why don't I fix you up with a friend of our family?" He'd been supportive to her and her husband during the difficult times following the loss of their son. I was thinking a nice guy to date with a personal recommendation might definitely be welcomed, if he wasn't a work-in-progress. I mean, we're all works-in-progress and we all have our "mishagoss" (Yiddish for eccentricities, crazinesses). It's just that some of us have more mishagoss than I'd be okay with in a potential partner.

Then Lois said, "I'm going to check with our friend, but he may be a nice man for you. He's a widower," she said. "Just be careful not to fall in love with him." And that made me curious. *Who was this unattached male who is so desirable that women fell in love with him right and left?*

And as I socialized with my friends Julie and Lois and others and we girls danced together, I had a really good time at the reunion—and I wanted to thank Myron, who I saw talking to another single woman classmate, and as I got closer, in order to say goodbye and thanks for the rose, I heard him telling her about having a crush on her in high school, too. So, I simply left his pink rose for his next prospect and waved goodbye.

It was a nice reunion, after all, and I wasn't the only one who was alone in my late-sixties. Julie and I found one another and returned to our room. We ordered a bottle of wine from room service. We had a lot of laughs, reminiscing about the time in our junior year of high school when we got lost in Peoria. I guess I don't have to say who was driving.

CHAPTER TWENTY-FOUR

The Heart Attack First Date

One of the advantages of living in my old hometown was that I had former high school and college friends who lived there too. The friend I reconnected with at the class reunion, Lois, who also warned me about Myron, set me up with Mel, a friend of hers and her husband's. She said she would give him my phone number, but she cautioned, "You'll probably fall in love with him, but be patient. Mel's kind of a commitment-phobe."

Commitment? At my age? I really wasn't sure what commitment might look like at this point in my life —The gravesite next to his is already taken? Should we continue to date, would we need to promise to keep our respective pensions for our kids? And I wasn't even sure how to go about this relationship thing again, should we happen to mutually like one another. And, here, Mel and I hadn't even met.

I mean, back in the day, there were only a couple of goals we girls had around dating. Usually, they were the following: *Do I want this guy as a boyfriend?* Or, *Would I want this guy to be the father of my children?* These days, my goals changed to having a guy friend as dinner company and a partner for dancing or having a boyfriend I can trust to be exclusive while he is my boyfriend, so that we can add sleeping together to our cache of fun things to do.

And much as I have whined about being lonely, wouldn't I miss my having-it-my-way life? The dirty little secret we single women have is that if we have any resources, when we want to do something, go someplace, spend something, however unwise, we can do it and enjoy it and not worry about what anybody thinks. I liked that I could eat pizza for breakfast and oatmeal for supper or put a dent on my

Visa card the size of a Hummer and no husband would be lecturing me about it.

This is the stuff our grandmas, our mothers or our favorite aunts never told us about, when they were praying that we would find a loving (and, even, prosperous) husband who only drank at weddings and Bar Mitzvahs, so that we could produce a little cherub for them to cuddle.

The hard part of living alone is being lonely, but if you have cable TV and/or Netflix, the selection of movies and shows are endless and, thank God, so many of the characters we find there are in much worse shape than we are.

Another plus: think of the time I save *not thinking* about how to change some guy. No need to come up with ways to help him cut down on his beers, eat something that *isn't* fried or keep any gas-passing relegated to the bathroom.

And, another piece is having and making friends; people to be there when you needed a ride to the airport or your car broke down, people to do things with, because it "doubles the pleasure" (like in the old Doublemint gum TV commercial) in that you were sharing the experience with someone else. When gals have a man in their lives, the man tends to take up the time we would be sharing with friends.

I could finally be all about me, moi, myself—-without guilt or blame because I had no partner to care for nearby. But, I guess everything in life has its trade-offs. Even as an "older woman," now in my late sixties, I still had a vague dream that I would meet the right guy.

The whole "relationship thing" at *my age*, an age which _I_ think of as a plus, many men think of as, "Eek, it's my mother!" Or, "If *I'm* with *her*, this means *I'm* old! NOOO!!!"

For me, when dating was fun, it was like that Carly Simon song before she sold it to Heinz Ketchup; it's all in the (please hum along if you know the tune) *An-tic-i-pa-tion*.

In a dating-situation, even as a Sager, I am filled with the same hopeful anticipation I was when I was sixteen, primping for the prom. Of course, this is before I know that my date might look less well than my Uncle Sid on his deathbed or that he's soooo boring that he could sell his droning story as an alternative to sleep meds. Before meeting a fellow, especially if he's been introduced by friends, I could hold out hope that my date would be an attractive, yet not entirely self-absorbed man, masculine, but in a quiet, chivalrous, kind-hearted and generous way.

And what woman couldn't do with some lovemaking or the fantasy of finding her true love even at this point in her life?

Interesting for me, was that if I told my friends or my sister I was cast, along with Dame Judi Dench, in the third version of "Best Most Exotic Marigold Hotel" or that my book was about to make the New York Times Best Seller List, then to become a Gengi Cohen-produced television blockbuster (Gengi Cohen? Producer of "Weeds" and "Orange is the New Black"?)—all of them would be happy for me. But never did I get as much interest from the people I knew, as I did when they heard the following words: "I have a date" or "I'm seeing someone."

The Dad-in-my-head would say, "Don't chase the boys, let the boys chase you." Marina (my very practical Russian-American friend and condo-rental neighbor) told me, "Do whatever you feel and if you like him, go after him. I did that with Mischa." (And they are happily married for around thirty years.)

The thing is that, with the exception of not getting any exercise, I tried to remain youthful for my age—-Still, I wondered if this might be my last chance in this life to make love or, as my friend Elaine Soloway wrote in her blog, to be *adored*. Okay, I was a failed-feminist for it. I'll have to live with that.

And yet, invariably, for me, the dating site thing never seemed to work. And I was way past the point of dumbing-down so as not to threaten an insecure guy. Or to worry about whether to call him or not to call him. Did I really still have the mental or physical energy for all that?

I had my own important goals and less time left in my life to achieve them. So, I didn't want to fritter away my time on some guy who wasn't a good fit for me anyway.

I wanted a life-partner and if I couldn't have that, I wanted to be invited to couples' gatherings, to be able to go to movies on Saturday night with a date (Okay, okay! So I'll turn in my National Organization for Women Card!), to get special attention for birthdays and someone to share holidays with and to care whether my plane landed yet. As Aretha Franklin sings, I wanted to feel like a *natural woman*. (And, *please go away* if you don't know who Aretha is!)

Getting back to Mel, eventually, he called and we made a date. At least I had a friend who knew him and what she said about him made me curious enough to want to meet him.

On the Sunday night of our date, my buzzer rang at exactly 7:30, the appointed time for our meeting. And I fiddled with the buzzer to let him in, but eventually gave up and took the elevator down to the building's door to let him in.

He looked nothing like my uncle Sid on his deathbed. He actually turned out to be an attractive guy with a good sense of humor. We left for our dinner.

We both ordered the broiled whitefish and he wasn't boring or a braggart when he talked about himself. He actually seemed to be paying attention when I talked about myself, too.

And when the check came, he gallantly paid it. I didn't know his financial circumstances, but I find it generous when a guy pays for my meal.

Sidebar: *Being poor* is different from *being cheap*. Cheap is a soul-disease. Cheap says: I can <u>afford</u> to pay for both of us, but I am saving my money for *me*. Ehhw!!!! Not so attractive a quality. (Advice to guys without a lot of dough: Just tell the woman in advance of a date, "I'd love to take you to dinner, but I don't have much money, so we'll have to make do with meeting over a cup of coffee or a glass of wine." If she balks, you've separated the womanhood equivalent of the wheat from the chaff. But, if, when the dinner bill comes, you tell her you left your wallet at home, you can expect that you'll never see her again, *and* she is likely to tell her friends that you are a dickwad!)

After a pleasant meal and some good conversation, Mel came back to my apartment because I trusted him. He was a friend of friends of mine.

And he behaved like a perfect gentleman, acting interested, but not grabbing at me. (Ben Franklin said something along the lines of *have an affair with an older woman, they are so grateful.* That may be somewhat true; but go fly a kite in a lightning storm, my bespectacled and very dead friend, if a guy isn't respectful!)

So, Mel and I were back at my place, having a conversation about I-forget-what and my cellphone rang. I told Mel I would ignore the call because I was trying to set appropriate boundaries with my therapy clients.

Although, truth be told, were I alone, I would probably have answered it, just in case someone was going through a crisis. I know. I'm a sucker.

A few moments later, I heard the whoosh of a text on my cellphone. Yikes! It was not a client, it was my neighbor, Dina, from across the hall! "Emergency!" she texted, "I think I'm having a heart attack!"

I texted back, "I'm coming to your door right now! And we'll get Marina and Mischa to check you out!" I excused myself and stepped across the hall. When she opened her door, I read her the text that Marina sent in answer to the one I sent after getting Dina's plea for help. "Five minutes away," Marina's text said. Dina and I knew that Marina and Mischa are registered nurses. Mischa actually specialized in cardiac care.

Dina came to the door in her robe and slippers, looking terrified. I ushered her into my apartment and told her to sit her down on the couch. She had already taken an aspirin, the universal helper for a burgeoning heart attack. Then I introduced Dina and Mel.

In what seemed like a flash, like a team of paramedics, Marina and Mischa arrived at my door, medical bags in hand. I introduced them to Mel.

Marina knelt down in front of Dina to take her blood pressure, while Mischa sat on a chair directly across from Dina. I could see he was carefully observing her. Both spoke in their very calmest voices. Mischa asked questions about any medications Dina might be taking and what made her think she was having a heart attack.

At the same time, Marina took Dina's blood pressure for the second time. Marina looked up from her blood pressure cuff and reported to Dina, "Your blood pressure has gone from 160 (which is high, but not call-an-ambulance high) to 140. Much better."

Both Marina and Mischa agreed that Dina was most likely not having a heart attack, but Mischa suggested, "Maybe you should go to the E.R. and get an EKG, just so you can sleep tonight."

Mel, trying to lighten things up, said, "Yeah, let's grab a bottle of wine and all go with Dina!" Everybody laughed, but it wasn't such a bad idea. I could picture us all in a clown car, arms and legs akimbo, howling with laughter, driving to the nearest hospital.

In a matter of minutes, Dina reported feeling better.

I said, "Dina, you can sleep over here, just so you won't worry," adding, "Mel's about to leave anyway. We both have to get up early tomorrow."

Dina said, "I really feel better, so I'm going back to my place and getting right in bed." Looking relieved, she went back across the hall. And Marina and Mischa went back down the hall to their place.

Mel was getting ready to go, but as I walked him to my front door, I was facing Dina's door, which was directly opposite mine. So I said softly, "I wonder how Dina is feeling?"

And Mel, who it was clear was being a goofball, whispered, "Why don't we ask her?" and he gestured with his fist like he was about to pound loudly on her door, as he whispered, "I'm comin', Elizabeth!" which was a line from the old Redd Foxx television show, where Redd plays a widower, who, at any sign of trouble, would hold his chest with one hand and reach up with the other to his dead wife, yelling, "I'm comin', Elizabeth!"

Okay, all of this was not much fun for Dina, who, by the way, turned out to be fine. She told me later the next day that she went for an electrocardiogram and a stress test and the outcome was that she was healthy.

Yet, it was such a sweet evening, partly thanks to her.

I don't mean I knew whether I liked Mel as a boyfriend or even a friend yet or that I enjoyed Dina's frightening experience. But, for me, when we were all there together, Dina and Marina and Mischa and Mel and me, it felt like I was in the middle of a caring community, right here on the third floor of my rented condominium. That was when I realized that community was a big part of what I'd been searching for since I left my parents' home and my kids grew up and left mine.

Marina and I had a five-dollar bet going: I bet her I wouldn't hear from Mr. Commitment-phobe again. She bet I would. I didn't really care about the five bucks or about Mel. I just felt all warm and fuzzy, that I had a kind of a family right there on the floor where I lived.

I won the bet with Marina. I guess it was instinct, but I kind of knew he wasn't looking for someone to date, or at least he wasn't looking for me. Marina's such a generous sweetie, that I never reminded her of our bet. And she was too kind to ask me if Mel ever called. She knew I would tell her if he did.

Thinking it through, even better than a call from Mel, I now knew that though some women never had this I-Am-Nothing-Without-A-Man imprint, for me to feel I was just fine by myself was an enormous growth step. Here, I felt, not isolated, but with important heart-connections to others that gave me a sense of joy and community right here in my building.

CHAPTER TWENTY-FIVE

Happy Trails to Me

It's said that all good things must come to an end. Just as I was getting comfortable in my rental condo, one day in late November, I got a call from Louis Chen. "Mye has to sell the condo," her realtor informed me.

"What?" I said, not quite sure that I heard him correctly.

"Yes, she needs the money, so she has to sell the condo."

"But. . . .but Louis, I just moved in…I just decorated. . . ." I said, my eyes welling with tears. "Where will I live?"

"She needs you out by June 1st, the latest," Louis snapped.

"So, wait. I pay rent since last June, move my furniture in and decorate in July, start living here in September and am fully furnished in November. And now, in almost December, after I've prettied the place up, Mye is giving me a few months to be out?"

"Sorry," said Louis, sounding not one bit sorry. Then he said, as if the two of us were cooking up a scheme he just thought up for my benefit, "Maybe, if you can move before your contract is up, I can get Mye to give you not only your deposit back, but a little incentive money, like a few thousand dollars."

I needed the money, but where would I live? All that packing and moving. This was going to be the third time in as many years. I felt sick to my stomach. It wasn't easy to find this place. How would I do it again? Here, once I got Mye's condominium all ready for showing on my dime, she was flipping it. I wondered, *Had she and Louis Chen been planning this all along?*

I called Olivia, who said she'd start looking for another place for me immediately. She suggested, "Why don't you make an offer on the condo?" But I told her, "I don't have the money."

"Well," she said, trying to console me, "maybe they'll make it worth your while, like sometimes owners will give a renter a cash bonus to move earlier."

I was devastated.

When I told Marina, she said, "Find another condo in the building. I know there must be some for rent."

I told her, "The rent is high and who's to say this won't happen again next year?" Plus, it occurred to me that the main thing I really loved about living in the condo was having Marina and Mischa right down the hall.

It took some time for the news to sink in, but then, over the next few weeks, my dark mood lifted and I began to deal with the situation on hand, however imperfect. I do find that once I take action, whether it works out or not, I feel less helpless or victimized. I said to myself, *This is hardly the end of the world. There are women all over the world just trying to survive and not to be raped or stoned on the streets. How dare I complain!*

And so, I formulated a new plan: I would stop acting like a baby about what one of my friends would call White People Problems, and with my sister's permission, I'd put all but a few essentials in storage and live with her till I found something of my own. Ugh, how I hated the thought of being dependent on or beholden to anybody, even my sister or my children.

In the next months, Olivia and I looked all over the northern suburbs of Chicago for a place. No, a tiny apartment close to work wouldn't do, I'd be too lonely, far away from the friends I moved to be closer to. A fancy rental with a pool would be expensive, and it felt too much like an Independent Living Center that had a nursing home conveniently next door. And, since I'd been burned renting this condo, another condo rental would make me feel too vulnerable. After all, who's to say its owner might not decide to sell again in the same way Mye had.

Not finding anyplace even close to resembling what I wanted, I signed a contract with a nearby storage facility and started putting aside work items and the things I would need to take to my sister's for immediate use, like clothes and toiletries.

I was totally resigned to sleeping on my sister's couch till I could find a place to live, when I got an unexpected call from Olivia. She said, bubbling with excitement, "I found just the place for you."

Exhausted from all the condos, apartments, luxury buildings and townhomes we traipsed to every weekend and some weeknights, I was certain we would be wasting our time. Still, I begrudgingly planned to meet Olivia the following Sunday at this rental she thought was so perfect for me.

At the appointed time, I drove to an attractive apartment complex in Highland Park, a suburb only twenty minutes from where I was now, and I parked, but I didn't see Olivia's car.

Then Olivia called on my cell, "Hey, I just saw your car drive by. I'm out on the front porch at the house west of you and across the street."

"House?" I replied. "I don't want a house, that would be too big for just me and probably much too expensive."

Olivia said, "Nope. This one looks just like you. It's charming and, I'm told, the second floor is rented to some lovely tenants, a very sweet and quiet family. The price seems like something you could handle and it has a garage and an indoor washer and dryer."

Sure enough. Once I turned my car into the driveway and stepped inside, it was love at first sight. A house with a fireplace and wainscoting, the longed-for washer and dryer in the basement and a detached garage with an automatic garage door opener.

"I'll take it," I said.

The week after the new contract was signed and I moved out of Mye's condo, Louis Chen and I met at a Starbucks, so that I could collect the $3,500 he promised in exchange for making special arrangements to be out of my condo well before the contract was up.

Louis sat at a table, holding an envelope, which was to contain my promised incentive money. When I opened the envelope, it held a check, not for the promised $3,500, but for $3,000.

"What about the additional $500 you and Mye promised me?" I asked.

Louis responded, "Mye is in a terrible place financially right now. She will have it to you as soon as she can."

Once I moved out, Mye and Louis sold my former condo for a pretty price. I never heard from either of them again.

With Mye, I was "judging a book by its cover." When I first saw her, I had assumed she was sweet and naïve. But I soon learned that there are bad apples in every bunch. I think poet John Ciardi said it best, "Beware the power of the victim." Or, as Rabbi Hillel once wrote, "If they're on their side and you're on their side, who's on your side?"

CHAPTER TWENTY-SIX

The Queen of Failure

Before I found my new home, I had a whole other confidence crisis to deal with. I sent three of my stories to Chicago's version of "The Moth," where people submit their real-life stories and, if their stories are accepted, the writers get to read those stories aloud in a cozy Chicago wine bar.

All three of my submissions got rejected. And so began my inner-critic. *You are a Failure: failed marriage/s, failed writer, failed money manager/moneymaker, failed mother.* (My boys-who-are-now-men live far away: *Is it something I've done wrong or not done when I should have?*) *Yes, I've done it* all *wrong!!!,* screamed my heartless inner Cruella Deville. *You are, in fact, the* Queen *of Failure!*

My sister and I dub our shared tendency to let one disappointment create a plethora of negativity, "lumping". Nine good things can be going on in our lives, but the tenth—in my case, the rejection from Chicago's storytelling venue—had me tapping into my often dormant, but now awakened, feelings of negativity.

You know what I'm talking about? For me, I believe these feelings came partly from my attention deficit disorder before it was a thing. Back when teachers and peers just thought I was "lazy" or "a daydreamer." (To their credit, my parents loved me anyway, though I don't know how I would have fared if I were a boy, expected to earn a living in the world, rather than, as the culture then believed, to marry someone who would do it for me.)

In the fifth grade and beyond, a girl could get along not doing well in school or anything, *if* she was cute and/or popular. I was neither.

I looked like a schmoo, a funny-papers cartoon character created by Al Capp, the cartoonist who became well-known for his "Lil Abner" comic strip. Schmoos had roly-poly, pear-like appearances.

In addition, I was unremarkable in any way—straight "C-minus" student with no recognizable or marketable talent in anything that anyone might notice.

Thus, when I received my rejection e-mail from Chicago, my inner-Queen reemerged in all her horribility. At these times, the tubby childhood-nerd would bring out my inner-Queen, wearing her "loser" robes and sporting her baby-fat coat, the words, "Oh, Just Give Up Already" etched in her brain. After the no-go-Chicago e-mail , I heard the familiar refrain of the Queen. *You're too old. It's too late. What were you thinking to even try?* It was as if this latest rejection and all that lumped in with it put the final shovelful of dirt on my attitude coffin.

And so, as usually happens when I am really feeling down, I was hearing the siren song of my drug of choice: binge-eating (and we're not talking carrot sticks here!). And I happened to be driving. But, before I got out of the car, I heard the faint sound of my alter-ego, "I kin do anything better than you kin. I kin do anything better than you." And I knew it was Annie, and hearing her confident voice, I knew enough to grab my cell phone and call for reinforcements.

"Mary?" I whined into my cell, relieved to find my own emotional 911 at home. Then I parked, locked the car, and cell phone in hand, grabbed a shopping cart from in front of the store, and I, as if possessed by demonic spirits, compulsively made my way into Trader Joe's.

I can't just talk to anyone about feeling down when I do, because as a therapist, I'm not supposed to have the same problems and feelings that everybody in the world has from time to time. I'm not expected to have the questions, I'm expected to have the *answers*— and I sometimes do, for people who are not *me*.

Mary and I have been through one another's heartbreaks and periodic downer days for years. She gets it. She doesn't judge. She's a good listener. She even asks the pertinent therapeutic questions. Mary asked, "Are you eating right?"

I answered, "No."

Mary asked, "Are you hydrating enough?"

I answered, "No."

Mary asked, "Are you exercising?"

I answered, "Do you *know* me?"

Another friend might say, "Well, then, what do you expect?" And this was precisely why I did not call another friend, because that response was just what I did not need to hear.

But Mary didn't lecture. She didn't laugh. She simply let me vent.

"Mary, I think with all my attempts to earn a living as a therapist and still write and develop my radio gig, my couple of Chicago tries being rejected brought me to my wit's end! So, today, for lunch, I ate two bags of Cheese Nibs, which I don't even *like,* with a side of jumbo Snickers bar! And I called because, despite feeling nauseous, I was about to top it all off with a dinner pint—possibly a quart—of Ben and Jerry's Cherries Garcia at Trader Joe's!"

Mary said quietly, "Trader Joe's doesn't carry Ben and Jerry's."

I can always count on Mary for sound shopping advice and assistance. One fall, she combined a Boston Store sale with her " 'seniors' discount" and some newspaper coupons to help me buy a fifteen dollar navy pea-coat! Fifteen dollars! And to this day, I still use that pea- coat.

I continued, "Also, I have to pack fast, though I've found a rental to live in, because Mye wants me out by the end of the month and I'm overwhelmed." By this time, I'd reached the freezer department.

Mary said, "Well, while you consider how to get it all done, would you want to make a salad for yourself for dinner?"

At this point, I passed the "Healthy Dinners" section and begrudgingly plopped a gluten free "light" frozen ziti dinner into my cart. Here, I noticed that my jonesing for ice cream was slowly easing up.

Then, wheeling my cart over to the fruits and vegetables section, I picked up a pre-packaged salad, since salads are things I tend to be uninspired to make myself. Once among the fruits and veggies, I spotted the Cara-Cara oranges, and recalled that their sweet-tooth killer flavor tends to end my cravings for more sugary items. So, I plopped a few of the oranges in my cart.

I breathed deeply into the phone. "I think I feel better," I said to Mary, as I found my way to the check-out line.

Mary asked, "Should we talk on your way home?"

And I answered, "No, I think I'm pretty okay now."

When my inner Queen of Failure emerges, I have to reach out for help to remain encouraged and focused.

Hope is all I need—and sometimes because I can't always seem to find it within myself, I call for support. I've come to the conclusion that the biggest strength a person can have is to realize that they can't do it alone and that asking for help is not a weakness, but a strength.

After all, who's to say the therapy work I love won't become more than a passion, but an important financial asset in my future? Or that my radio essays won't get aired somewhere again?

It's even possible that these writings might get published and that people will read it and be helped by it; that I could add to some positive changes that are well overdue for older women with my little musings. I could even envision a television show. *Gray is the New Groovy,* I thought, as I laughed at my little fantasy.

I don't need the certainty, just the possibility that a dream could happen. And, even if I eat right, drink plenty of water, have a wonderful space to live, enough money to live on without worrying, my kids are all right, and I have a partner to love me, I will always need that hope.

Some of my dreams may become realities and others may just be intriguing ideas I'm following. But to park the tiara of Failure Queen, I need my possibilities—and a friend to talk me through the dark moments till I believe that, even if some of my dreams change, that some could actually happen.

As I settled myself down, no Ben and Jerry's in hand, and about to continue the journey toward my place, I pulled over into a strip mall and grabbed my cell phone to share my insight about possibilities with Mary.

CHAPTER TWENTY-SEVEN

A Tale of Two Sisters

My younger sister and I text one another often throughout the day. We are both therapists with busy practices, both writers who are writing in our non-therapy-hours. So, the way we maintain our relationship is by text. But, one day in February, I got this call from her. Usually, when I get a call from my sister, it's something important. I felt like saying, like the Olympia Dukakis character in *Moonstruck*, "Who died?" I picked up. Sue took a moment, then she said, "Lin, I found a lump in my breast."

I swallowed in shock, and automatically said that annoying thing people always say when you tell then something frightening. "It's probably nothing." Although, the tears welled up as I recalled, *Uh oh, several of our cousins and aunts had breast cancer. Some had lumpectomies. Some had mastectomies. And some died.*

Sue took a breath. "The doctor scheduled a biopsy."

Then, trying to hide the tears, I asked, "When?"

Sue said, "In two weeks."

"When did all this start?" I asked.

Sue said, "I didn't want to alarm you, so I didn't tell you till I knew for sure. I found the lump in my breast myself. Right afterwards, I scheduled a mammogram. Then, the radiologist scheduled an ultrasound and an MRI, which confirmed that I probably had cancer and that it was very likely caught early, but that I needed a needle biopsy followed by a lumpectomy."

Hold the phone! I thought. *I'm not ready to lose my sister*! The wells of tears I was holding back overflowed and streamed like a tiny river over my cheeks and down the hollows of my face.

Susan is my baby sister. My only sibling. The brown-eyed curly-headed kid whose birth de-throned me from my princessly only-child position. And, though I long held a grudge about that, she is very, very dear to me. She holds my past, accompanied me through my childhood, and shares both my taste and my sizes in clothes and shoes.

She was with me in New York when my first husband proposed. She was the one holding down the fort on that Chanukah/Christmas where I left my own party to go to meet Isaac Bashevis Singer, and she was there when, years later, wearing new glasses, I tripped on the steps of my then apartment with Noel in Milwaukee, and stood up and saw her face looking in horror at my bloody and bruised face.

As happens to me when I am in shock, scenes from the past flew through my head.

"The Sister's Song," I wrote for us when I was ten years old, she was five and we shared a bedroom:

My verse, sung to her, "Do you love me?"

Sue's verse, sung to me, "Yes, I do."

Sue, "Do you love me?"

Me, "Yes, I do."

Sue and I, together, "We both love each other because we're sisters. Mwah, mwah, mwah!"

Okay, so it's not quite ready for the Grammies, but, hey, I was only in fifth grade.

The time I lived in Highland Park, New Jersey and she lived in Highland Park, Illinois and we talked our way through the bombing of Israel together. (Israel is not our homeland, but as Jews, we do know if the world history of anti-Semitism were to repeat itself, Israel is the one place that would take us.)

We shared the awful time our mother had a stroke and we both dealt with it in our own ways. She by keeping maniacally busy. Me, the out-of-towner, staying daily at my mother's hospital bed, knowing that Sue would be left, along with our father, with the primary responsibilities once I left.

Then there was the time our parents were living in independent living with a private caregiver, and we discovered their caregiver was threatening them with, "If you lose *me*, you're going to a nursing home."

This was a particularly cruel and totally untrue taunt from their live-in nursing assistant, who I'll call Renata. And we did what our cousins came to call "Commando Sisters," where we got Renata out and had her replacement ready all in the same day.

Her painful divorce. My painful divorces. 9/11.

Visiting our cousin Sarri in Champaign, Illinois, where she was experiencing the signs of Peck's Disease, an Alzheimer's-like brain deterioration disorder, which took her brilliant mind and eventually, her very life. Susan and I wanted to give her husband, Randy, who was caring for Sarri at home, a break to play golf and not worry about our cousin.

We held hands through all the funerals. Those of our beloved parents. Our dear aunts and uncles. Our same-age or even younger cousins.

Happy times, too. Her meeting her fiancé. I remember going together, Sue's fiancé Barry and Susan and I, to our Auntie Shirley's funeral.

Shirley's daughter, Cousin Ellen's husband, Jack, addressed the mourners, as we three—Susan and Barry and I—stood huddled together, freezing, on one of those miserable, snowy and blustery artic-cold Chicago winter days.

Jack started the eulogy, "Shirley was a loving and generous person. Very likely, most of you here have one of her crocheted afghans."

As we stood there shivering, Barry whispered, "Would that we could have one of those afghans *now*," lightening the mood.

Sue inviting me along when I was without a partner to accompany me.

Us two, driving together to the neighborhood where we used to live on the South Side of Chicago, which changed into a scary gang-shooting type place. She could be fearless. Much more so than me.

We are different, my sister and I, and yet also alike. Once we got accused of cheating on the game, "Apples to Apples," where one player has to guess who thought up a particular answer. She knew my quirky sense of humor and I knew hers so well, almost telepathically, because no one else knows me quite the way she does.

She's not quite the ruminator I am, picturing worst case scenarios and horrible outcomes. And though we are Jewish, she leans toward Kabbalah for her spirituality, while my practice is more "Booish", as my children call it—being a combination of Buddhist and Jewish.

She told me, after the needle biopsy, "My doctor said, 'You have cancer. Now we need to find out where it is and how extensive.'" In my head, I was (gulp) screaming, "*Noooo! My baby sister, this can't be real!*"

I suppose we all live with the fantasy that we will outsmart disease and death. My sister's diagnosis changed that fantasy for me. I knew one of us was likely to outlive the other, but I thought that would be her, not me. It still could be her that lived longer. I hoped so.

She told me not to tell anyone. But I needed my supports too. After all, she had her partner, her children, her friends, some of them breast cancer survivors, and her entire Kabbalah group of thousands, praying for her. So, I told my friend, Mary.

Then in my mind, I went through the ambivalence of a shared childhood. Was I a good sister to her? I teased her and excluded her many times in my own semi-depressed, chubby, attention deficit miserableness. But I can't complain about her. I think she probably admired me, perhaps just because I was the older sister.

"Now what happens?" I texted her, once I collected myself.

"Now we wait for the outcome of the surgical biopsy and hope that we caught it early enough and they get it all." she texted back.

For me, aside from calling and texting and seeing my sister more often, I scheduled to see my doctor the following Monday. I won't be dragging my feet about my mammogram and self-exams anymore. A self-exam is how she found her lump. I even scheduled genetic testing, which predicts the likelihood of BRCCA-genes, reported to be inherited, especially in certain groups such as Ashkenazi Jewish women. The test turned out I was clear. My sister got tested, too, and she was clear as well. Good signs for us both.

I was with her the morning she awaited her operation. She'd been told by her surgeon that the pathologists found from the needle biopsy that hers was likely a Stage One cancer, the kind if caught early can be removed with a lumpectomy. But she was also told that they couldn't be sure until she had a surgical biopsy and definitive results.

She was so brave. She told me, "If I die. . . ." and went on to detail how she wanted us to pull the plug if her brain was dead. And that she figured Barry, being a lawyer, would be more capable of that than me, so she signed that he had Power of Health Care for her. Then, I sat in the waiting room of the hospital, along with Sue's close friend, Carol, and many other people waiting for mothers and fathers and siblings and children to be wheeled out of surgery.

After a couple of hours, I wasn't sure how many, when the operation was over, her doctor came out to speak to us. He took us aside to a small room inside some glass doors and separate from the waiting area. He told us, "We did a lumpectomy and took a couple of glands, just to test them and be sure. But it's good news. The frozen section shows that the lump was malignant, but it was in its earliest stages and I'm sure we got it all. The pathology department will examine the tissue and should confirm this by next week."

It was all I could do not to jump for joy! Literally! The three of us hugged and cried and waited for Sue to be wheeled into the recovery room.

After the surgery, my sister rested at home for a short time. Then she saw the oncologist and the radiologist. She was ordered to have radiation treatments, but no chemo after the surgery. I was so relieved!

She went through the surgery so bravely, my little sister. And in a very short time, she got to a point where she was having her mammograms and her sonograms just once a year. And none of them showed abnormalities.

I am so grateful that I still have my sister to share things with— bad and good, as we always did and still do. But, whew! Cancer sure puts things in perspective.

CHAPTER TWENTY-EIGHT

Homage to A Bodhisattva

Just when I am feeling overwhelmed with the "poor me's," there is one thing that, even more than cancer, can put it all in perspective: Death. (Wait, wait! Come back!) I know, we Westerners live in denial of it, but as my Aunt Alice used to say, "How bad could it be? It happens to everyone."

Here in my story of living through my sager years, I have not yet dealt with something that may never have occurred to us before this particular time of life. I have been in denial about the losses we experience as we age—-in particular, I have neglected to mention Death.

A little while back, my younger-by-twelve-years cousin Judy died. Yes, she had been sick, but all of us in the family believed that she would get better.

She had what people in-the-old-days used to call "The C Word." The world I grew up in treated "The Big C" as if it were a curse followed by imminent death. Things have changed for many cancers in our time. Back then, there was shame connected with having The C. Perhaps it was thought that cancer was contagious or inherited, or that news of it in the family would make the rest of us unmarriageable. Or it might have been superstition that silenced any talk of the disease, the belief that if you didn't talk about something, it didn't really exist and thus it could certainly never happen to you or someone you loved.

The amazing thing about my cousin was the truthful and open way she coped with her C. Here she was dealt what was often considered by others to be an ugly fate, but she transformed it into a lesson—a meditation on the preciousness of living and dying—

without leaving out the painful feelings and physical challenges she suffered.

So that, even through her losses, possibly because of these anticipated losses, she mindfully embraced the "little things" that aren't so little, the beauty in life that, many times, most of us can take for granted.

As my cousin Judy Sue ("The Other Cousin Judy," as she calls herself) said to me, "Judy must not have had the anxiety and depression gene that you and I share!" My cousin wrote her poetic and profound blog, "Word of Mouth," right up until her last days. In it, she documented her experience of hope and loss, never seeming to feel sorry for herself. In this way, Judy gifted those of us left behind with the legacy of courage and gratitude.

These blog entries became her voice when she could no longer speak. They became her way to connect with family and friends; when, though we longed to, we couldn't see or support her.

She wrote of the bud vases she created out of miniature apricot juice bottles and the loveliness of her garden and of the antics of Audrey, her cat. And she shared the joy she felt in carefully preparing a meal for guests, even after she herself could no longer eat solid food. She shared how she would put a little of her much-admired chicken soup or banana bread into the juicer, so that she could taste some of what she prepared along with her guests.

She spoke of her daily walks around the neighborhood and admitted (you can just see her impish smile here) guiltily plucking a lemon off a neighbor's many-lemoned tree. She reported that, just as she did, the lemon tree owner drove up in her car and yelled at her.

Now, if on a California summer day, you saw a woman with a pad and pen strung around her neck, atop a brightly colored scarf, my guess is you might take a moment, during which you might understand that possibly this woman had a challenging difficulty and that you could, perhaps, spare a lemon for such a person.

Judy blogged that she could not resist the urge to laugh. But she immediately wrote an apology on her pad, explaining that she was a neighbor and then writing, "If I had a lemon tree with *this* many lemons, I would want to share them." But Lemonwoman was merciless, shooting back, "I *do* share them, I share them *with my friends*!"

Judy shared her lemon-picking experience with her husband, Allen. And how she was adored by her husband and her children, her brothers and sister-in-law, her best friend Cousin Debra, and the whole family. Perhaps The *Lemon Tree Incident*, as some of us blog-followers have come to call it, reinforced her awareness that, despite her swollen cheeks, her inability to speak, and having a limited time to live, there were people in the world who were far less fortunate than she was.

On leaving Judy's memorial service, I said to my sister Susan, "You can bet that if *I* were given the diagnosis of a debilitating and disfiguring cancer that over a fairly short time, despite many operations, would eventually take my life, I'd be a royal pain in the ass! I'd be kvetching and obsessing and taking any numbing med I could.

She replied, "And that's why you and I are still here; we haven't learned our lessons on earth yet."

Hmmph! I really hate it when my younger sister is right, I thought, but avoided saying it aloud.

What I have most feared about growing older, personally, and thus ignored here in my story of my early sixties to my seventies (with a little backstory from my earlier days) was the very thing my cousin seemed to embrace.

Her way of living out her life, even with the challenges she faced, made illness and death seem not quite as frightening. Judy went through that first operation which altered her voice. Instead of bemoaning her loss, she shared being almost-tickled by her "practically English accent," as her sister-in-law Marlene dubbed it. And she dressed the long scar left on her throat with her selection of multi-colored scarves. The next operation took her capacity to speak at all and her ability to eat.

Given the person Judy was, I can't imagine the pain of the doctors who tried so hard to save her life, and yet had to give her the news that they could not do it. They must have gone home and wept.

Still, Judy was not to be silenced. She used her voice in her writing, appreciating the beauty in life and keeping concerned family and friends posted on her treatment status. Read her on a day you feel sorry for yourself and I dare you not to be at least a little bit embarrassed.

In this way, she was able to rise above a self-involvement that would have been understandable, if not expected. And, doing so, she continued to comfort the many who cared for her.

Once she lost her speech, Judy's pad and pen around her neck gave way to an erase-board, which was supplemented with a computer with its own voice. Even this loss, she greeted with humor, donning one board for her good days and one for her bad; teaching us that even in the most dire of circumstances, one can still laugh and not take ourselves quite so seriously.

I have to admit, I have too often, like most of us humans, not lived mindfully in the moment. Rather, I was very often preoccupied with some matter that seemed important at the time, worrying about this or that—some decision or event of the past or future—not taking notice of the new buds blossoming or the changing of the leaves.

Judy Samuelson did not have as many years to live as we tend to expect these days. But, for those of us who loved her, she left such an exquisite gift, especially in her last four years, from when her cancer was first diagnosed until the day she took her last breath. She lived a life rich beyond most and taught lessons that can only be taught, as our cousin Stu first noted, by Bodhisattvas; advanced souls who've come to teach us mortals great lessons.

In these last years, Judy used her sharp mind, her unscathed sense of humor and her creativity to assuage our pain in even comprehending her loss among us. In sharing her end-of-life experience the unique way she did, it was as if she seemed to instinctively know that with the lemons she had—though certainly not the ones she would have chosen, were she given the choice—-with these particular lemons—*still,* and maybe *especially*—she could continue caring for others, leaving us with some truly unforgettable lemonade.

Note: Apologies to those who shared some of these same thoughts at Judy's memorial service. I am sure that I wasn't the first to have these observations, proving how all of us are really connected.

CHAPTER TWENTY-NINE

I'll—Yes, I'll--*Always Have Paris*

I definitely needed cheering up. And my way to do this was to find an affordable flight to France, where Sam and his girlfriend Chloe lived, for Christmas that year. Me, a woman who at one time couldn't see a plane in the sky without dreading I'd someday be forced to be on one. I feared that of the millions of flights that safely landed daily, mine would be the one and only plane that would be detoured to a Taliban hideout where my head would be lopped off on TV or I'd be begging terrorists to throw small children out of the plane instead of me.

Since Sam and Chloe lived in a place not much larger than a toolshed, and they were about two hours outside of Paris, in Normandy, I booked myself at an inexpensive hotel. In France, people take their holidays seriously, so at my hotel, most of the potential guests and pretty much all of the staff were gone for the holidays. But, *clever me,* I thought. *I brought along my laptop and my iPhone, so that if I get lonely, I can always text, e-mail or call my friends.*

I had one problem: I didn't really understand Wifi yet and none of my techno-communications seemed to work in my hotel! There was surely some way to activate them, but I couldn't ask or understand in French how to go about it and who would I ask anyway, given my hotel was a holiday ghost town. My son Sam voiced his concerns that I was too dependent on technology, rather than being in the moment, so I didn't want to burden him with my technological questions.

I already finished the book I brought on the nine-plus hour flight *across-the-pond,* as the frequent travelers tend to call it. Thus, whenever my son and his "petite-amie" (French for "girlfriend") brought me back to the hotel, I was totally alone. No room service to call, no in-room movies to watch, not even a working telephone.

All I had with me was my French to study, and I expected it would make little difference in the brief eight days of my stay. Plus, the jet-lag was pretty tough for me to adjust to. When Sam and Chloe would come to get me, at 10:30 or 11PM, a perfectly reasonable, if not luxurious time to arise, it was somewhere around 5:30 or 6 in the morning to my Midwestern body! I didn't want to see the sights; I wanted to go back to sleep!

So, night after night, when I was dropped off at the hotel after a day of sightseeing beautiful castles and glorious churches, I was all alone with no one but me in that charming room of country-French furniture and inscrutable plumbing. I would have to fiddle with the knobs in the shower, so that the water didn't scald or freeze, but I did finally figure them out. At least I had my conversational French book in order to practice the language.

Seven days in, I awoke with vigor, finally feeling alert. Perhaps it was that my jet lag ran its course or maybe I knew this would be my last full day in France and Chloe's "Francais famille" ("French family") was taking us into the heart of Paris to see the Christmas lights on the Eiffel Tower and attend the Gertrude and Leo Stein exhibit at the Grand Palais museum.

I dressed in my black tights and sweater. Wanting to feel just a little more like a Frenchwoman, I took the long multi-colored scarf that I'd found at a local "*marche*" (market) and wrapped it around my neck. Then, I donned another thing I'd found in the marketplace, a beret.

The hotel where I stayed was not even close to the heart of Paris. I was in a small town in Normandy, a quieter section of the country, but not far from Chloe and Sam. I always need my coffee first thing in the morning and, while staying at the hotel, just as soon as I woke up, before my pick-up time, I threw something on and stumbled to the café across the street.

But this day, dressed in my Frenchish best, I saw that fellow café-goers stood outside, smoking and talking. The sign in the window said the coffee shop opened at 9. It was now 9:15. Curious about what would keep customers outside in the cold, I peered into the storefront glass and saw that the shop's manager was taking his time washing the floor.

Somehow, the people who waited outside just waited politely in the cold, smoking and chatting, as it began to snow. I was astonished! Imagine local Starbucks patrons waiting outside for their morning dose of caffeine because the floor needed mopping up! Unthinkable! *Perhaps,* I concluded, *this odd patience and way of doing business was a very different French custom.*

One man, who seemed closer to my age, saw me with my backpack and he asked (in French, of course) if I was driving. He seemed concerned, perhaps because of the snow and my accent and age, and I understood him. And then he whispered conspiratorially, *"Il y a un autre café au coin de la gauche."* (Which I slowly realized meant "There's another café around the corner to the left.") I understood the word *"gauche"* for left and I already knew what a café was and he did point and gesture, making it clear he meant "around the corner".

So, I thanked him and walked down the street. And *Voila!* I saw, sure enough, there was a teeny tiny, but cozy cafe that was open! Once inside, seeing that there were only a few tables, I thought, *I'm alone— why take up a whole table when there are people who want to sit together?* So I found a barstool at the counter, near where the owner was bustling around, preparing orders and collecting euros.

The owner looked friendly and he smiled at me. In Paris proper, many people, particularly shopkeepers, spoke English, but in this part of Normandy, few did. He asked, *Vous desiree?* (which I understood as, "What would you like?") And this was one thing I was sure about how to say in French, *"café crème"* or "coffee with cream."

Anticipating my morning coffee, I was delighted. I was feeling a little more confident, having broken the conversational ice with an actual Frenchman. Venturing out to this new café and ordering my coffee—I took a chance that I might not do it perfectly and so what? Everyone has to begin somewhere, right? So, I began to speak French.

I told the owner that I lived in the Midwest of Aux Etats Unis (my best version of the United States) and that there were cows (*des vaches*) much like the French countryside. I also told him that where I used to live was *"Chez Harley"* (the home of Harley, one of Milwaukee's claims to fame)—and I did the "vroom, vroom" thing with my hands and my voice. The owner laughed and brought his wife over to introduce me.

And, soon enough, everybody in the tiny café seemed to be talking to one another and to me in, of course, French and I was feeling totally and unselfconsciously a part of it all.

I texted Sam and Chloe to let them know which coffee shop I was at (I finally figured out how to text in France). My son said the scene looked like a French version of *Cheers*, the American television show, with me as Norm, one of the regulars at the bar; that I looked comfortable and right at home.

Then, in walked the guy who directed me here and, recognizing him, I waved. *Had he gotten tired of waiting or was he coming to continue our conversation,* I wondered. Chloe told me later that she heard another café patron, who must have known my coffee-savior, say, *"Bonjour, Monsieur Celibataire!"* or "Hello, Mr. Single Guy!" and saw the friend motion his head toward me. I felt pretty amazing, fantasizing that *Monsieur Celibataire* and I would meet and marry and live in this little town someday and my French would get better and better. (Alas, I never saw him again, but my French did improve.)

As Sam and Chloe and I left for our day in Paris, I thought I looked pretty Parisian, with my long scarf wrapped around my neck and my boots and long sweater with tights. So, straightening my beret with resolve, I told them, *"Aujourdhui, nous ne parlons que Francais!"* which means something pretty close to, "Today, we speak only French!"

And what a day it was! First, the friendly people in the café who seemed to actually understand my French and then the rest of the day with Chloe's lovely family.

So, all day, I spoke *le Francais*. Oh, I made tons of mistakes, which Sam or Chloe or her mom or dad would correct, and I would try it again. So what?

And then I thought, *As I've grown older, I'm not as concerned about what other people think. And I've survived some of life's tough moments—and every life has them—I just need to really* take risks *and* be present *to truly relish the good moments.*

It was breathtaking, driving into Paris, with the lights of the city and the Eiffel Tower all lit up at the center of it all. I had to pinch myself to really believe that I was actually there!

More than the twinkle lights on the Eiffel Tower or the Gertrude and Leo Stein Exhibition at the Grand Palais or even the beautiful classic French Christmas I was part of at Chloe's "Famille Bisous" ("affectionate family"), I had this amazing revelation: I can be alone, take risks and have a wonderful time of it! And, as I do, life on my own can be pretty exciting! No sparkling bauble or new computer gizmo can even come close to the epiphany I was gifted with on my Christmas in France!

CHAPTER THIRTY

Face Work

My face was all blue and I looked like a Smurfette. The thing was it was my own fault. I did the deed, or as Hollywood calls it, I had "work". Whenever people say about a woman from her middle years to her nineties, "How does she look so good? So young?" I may not say it out loud, but I always think, *How? She's had some "work", that's how!*

Living, as we do, in the land where youth and attractiveness reign, it's not easy to grow old. But for a woman to "look old" can feel like a particular loss. Not for all women. I know many friends who could not give two shakes about the way their bodies and faces change as they age. Often, I've envied them, as they seem to have been born with so much more confidence than I have, or perhaps were more immune to our cultural messages. And it's a little baffling how I often feel so much like the chubby ADHD kid I once was. But, still, the natural effect of years on our faces and bodies seems to matter to me.

I'm kind of embarrassed about it myself, as here I am writing a book on women and aging and the superficial, youth-worshipping world we live in. But, at that time, my rationale was, *What will empower me most right now and make me feel better after feeling old, discarded and over?* And for me, at least at the time, the answer was *Face work!*

I mean, I'm terrified of losing my life before I'm ready and I'm a big baby about anesthetic and possible strokes or any debilitating brain stuff that might happen in surgery. Also there was the expense part, as well as the very real fear that this face work thing would turn me into one of those women who looked worse after the surgery than they did before.

I see women all the time who've had too much "work," and their faces and their bodies don't seem to match. No offense, but I thought of Phyllis Diller, the popular comic of the 50's and 60's, who made no secret of her face work or the comic Joan Rivers, whose frequent plastic surgery was the butt of many jokes on talk shows of her day.

This reminds me of a joke.

This woman goes to a plastic surgeon to inquire about his newly discovered facelift that will, he claims, end any need for another.

"This facelift is revolutionary," the doctor tells the woman proudly.

"Really?" asks his patient with excitement. "Tell me more about it!"

"Well, I call it The Knob," says the doctor. "You see, I install a knob at the back of your head, under your hair, and whenever you feel that your face needs a lift, you just give the knob a windup. Bingo! It tightens up any excess skin."

"I'm in!" says the woman. And she proceeds to schedule her Knob procedure.

The operation is a success, and for several years, the woman is delighted. But, then, she calls the doctor's office with a question and is told to schedule an appointment to see the Knob doctor. Once in his office, she says, "I don't understand why I'm getting these big brown lumps under my eyes."

The doctor says, "Well, those would be your nipples."

"I see," says the woman. "Then, that would explain the goatee."

Before I went ahead and scheduled my facelift, sans knob, I discussed the idea of doing the procedure with my sister. "Are you sure?" she said with concern. "I mean, that seems pretty extreme."

I guess she was worried about me. *Hmm, maybe I should give it more thought.*

I waited a while and then told my friend Mary and she said, "If it's that important to you, then do it!" Now, that was the answer I was looking for, I guess, because very likely, inside myself, I was already determined to do it and get it over with.

I wish I was like Meryl Streep or Gloria Steinem who haven't let the Hollywood youth-worship get to them. But, frankly, I'm not. I've been insecure about my appearance since I had three chins in fifth grade and I have probably suffered from a mild case of body dysmorphia ever since. All my life, after fifth grade, I'd go up and down ten to twenty pounds, which is a lot for a short person with small breasts, and I thought I was shamefully horrible-looking; almost as if I should stay inside till I took the weight off and could respectably be seen in public. And I sadly wonder if age-shaming isn't why Greta Garbo, the glamorous 30's and 40's Hollywood movie star, is quoted to have said, "I want to be alone." Some say she was misquoted, but it was true that she did isolate herself as she grew older.

Hey, my ancestry is all Eastern European Jews and we just aren't made to be Nordic—tall, slim athletic people! But, oh, how many of us would like just that! Our DNA dictates the chubby, short folks that many of us still are. I would've liked to be that person who didn't give a damn, but the truth is, I'm not. Bad Feminist! (Hand slap here!)

I was always excruciatingly self-critical regarding my appearance. But when I began to look in the mirror and see wobbly skin under my chin, just hanging there, I thought, *I know that my wobbly neck is a natural part of aging, but I hate it!*

I imagined that I could just have it tightened up. *Probably a couple of stitches on either side of what I considered my unsightly turkey wattle should do it,* I thought.

I figured why not give myself a little "freshening up," as the people who work in aesthetics call it. I thought it would give my self-confidence a much-needed boost. Yes, this is "The Dirty Little Secret" that many women share (though plenty of men have "work" too). I always feel like the "looks wonderful' s" have not just gotten more sleep or returned from the health spa; it's that they've taken the step that nobody (but me and Jane Fonda) cares to admit, to make themselves look what they think of as more attractive.

I have friends twenty-five years younger who have had the parentheses around their smiles or the laugh lines close to their eyes botoxed. So many people I never thought of as vain take steps in this direction, that I've come to think of face work as a cultural phenomenon. I even predict that face work will be to tomorrow what cosmetic dentistry is to today: just good grooming. I believe that no matter how much we embrace ageing in the future, and I hope it will be a lot more than we embrace it now, face work will be to the middle-aged and older what braces are to middle schoolers and teeth-whitening or capping are to divorcees.

After all, long before dentists and caps were just a part of good oral health care, it was probably considered self-indulgent to get replacements for one's bad or missing teeth. Plus, who could afford such luxuries? I mean, there was a time not all that long ago when I thought having a Blackberry or a cell phone was totally pretentious. And now, seeing me without my cell phone 24/7 means I have it in my purse or have lost it.

I covered what I considered to be the eyesore beneath my face with scarves of many colors, even if it was ninety degrees outside. To make matters worse, I would (ick) pull at my neck during my clients' therapy sessions, as if exercising the wattle would somehow tighten it up. In short, my loose neck flesh was bothering me, and I wasn't getting used to it one little bit.

So, I started squirrelling away some money for a year or two. When I had enough, off I went to the plastic surgeon, for my free consultation about ridding myself of the turkey neck I saw every time I looked in my bathroom mirror and thought, with surprise, *Oh my god, that's not my mother; it's me!*

Although I assumed all it would take is a couple of stitches on either side of my face, it turns out when I had my consultation with the plastic surgeon, he laughed and told me that this two-stitch idea could not be done. He told me only "a partial facelift" would rid me of my extra neck skin, but he did go on to explain why a stitch on either side would not do the job.

The doctor told me if I decided to do it, I would have a nurse-anesthesiologist, who would give me medication that would put me to sleep. Then, I'd need at least two weeks of recovery time, as my face might look bruised for a while.

Being an occasionally positive person, I went into complete denial that the anesthetic could have unpleasant and lasting side effects, such as being in an eternal coma or, perhaps, the most lasting side effect of all: Death. Nor did I consider the possibility that I could awaken to find myself looking like a circus freak. I only thought, *The fooling with my extra neck skin was rather like biting one's nails: I was not even aware I was doing it.* And how distracting and undignified to have your therapist playing with her neck during sessions, right?

The morning of my "procedure," as the doctor's staff called it, the doctor's outer office looked like an ER waiting room dressed up as a living room. Comfy couches, pillows and coffee tables adorned the place in soothing blues and greens and velvet or silk fabrics.

I almost wanted to say, "Where's the television set?" or "Pass the chips and salsa!" The only thing that was unusual about this waiting room/living room was that it was filled with people who looked as if they just survived a horrible disfiguring car crash, all bandaged and sunglassed.

Some soothing Chopin etude was playing through an invisible and probably pricey sound system. And the doctor's staff, having had the surgical perks of working for the doc themselves, were all so matter of fact and cheery and glamorous-looking. Although a couple of them looked painfully thin, there wasn't a turkey neck among them.

Except for the bruised and bandaged all around me, the ambiance in the plastic surgeon's office was comforting. Still, I was terrified. I had to remind myself, *If I let everything that terrified me rule my behavior, I would never have left Skokie, Illinois, never have gotten married,* twice, *never have had children, never have gotten divorced.* And, ultimately, all of these decisions turned out well for me.

My sister drove me there and we waited, until a perky nurse assistant came out and called my name.

I followed the nurse to a room, which looked a little like a bedroom, all soft colors and the same calming piped-in music as the waiting room. What made this room different from a cozy little guestroom was that this place had a dentist's office type recliner chair with Frankenstein body straps, gigantic overhead lights and magnifying mirrors, and it exuded the odor of disinfectant.

I wondered why the anesthesiologist, the office assistants and the nurse here seemed not at all alarmed for me. They smiled and cooed and nobody acted as if in a few moments, I could very well be wheeled out on a gurney to languish in a coma for the remainder of my life or be removed by the coroner's office in a body bag. Although these possibilities were not lost on me, once I was determined to do something, I just had to get it over with, whatever the possible consequences, praying that they wouldn't happen to me.

After all, I told myself, *why would the nurses and the front office staff all have the "work" themselves, if they expected to be permanently unconscious or to appear on the cover of People magazine as terrifying examples of botched plastic surgery?*

After they strapped me in and said some comforting words, the nurse-anesthesiologist put the IV in, and I soon fell into a dreamless sleep. Though it actually took hours in total, it seemed to me only moments later that I was awakened in the recovery room, where my sister waited. Seeing her somewhat worried-looking face, I asked, "Is the surgery over? Was everything all right?" She reassured me that all was well. *Okay,* I thought, *I'm alive and I'm not in a coma! Anything else can probably be changed or lived-with.*

Though covered in bandages, my face felt swollen and my throat felt sore and I was very dry-mouthed from the anesthetic. Reassured, I must have fallen back to sleep, and then the doctor came in to admire his work and give me my marching orders: bandages were not to be removed for twenty-four hours; no washing my hair or getting my face wet for forty-eight hours; he gave me pain meds enough for a few days, should I need them; and I was to return for the removal of stitches and a recheck in a couple of days; also, to call his office, day or night, if I had any problems or concerns.

Then, my sister drove me to her house to recover.

It was the next day, when I slept off most of the anesthetic and the bandages were completely off, that I went into her bathroom and looked in the mirror and saw my moon face, all swollen and blue. "Nooo!" I screamed. "What have I done?"

Once the initial shock was over, I comforted myself with my best looking-on-the-bright-side self-talk: *At least I lived through the surgery and I'm not in a coma. . . .My face will look better in time! And if it doesn't, aren't there these guys who fix bad face work?* I mean, hadn't the doctor warned me that there might be swelling and discoloration for a while? I was counting on that "for a while" (rather than "forever") part.

I stayed at my sister's for a day or two, and once I saw the doctor for the stitch removal and re-check, I felt more myself again, and I drove myself back home.

When I got back to my place, several of my friends stopped by, wanting to see how I was doing. Though I knew they were concerned, possibly there was some curiosity, as well. Perhaps, if my face looked good enough, they might consider it themselves.

Once the blueness and swelling went away, I had a kind of "high"—maybe it was about having survived something that had the possibility, however small, of being dangerous. And I didn't miss my old neck at all. 'Didn't have to replace my neck-playing by taking up knitting or smoking to do something with my hands.

I stayed at home for about two weeks and covered the remaining bruises with make-up. My face felt a little numb, but not painful. And I slept through the night. Once the bruises healed and I felt less self-conscious, I was getting used to my new face. Though, to me, it didn't look all that different than my old one, except for my neck. Now I could give away my extensive collection of scarves and know that summer in the humid Midwest would be that much more pleasant without wrapping my neck in one of them.

I was reminded of how a girl I knew in high school had what we used to call "a nose job" and her new nose looked as if she'd been hit in the schnozz with a golf club, causing her nostrils to point upwards, as if they could catch the rain in a downpour and they kind of resembled a pig's snout. But she felt beautiful and way more confident. I wondered if this was the same with me. Did my face look the same or worse (except that the neck-skin was tightened up), but having spent the time and the money, I just *felt* more confident?

However, when I went back to work, people gave me that compliment about looking "refreshed" and asked if I'd been on vacation. Also, when I had reason to tell someone my age, they would look surprised and say, "You look at least ten years younger!"

Still, I felt a little guilty, as if I should be showing them the "before" pictures or keep wrinkly-neck remnants in a pendant around my neck to show them that I deserved no personal credit. I didn't want them to get the false idea that I was from some magic gene pool that kept me from aging naturally.

What I would say when people gave me those kinds of compliments was, "I've had some help," and that makes me feel more honest and less too-much-information about my appearance. If they asked further, I answered. If not, we dropped the subject. I guess this was how I made my peace with being a feminist writing a book about women and aging and, at the same time, being "out" about my facelift.

And, sometimes, like one of the characters in "The Best Most Exotic Marigold Hotel" who does a little confidence-wink in the mirror before she goes out, I wonder if, on a day I was in a good place, would I have eventually gotten used to my neck just the way it was?

CHAPTER THIRTY-ONE

I Lied to Mary: The Shame that Kills

One day, I called Mary with my daily list of kvetches. And after she listened carefully to my moans and groans, she asked, "Are you taking your medication?"

I lied, "Yes." And I had the distinct feeling she knew I was lying. But, somehow, I just couldn't admit it.

As a therapist, you would think I would know better. There is already so much shame out there and, unlike taking meds for diabetes or even a headache, there's still a bit of a stigma that accompanies taking meds for a condition of the brain or the nervous system or our situations or social systems (like money worries, loneliness or losing our sense of purpose in life) .

I have tried many new age remedies for my ADHD, depression and anxiety. But the only things that work for me are the combination of medication and regular sessions with my therapist.

I usually do the steps I advise my clients to do. But depression can come from a number of sources. It can be the very medication one is taking (and I take medication for my ADHD. It could be that when this medication has run its daily course, I have a mood-slump that feels almost exquisitely unbearable to me). Depression can be hormonal or situational, such as stressful life transitions, even good ones, like buying a new home or having a baby. But a part of it may be genetic and some folks are just more sensitive to the ups and downs of life.

There are various theories about depression, but one thing that still exists in our culture is the shame that accompanies taking psychotropic medications.

• • •

I've made so much progress in my life, though it may not have seemed like progress at the time: leaving marriages which were no longer working; starting all over in a new city, then moving to another; developing new friends and interests. Still, there have been times I feel down in the dumps. Not just a blah kind of day, which we all have, but a seriously down period of time. It's just that, at times, I feel a little bit guilty and ungrateful about having a pretty damned good life and still feeling blue. At times, I sometimes remind myself of the old story about the hat:

A grandmother takes her little grandson to the beach. It's a beautiful sunny day as they throw the beach ball back and forth. The little guy, who's about two years old, is giggling and chasing the ball in the shallow water and having so much fun. Then suddenly, the sky grows dark, there's a thunderclap, and a huge wave comes and sweeps the small boy away.

Of course, the grandmother is beside herself. She raises her hands to the sky and yells to God, "He was only two years old! Why did you have to take him? My daughter-in-law is going to kill me!" She carries on like this for a long time. And then, gradually, the sky grows clear and the water calms and a perfect wave comes in, depositing the small boy at his grandmother's feet, not a hair on his head harmed.

Whereupon the grandmother looks up, raises her hands to the sky and shouts, "He had a hat!"

I considered my accomplishments and all the good things that have happened to me. But, in addition to the changes in my life, and what I had done to adjust, and I remembered my aunts and my mother at my age. Our sixties and seventies for women a can be a time of loss in many ways.

The book, *Lost Connections: Uncovering the Real Causes of Depression—and the Unexpected Solutions,* author Johann Hari names at least nine reasons for depression and anxiety:

1. Loss of connection with other people;

2. Loss of connection with community;

3. Loss of connection to meaningful values;

4. Loss of meaningful work or purpose in one's life;

5. Loss of connection to sympathetic joy and overcoming self-absorption;

6. Lack of processing childhood traumas;

7. Lack of a sense of hope for the future;

8. Loss of status and respect;

9. Disconnection from nature.

I might also add,

10. Disconnection from one's creativity and

11. Disconnection from one's Spirituality, or a personally meaningful connection to something outside of oneself. (This could be a religion or a Higher Power, but one could still have a spiritual connection with no fixed belief at all.)

Hari also has a chapter in his book called, "The Grief Exception." Actually, when I think of my mother's generation and my own, I see a lot of "The Grief Exception."

In my life, and I expect for most women in our culture who've lived fairly traditional lives, there is a lot of loss one that women may experience in growing older. First, women have been admired for our physical beauty (and the word "beauty" in our culture has become synonymous with "youth"). As we grow older, we find ourselves losing that quality that opens doors and interests potential partners. Thus, for no other reason than aging, we lose opportunity and status. Is it any wonder most of us fear growing older and we give up, since often partners and potential employers lose interest in us with the years? I mean most of us are no Justice Ruth Bader Ginsburg or Dame Agatha Christie, where our lives have never focused on our youth or our looks, instead we've led with our gifts and our work and we would be likely to continue doing that for as long as we live.

So, in the world that we women live in, aging may feel like we are stripped of our status, often our connection with community, meaningful work, financial independence and empowerment, and partners or potential partners. Right there, we've covered over half of Hari's reasons for depression.

For myself, I worked hard to build or re-build the connections I once had as a younger woman. Still, I believe I was grieving the empowerment and status of my youth. Even though I never felt especially physically attractive, it could buoy up my spirits when others found me so. Though I left a marriage when I felt unloved, I did have my now-grown children and meaningful work and I was using my creativity both in my work as a therapist and in writing my *Psychobabble* segments for radio. Still, except for my therapist, my friend Mary, and my sister (since my sons lived so far away), I felt pretty disconnected from others. My assessment of my loneliness problem was that I was a social person who was not being social.

I did try to connect, joining a dance class, trying a screenwriting group, going to hypnotherapy gatherings, and attending a mindfulness meditation group near where I lived. It just seemed the connections I made were very temporary. The class would be over and many of us would plan to keep meeting. But, then, over time, we'd lose touch. The 12-step group I loved in Milwaukee was wonderful when I went to meetings, but I couldn't find one I felt as comfortable with in the suburbs of Chicago. Perhaps, unless one was really actively participating in ways such as volunteering to chair events, taking charge of the collection basket or keeping track of the reading materials, it was difficult to make meaningful long-term friendships.

Since I felt overwhelmed already, working and writing. In retrospect, I was probably frantically looking for friends who would "get" me, and dependence is always a recipe for failure.

For me, the loss of a group of friends or a mate was difficult. Still, I'd grown a lot since I left New York. And when I was unhappy about my social situation, I was also irritated with myself for being unhappy.

As my favorite Buddhist nun, Pema Chodron, says, "This Moment is the Perfect Teacher." In other words, every moment, especially the tough ones, are lessons we are learning. Unlike the grandmother in "The Hat" story, maybe the real joy in life is taking some time to appreciate the little and not-so-little miracles all around us and in weathering the missing hats.

Now, Johann Hari claims that we've been sold a bill of goods by Big Pharma. He cites flawed and skewed studies which put into question the push-button cure that antidepressants promise. I agree with most of what he says about our alienated society and the meaningless values we've bought into, which cause much of our unhappiness. I especially agree with something wise told to him by a Vietnamese doctor, *You need your pain to tell you what's wrong, or else you can't fix it.*

And his research may be absolutely spot-on, that antidepressants don't work for the reasons the companies give us. But even so, I find, when I do use medical mood-enhancers, my energy increases so that I can get to the therapist and figure out what's missing in my life or they work to help me get out and exercise and, as a sort of jump-starter when I'm feeling stuck.

Depression (and grief, as well) can be deadly. Not only in direct ways, such as people who lose hope and are in so much pain that they choose to take their own lives, but also by our not taking good care of our health or doing the things that boost our mood and, thus, we would be more likely to attract others.

Psychopharmacological medications do not work the way antibiotics do. With an antibiotic, you take it, and five to ten days later the infection disappears. With an antidepressant, once people notice they are doing better, perhaps there are positive changes, at least for me, in my general outlook and more energy to get things done, which then brings an upward mood spiral, that tends to get me thinking, "I'm cured". And, much like alcoholics who think they can resume drinking safely, I will think, *I am an exception. I don't really need these pills anymore. I'm happier and less stressed now.* Sometimes, we therapists can be wise for other people, but not very wise for ourselves.

Many people still feel a stigma in seeing a therapist and/or taking medication. Sometimes, these folks will wait till their partner leaves or they lose their job or both before taking the steps that will help them to feel and act differently. I mean if you were choosing a colleague or a friend, would you be drawn to a Debbie Downer?

Oh, and, by the way, not long after I started taking my meds again, I called Mary, and told her, "Remember when you asked if I was taking my medication? I lied to you and said I was." And, I wasn't terribly surprised when she quietly answered, "I know."

THIRTY-TWO

Two Orange Coats: Not Every Dream is A Nightmare

Remember my dream about the two orange shirts that foretold the unexpected journey I've shared here with you? Well, later, I had a dream which may be more positive in terms of predicting whatever's to come in my life.

In this dream, I was at some dating event with lots of other women. A man at this event had to choose among us and he didn't much like any of us.

This me with dark hair (like Marlo "That Girl" Thomas?) left the man-chooses-the-winner contest and took all the other women with her. A plane awaited our escape right outside. But there was no pilot in the plane.

I actually used to be afraid to fly. I was frightened to, not only fly this plane, but pilot it too, but there was no one else there to do it except me. So, I flew the plane and all the other women held hands with one another, securely holding onto the plane and forming a kite-tail in the sky. And I landed the woman-kite craft safely at a New York City subway station.

Then, the women and I got on the subway train and before it even left the station, I had this wild idea of placing all these charms I owned, like the ones you see on a charm bracelet, each signifying a life-experience or a place I lived, up above the advertising billboards on the train. I realized that leaving my charms in a subway car could mean they would fall or be stolen, but somehow, I didn't care.

So, in my dream, I was balancing each of my charms up above the usual subway ads. Then, I became aware somehow that a reporter, as well as Oprah Winfrey, were somewhere in the subway station. Next, I got off the subway, following a friend home. And all of the women came with me.

In the second part of the dream, I had two orange coats, the same color of the coats as those shirts I packed in my suitcase, when I had that dream that became a prophecy.

Dream interpreters say that the only one who can really understand the symbolism of a dream is the dreamer. So, I'll do my best to interpret mine.

I think this dream was telling me, "Your life may not be the one you planned for yourself in your younger days, but it's been a rich one. You've piloted your own way and still are, and maybe you'll even inspire other women to pilot theirs." The subway might be symbolic of the underground of my mind, my subconscious. And the charms insecurely placed on the subway walls atop the ads could be my many experiences, which, whether good or bad at the time, ultimately added to my life experiences and wisdom. And the fact that I didn't care if the charms were stolen, might mean that nothing that's real can be taken away and that I would keep whatever was valuable in my mind and my soul and not as corporeal things. (Ads are for selling *things*, but memories and wisdom and feelings and experiences can't be sold.)

Maybe the reporter and Oprah being in the subway station were symbols that I would have assistance in publicizing the cause of other sager women and preparing younger women to become sagers themselves someday.

When I woke up, I felt this was a good dream and, perhaps again, a prophecy. It spoke to me of my daytime dream of changing the meaning and treatment of older women; of women no longer being pitted against other women for men. Instead, if the prophecy of the dream was correct, I would help the cause of women living our own dreams, with sagers included.

In a way, these things are happening now, with women having more opportunities in the world and realizing their dreams. We see our Maxine Waters, our Leslie Stahl's, and our Jane Fonda's, but not often enough. Not representative enough of our actual population of aging women. Yet, life for some older women seems to be improving.

I've had an issue with ageism since I was in my thirties, but I didn't experience it myself on a deeper level till I moved into my own sager years.

I have long hated the world of women against women to please men. I saw it as a beauty pageant—women being pitted against one another like prized pigs in a country fair. Which one had the best legs? The best breasts? Even in love, was this what real love was? If so, how does one value a sager woman whose youthful looks are changing. Do we put her out to pasture and replace her with a younger model?

But in this dream, I flew my own plane, taking other women along, rather than leaving them behind. All my life, I made stabs at this dream: in my thirties, I had a feminist radio show; In my forties and fifties, I compiled interviews with women who were in their sixties and beyond, women who didn't buy into the stereotypes that life for a woman was over once she was "no longer young."

What I know, as a therapist and a woman, is that *taking action* is what tends to help people feel their own power, at least it has worked that way for me.

This is different from the way I and so many women of my generation absorbed cultural messages, such as, "Wait, be a good girl, and your prince will come to save you." That's a lot of pressure for any prince! And what if he doesn't come? Who will save us then? What if he changes his mind? Or what if we have to save him?

As in my piloting dream, taking other women along, in an updated model of woman-power and helping one another seems so optimistic. And my dream gave me the feeling that I will be safe, turning the orange shirts of earlier, the symbols of unwanted choices, into orange coats, symbols of protection, and making the tough stuff of life into the parkas to keep me and my sager sisters warm.

Orange pigment converts light energy that carrots, pumpkins, sweet potatoes, and oranges, among other plants, take in from the sun and turns it into chemical energy for growth. In Confucianism, orange has been seen as the combination of the male, yang, and the female, yin. Yellow symbolizes perfection and nobility and red, happiness and power. The two in combination, which make orange, are like light and fire, spirituality and sensuality—which might seem, to some, oxymoronic. I see it differently. I think my dream gave me the feeling that we could put both sides together and create a powerful synergy from their integration. In my dream, I was a part of turning a woman's sager years from Death's Waiting Room into transitional moments to anticipate with joy and courage.

Awakening from this dream, I felt happy. The dream gave me the feeling that these long-awaited changes would finally become realities—and that I'd be a part of it all.

CHAPTER THIRTY-THREE

A Much, Much Younger Man (And French!)

I know nothing stays the same. But it seems to me lately that my world is always in hyper-flux. Sometimes I focus on my fear of the future: being alone as I grow older, possibly descending into some kind of decline, and/or living in potential poverty (which I wouldn't be good at!).

And then there are just the losses or changes we naturally experience as we age (unless we are enlightened beings): maybe annoying people saying "What? What?"---rather than admitting the need for hearing aids. Then, there is the feeling one gets of being kind of invisible, as if love is out of the question, even silly.

It's a lot to take in. People I have known and loved, people my own age or younger, have died. My parents' generation is mostly gone. And they were my buffer. Now I am standing on the front lines, awaiting the firing squad of death—maybe not this year or even in twenty years, but someday.

Especially as I age far from my children and without a partner, I ask myself, *why is this not what I expected?* This is not the life I imagined for myself.

But now, for me, there is a little man, a just-born little guy, Nathaniel. My son Sam and his wife, Chloe (who married in a civil service in France) gave birth to a little grandchild, the sweetest little man in the world. And I love the thought of visiting him and watching him grow.

He's too young to understand, and he's French, so we don't speak the same language. But my son Sam calls me regularly on Skype so I can read Nathaniel stories. And soon he'll be old enough to come to visit me here in the States, too.

My old negative brain says, *How will I be a part of his life, when he lives far away?* I have some ideas. But, of course, they would involve trade-offs and change. I could stay in one place and try to work as much as I can so that I can see him a couple of times a year. I can perhaps move to France for chunks of time, to bond with my new little grandson, babysit, see his first tooth, have him know me—and not just on Skype. And, yet, I am so grateful and looking forward so much to meeting him in person.

So, here I only moved to Illinois a short time ago, thinking it would be my mecca, I found a cozy place to live, not that far from my office and my sister and a couple of good friends nearby. If I took steps to live in France for a part of the year, there might be another plan altogether. Perhaps I should write a book about my traveling around in my late sixties and seventies and call it, "Eat, Pray, Die."

There's that part of me that wants to grow old around the people who know my history, people who accept me, warts and all. And there's a part that wants to fall madly in love again and live near my family and stay that way till death do us part—literally.

And then, I wonder, how will I have enough money to live in my eighties, nineties or beyond, when I never really was very good at earning or saving in my thirties, forties, or fifties?

My dream was to start a family or attract my family to a wonderful business in which each of them played a part. Plan B would be to round up a group of people I like and all live together in one place, but not be marginalized. Kind of develop my own Best Most Exotic Marigold Hotel, only in New Mexico or on the California coast. We could each have our own separate homes, but gather for meals or to do something spiritually fulfilling or something to help others or simply something we enjoyed.

But back to my little Frenchman. I had to see him, at least two or three times a year. His little blonde hair, his dimply face and his bright blue eyes looked exactly like his beautiful mom, but his ears resembled mine. I haven't yet alarmed my son by telling him—that noses and ears continue to grow throughout our lives. The Eastern thinkers believe that big ears are signs of wisdom. It's a nice trade-off for my auditory structures, which I usually hide behind my curly, medium length hair or adorn them with fun earrings.

I booked a flight for Christmas through New Year's to France when Nathaniel was barely six months old. Sam and Chloe and Nathaniel (I just love long names for tiny children) live in the countryside now, only a couple of hours from the airport. Chloe's charming parents picked me up and we spoke our own blend of English and French, a kind of Franglish, as we drove to see our mutual grandchild.

When I got to the house, everyone was getting ready for Christmas there, fussing and planning and hanging decorations all over. Nathaniel, my little grandson, was about to have his first Christmas. And I, being Jewish, was about to have my first Christmas with him. (I'd celebrated with Chloe's family before.)

I couldn't wait to see Nathaniel, and as soon as I did, I covered his face with kisses. What I couldn't have known at the time is that I contracted a virus on the plane. I was told that Nathaniel wasn't a great sleeper, but he was a great screecher and his parents spent many nights without any sleep themselves. Chloe told me that, once, she and Sam even tried to let him "cry it out." Their next-door neighbors came over, telling them they'd considered calling the French version of Child Protective Services because they thought Nathaniel might be getting abused! This lack of sleep had everybody on edge.

In a relatively short time, I got so sick that Sam and Chloe brought me to the village doctor, who diagnosed me with bronchitis and, in that I was an American, immediately prescribed an antibiotic. I lived in terror that I had passed my infection down to baby Nathaniel. And, I knew Nathaniel's parents were concerned about using antibiotics so early in his young life.

Sure enough, not long after I was diagnosed, Nathaniel began pulling at his ears and acting very cranky. He developed a temperature and he, too, was brought to the doctor and diagnosed with bronchitis. In France, doctors don't tend to give antibiotics to small children unless there is no alternative.

But I was terribly worried about him, and Sam and Chloe were already feeling exhausted and frazzled, They had the antibiotics on hand, in case a fever got worse during the night, but I already felt like the devil incarnate for bringing bronchitis to my little grandbaby. Now, my son and his wife were not only worried about me, they were worried about their tiny baby.

Feeling weak, I stayed upstairs in my room, as my French family decorated and cooked for Christmas. I felt as if my very being there endangered my grandson and stressed out my dear Sam and Chloe. I felt all would have be better if I had not even come! I managed to join the family for Christmas dinner, but took to my bed as soon as I could, feeling chilled, feverish and tired.

New Year's Eve was a little better, And, when my son did take me to the airport, I asked him to keep me updated on how Nathaniel was doing. More than anything, I wanted him, exhausted from lack of sleep and worry, to make the hour and a half drive to the airport and back safely and then text me that Nathaniel was alright.

My entire flight home, I was still feeling ill; but most of all, I was thinking and praying that Nathaniel was getting better. Being on a plane, at that time, I had no information that could confirm my wish.

My plane to Chicago connected in Charlotte, South Carolina, but somehow I missed my connecting flight, and I had to stay at a motel near the airport. I tried to reach Sam and Chloe to see how Nathaniel was doing; but, somehow, I couldn't. So it was nine hours from Paris to Charlotte and then overnight at the airport motel, where I didn't know whether Nathaniel had broken the fever or gone to the hospital! I was a wreck!

As soon as I checked in at the motel, I got a decongestant at the little store off the front desk. Then, I schlepped my suitcase to my room, took the decongestant and jumped into a hot shower. After that, I fell into bed.

Finally, I got a text from Sam and Chloe that Nathaniel's fever had broken, so he was on the mend. What a relief!

In the morning, I took the transport bus back to Charlotte's airport to get my flight to Chicago. I was so glad that I had seen my little French grandson, but especially I was relieved and grateful that he was feeling better. Being a grandparent, as wonderful as it is, has its challenges. Perhaps my big-eared wisdom will grow even bigger, as I learn from my early grandparenting experiences.

CHAPTER THIRTY-FOUR

Writing for My Life: Synchronicity

"When the student is ready, the teacher will appear"
–Tao Te Ching

When I moved back to Illinois, I missed doing my radio segment, "Psychobabble," yet I didn't know how to begin to find a home for it in Chicago. One of my friends suggested I come to a Chicago professional women's networking group. Despite doubting that I would find a network at a businesswoman's meeting, I went.

The buffet lunch at the meeting was excellent. But as I looked around, I felt my inner-shy and wondered how I could do a good enough elevator pitch to network with someone in Chicago who could help me air my radio essays.

A woman got up and spoke about the organization and then she explained that we would change tables, so that each of us could meet the others, exchange business cards and see if we could help one another or trade services.

At the first few tables, I felt as if what I was interested in was not to be found at this meeting. While other women exchanged cards enthusiastically, there seemed to be no one there directly related to radio.

But then, one young woman introduced herself as a publisher who was launching a new Chicago women's magazine. I turned to her and said, "Would you be interested in a column, something I've done on radio, which combines a little advice with some humor?"

And she said, "Why don't you e-mail some samples and your bio to my editor?"

After a few e-mails back and forth with the editor, I was asked to write a column on setting appropriate limits with your children. This, I knew my sons would find hilarious, as I was a complete what-not-to-do at limit-setting, even to this day. *Oh, well,* I thought. *We teach what we most need to learn. The shoemaker's kids have no shoes, right?*

After approving the finished copy of my column, the editor said, "You'll need a professional picture."

I said, "I have some shots on my iPhone, I think."

"No, that won't do. You need a *professional* headshot."

My friend, Elaine, had the cutest picture of herself. She'd given me her photographer's name and number maybe three years ago. I couldn't find it, so I texted her to ask and she sent it to me right away.

I scheduled a photo-shoot at the studio of Elaine's photographer for 11 AM on the following Sunday morning.

And, without worrying too much about it, the night before the photographs, I went dancing with my sister and her fiancé and some girlfriends. I stayed out till 1AM having dinner and drinks and I had a great time dancing with "m'girls."

The photo shoot was in Chicago, which was about a half-hour's drive from my place on a Sunday morning. The photographer suggested I take a choice of clothing and accessories; a business suit jacket, a couple of tops, some scarves, maybe some necklaces.

When I finally found the studio and met Ron, the photographer, he looked through my clothing choices and led me to the changing room, where I put on my most professional-looking outfit, a black suit jacket with a red "pop" color top underneath it.

Throughout the shoot, Ron joked and flirted. I said, "I'll bet you always flirt with women you're shooting. That's how you make them smile."

He shot back, "I never mix business with pleasure." He continued to joke and talk and have me change from my different wardrobe choices—with the scarf, without the scarf, Annie Oakley faux cowgirl jacket, and different tops. The shoot started at 11:30 and ended at 4:30.

I was feeling pretty loose that day, having danced up a storm the night before. Ron had smooth jazz on in the background and I was dancing around. Somehow throughout the shoot, he let me know he was single and not dating anyone.

He said, "Would you stop dancing and hold still?"

I said, "Don't you dance?"

He said, "White men don't dance."

I said, "Gay white men do."

He said, "Ron Gould doesn't dance."

Feeling pretty uninhibited and comfortable with myself, I said, "Do you slow dance?" And we did—and it felt very nice to be held in his arms.

We spent four and a half hours, laughing and talking and taking pictures. And noticing it was now a little after 4PM, I said, "You must be a real perfectionist! How long does your average headshot take?"

"Twenty minutes, thirty, tops." he answered.

I felt hopeful. Here was a guy I was attracted to, felt comfortable with, a nice guy who came with stellar recommendations (He'd been my friend Elaine's photographer for thirty years!) And he seemed to be interested in me, too. But I wasn't sure yet if I was misreading this.

I tried to maintain my cool. I got dressed in my jeans and tee-shirt and then sat at his kitchen island-table to write him a check. "How much do I owe you for your services?" I asked.

"Well that depends," he answered. Was he making a move on sixty-nine year old me? *It was a compliment*, I thought, *as a lot of men his age, whatever that was, would find my approaching seventy a daunting thing.*

"How about instead of sending these or e-mailing them to you, why don't I bring them myself when I pick you up for dinner any evening this week that works for you, at any place you choose."

I liked this guy. He was direct and funny and he seemed to like me. I thought about it and said, "How's this Wednesday?"

"Works great for me, he said, "You find the restaurant and I'll bring the pictures."

Now feeling especially comfortable, I said, "I'm hungry, have you got anything to eat?"

He looked into his bachelor refrigerator, which was surprisingly clean and came up with a brick of gouda cheese and muenster slices.

Then he found some crackers in the cabinet above the fridge and some bottled water.

We continued to talk, finding out that we both came from Skokie, went to the same elementary and high schools, though our paths hadn't crossed. Turns out we had lived maybe five blocks from one another; both been on the school newspaper, he as the newspaper photographer and me as a cartoonist. Also, he could remember all of our junior high teachers.

Sometimes people tell me I look younger than my age, so in order to be sure that he still wanted to have dinner, and he understood that I was older than he was, I said, "I'll bet you were in my sister's class."

"Your *older* sister?" he said.

"No, my younger sister," I answered. We then compared graduating classes. We realized that I was four years older than he was, but it didn't deter him from our dinner plan.

I gathered my clothing choices and headed for the door.

"See you on Wednesday," he said with a smile.

As soon as I got in the car, I called Elaine. She's usually pretty busy, but this time, a Sunday, she picked up. "I just did my photo shoot with Ron Gould and it went really well," I reported.

"Yeah, he's been our family photographer forever," Elaine said.

"I like him," I said.

"Well, everybody does," she said.

"No, I mean I *like* him, and not just as a photographer. We have a date this week."

"Wow!" she replied.

Ron and I have been dating for over five years. We moved in together in his work-live condominium two years after we met.

Had I met him at a different time, when neither of us was divorced or one of us was dating someone else or one or the other of us was in a "downer" mood, maybe we wouldn't have connected the way we did. But we both were at a place of acceptance with the idea that we would probably be living out our lives without a mate, even though neither of us preferred that option.

The magazine used my article with the business suit/pop color photo, but never responded to my offer to write other pieces.

I figure, you never know what's going to happen when you get out of your house and your head. My radio segment might be still looking for a home, but I'm not. Who would have guessed that the women's networking lunch would lead me to the man who would, as Leonard Cohen sang, "Dance me to the end of love"?

Oh, and the photos came out great. I especially liked the one where I was throwing my head back in laughter and another where I was dancing. And, in case you were curious, Ron never did charge me.

CHAPTER THIRTY-FIVE

Elaine Soloway:
Caregiving, Widowhood and Risk-Taking

Elaine Soloway celebrated her 80th birthday with a tattoo she calls Graciella on her upper arm. She is the author of *The Division Street Princess, She's Not the Type, Life After Loss, Bad Grandma, and Green Nails and Other Chapters in a Life Lived Out Loud,* as well as four well-read online blogs, all of which she wrote in her sager years. *The Huffington Post* published her article, *Why I Chose to Get a Tattoo Instead of a Facelift for My 80th Birthday.* Most recently, political activist Elaine organized a gathering of women called, *What*

Black Women Want White Women to Know, where she invited women friends of color along with white women friends to have a conversation around what it was like for black women; to help white women understand how life felt for women of color.

Her two daughters, Faith and Jill, wrote and produced the television series, *Transparent.* A character based on Elaine was played by actress Judith Light. Elaine even got a cameo in the second season.

My interviews with Elaine took place in her garden apartment in Los Angeles, where she moved for a time, and in downtown Chicago, the home city she returned to. I started by asking about the losses she faced in her life and how she survived them.

Linda: I wonder what you've done that helps to ward off depression in the losses that typically come to us all as we age. It seems to me that every time you've faced a loss, your first husband leaving you, then your second husband's illness and death, caring for him and then adjusting to changes in your life around his loss, you've always turned your experiences into something useful to yourself and others. I find too many women in this sageing phase of life, understandably get stuck in depression.

Elaine: Of course there are times when I get depressed. I'm normal. But I have found for me, action is preferable to limbo. I find if I take steps, even if they don't turn out exactly right, I feel better. It gives me a lift to do something. My theme for myself is, "If it doesn't work out, I can always move back." That's one part of it. And the other is, I like to take risks. Many people assume if you take a risk, it's going to fail. But I think, What if it's better? So, I guess I'm an optimist.

Linda: Why do you think that is?

Elaine: I'm not sure where it came from, maybe my father was an optimist. And I'm not sure how one changes into being optimistic. I think some people are concerned about taking a risk, fearing embarrassment over, "What if it doesn't work out?" I guess I have very little embarrassment. In fact, for me, embarrassment is fodder for my writing, because I find that self-deprecating writing is much more enjoyable for people to read than "Oh, aren't I great." Honesty has always been helpful to me. People love it when I say, "I made this mistake," because they can see I'm human just like them. And I am not afraid of trying things and making mistakes. To me, these things are very minor. As for optimism, somehow I always felt that I'd land on my feet, that I'd be okay.

Linda: I see it in your writing. For example, you wrote about the real things that happened to you: the surprise of finding out your first husband was transgender...

Elaine: Well, I had no idea during our marriage. I found out after our divorce. He left me for another woman after thirty years of marriage. But I was not unhappy about him leaving me. Perhaps it was kind of a relief. And it was a sad divorce, but not angry. We were never angry with one another.

Linda: And I understand that, in time, you became friends.

Elaine: We are friends. We talk on the phone and help each other out, like recently I went to a doctor's appointment with Carrie (Harry, who has transitioned, is now Carrie). We've been good friends to one another. But right after we separated, I was crying a lot, so I went to therapy for a while. And I would say to my therapist, "Why am I crying, when I'm happy this is over?" and she said, "Well, it's been thirty years."

Linda: So the crying was your expression of grief at the end of your thirty-year marriage?

Elaine: And I survived it, but then I was single for about six years, before I met Tommy.

Linda: Your second husband.

Elaine: My beloved second husband. I was in my sixties, I wanted to be married again. I wanted to be part of a family. I wanted to have somebody in my life who had friends. I really hated being the third wheel. But it took me a while to find Tommy and we were very compatible.

Linda: Do you mean you were very alike?

Elaine: In many ways, we were different. He never went to college; he was self-taught. He read a lot and was a really, really smart guy. He had a lot of wisdom and love in him. His interests were different than mine. He had his own interests and activities. He loved sports and working out and jogging and golf. My first husband was more of an intellectual, so I had that, and I saw that though we were alike in that way, that wasn't what made me happy.

Linda: Some women might think, "Oh, we're too different to be happy together, but as you said earlier, you are very open to give something or someone new a try.

Elaine: When Tommy and I met, it was a pretty fast romance, because we were so compatible. And it seemed like this would be an easy kind of marriage and it really was. And then when he got ill, at first, I was mystified by his behavior because he changed so dramatically. He didn't leave me love notes anymore, he made inappropriate remarks on the street, he became aggravating. I went to a therapist to see—I was going to leave him. But then, he started having trouble finding words. And the therapist suggested we see a neurologist. And the neurologist confirmed that he had Frontotemporal Degeneration.* And when I learned that all of his symptoms were part of this degenerative brain disease that would typically make him decline gradually and not have long to live, and he couldn't help it, I became compassionate. And he lived for about three years after the diagnosis.

Linda: And you took care of him at home.

Elaine: I did. But he was an easy guy to take care of; he was a good patient. I kind of felt blessed to have that opportunity to take care of him.

Linda: And you started your blog, "The Rookie Caregiver" which became part of your book, *Green Nails and Other Acts of Rebellion.*

Elaine: I think that having the blog saved me. I had some tough moments when Tommy got ill, and I knew he wasn't going to get better. That this disease was going to kill him. I could blog about it, hoping to help others in my situation. And, in fact, it helped me to get it down on paper. And some of the readers of my blog who were also caregivers would write that they felt I understood, and the blog helped them as well. So, it didn't feel like I was going through this alone; it felt as if even this horrible experience could make a difference for someone else, knowing they weren't alone.

Linda: Here's an excerpt from Elaine's blog, *The Rookie Caregiver.*

I'm in the kitchen preparing dinner. A pot of spaghetti is nearing its boil on the stove. I remove a colander from its place in a cabinet and set it in the sink. When the timer rings, signaling al dente, I lift the pot by its two handles and turn around to dump pasta and water into said colander. Alas, the pockmarked utensil has vanished.

In his fancy step, while my back was turned, Tommy has removed the colander from the sink, placed it back in the cabinet, and exited. He has not done this to vex me; this I know. He just can't help it.

I remain standing—a tricky move because I am holding the caldron with padded gloves, steam is clouding my eyeglasses, and I have nowhere to toss its contents. I hold this pose for a beat, then swivel and return the steaming pot of spaghetti to the stove.

Early on, when I first encountered my husband's stealth move, I would try this: "Honey," I'd say, "Please come back into the kitchen and get the colander out of the cabinet where you put it. I need to drain the spaghetti." Tommy would return, a contrite grin on his face, and perform his well-practiced steps.

But I no longer make that request. I have memorized my moves: button lip, pot back to stove, retrieve colander, return to sink, lift pot, dump.

The reporter notebooks I use for Trader Joe's and Target shopping lists are invariably returned to a neat stack after I have separated and laid them side-by-side for easy entries. All it takes to cue my spouse is for me to turn my back.

"Don't you get mad?" I was asked by a friend. "Don't you want to scream at him? Tell him to leave your stuff alone?"

I answer, "I think it helps Tommy when I remain calm." I believe this to be true. My husband shows no rage in dealing with his illness.

To this friend, who has had her own frustration with a stubborn, aging relative, I say, "I'm a patient person. This comes naturally to me." But, I fear I lie. I can recall many instances when I am anything but patient. See me drumming the table of a restaurant until the wait staff comes for our order. That's me at the hot dog stand, stewing, while the proprietor chats it up with the customer in the front of the line. And yes, that's me fuming in any and all medical offices while waiting for my name to be called. So, how am I able to remain saintly with my husband? What good would it do to seethe or explode? His condition prevents him from veering from his compulsive, neat-making routine. The pattern of his dance steps is imprinted on his brain; he cannot do otherwise.

As for me—petite and compact—I'm quick on my feet. Over the years, I've been able to practice my moves. Sometimes, I stumble if the steps are too difficult. Often, I wish I could get one maneuver down perfectly before another is introduced into our lives.

Thus far, I've kept up with my creative dance partner. The trick is to let him lead.

And an excerpt from Elaine's blog, *The Rookie Widow:*

At first, sleeping on Tommy's side of the bed seemed like a good idea: It was a quicker trip to the bathroom and would eliminate the nightly toe stubs endured during my darkened path from my side.

But, in this new space, I hadn't had a full night sleep since my husband died November 2. At first, I blamed it on a sort of Post-Traumatic Stress Disorder following three demanding events: my hip replacement surgery, 10 days in the hospital with Tommy, and finally an additional 12 at home with him in hospice care.

Then, I dismissed the PTSD theory and fixed on this: Tommy, despite his journey to heaven, wanted his side of the bed back. The 11 p.m. and 2 a.m. wake-ups I'd been experiencing were really my husband elbowing me over to my side.

So, last night I obeyed. I returned my iPad to a charger on my bedside table, and lined up on the nearby windowsill, my water bottle, Melatonin pills, Tylenol, and Neutrogena hand cream—the same setup prior to my switch. I arranged a mini-memorial on Tommy's bedside table with his portrait, his beloved AM/FM earphones, the 40-year-old wallet he refused to replace, his wristwatch that displayed date along with time, and his wedding band.

Then, I scooted onto my side, pulled up the covers, and bawled. My partner was gone. His side of the bed was empty. He would never return for our nightly spooning, or our ritual of him patting me on the tush and me returning a mild pat to his head, and finally, our exchange of "Love you," before falling asleep.

On my side of the bed, I continued to wail as my stored up grief filled the room. I realized I'd been so intent on getting my life back together, that I hadn't allowed myself to mourn my loss. Oh, I had cried each time I left his thinning and weakening body while he was in hospice, and I cried when he finally gave up his last breath, but I hadn't cried over his absence.

After I could sob no longer, I turned over, clicked on iTunes, and slept for 8 hours. There were bathroom trips cautiously tread, but I willingly took this longer route, then snuggled into my old spot hugging his pillow as substitute.

Linda: You always seem to, as the saying goes, take a sow's ear and make a silk purse out of it.

Elaine: There was no silk purse, no happy side, to this caretaking experience, except that I felt blessed to be able to care for Tommy at home and grateful to have a creative outlet in the blog, where I could express my feelings, cry or bitch and moan if I needed to. I do get depressed, but for me, it only lasts about a day. And I switch quickly to saying, "All right, what are the good things in your life?" I talk to myself that way. And I can list so many of them that soon I can get past the things that are depressing me. One thing that helps a lot is that I find a project. I find that if I can fill up my day with something I can get passionate about, then I'm fine. The projects don't stop me from having low points in my life. But having things to do, taking action, and being open to changes, being open to looking at myself too and my expectations; these help me to stay excited about life.

Linda: Could you give an example of what you mean by your expectations?

Elaine: Yes, of course. I have a very clear example. When I moved to L.A. a couple of years back, my expectation was that my daughter Jill, who lived there, would be jumping for joy and include me in everything she did. Well, it turned out that my daughter was busy with her own projects and, also, she has certain activities that she doesn't necessarily want her mother to be at. Because they're her things. So, I had to absorb that, get angry at her and complain about her to every friend I had, and, finally, tell her what was bothering me. And we were able to talk it through.

Linda: How great that you could do that!

Elaine: I couldn't do that when I was younger. In the past, I was an excellent passive-aggressive person. I'd say I was a perfectionist at that. So, I wouldn't talk to her for a couple of days. What we came to was that in the old days, I always wanted more of Jill than she could give me. Rather than being passive-aggressive and having hurt feelings and expecting her to read my mind, now I get it and we can discuss it and see where it's coming from.

Linda: Wow, that takes a lot of courage on all sides. And a lot of times, what we find out when we reveal ourselves in the way you and Jill did, can be that not being included can just be a trigger issue from the past—say one's parents or siblings did things where we felt left out. Some small thing happens in the present may remind us of how we may have felt in the past. Once you two talked it over, and really listened to each other, you understood how one another felt.

Elaine: Actually, Jill was very helpful at getting me going on a few projects and building a community in Los Angeles.

Linda: What sorts of things did she suggest?

Elaine: She had the idea that I could join the Speaker's Bureau for "Transparent", because cast members were always being called upon to speak about the show. And who better to speak about it than those of us who lived it. That gave me confidence, that she thought I could speak. Then, she had a friend who taught a six-week TV pilot writing class. And I wrote a pilot for a television series.

Linda: What was it about, if you don't mind talking about it.

Elaine: Since I walked everywhere and took the bus in LA, I saw that there were so many homeless people. And I wanted to find out—aside from the weather—why that was. So, I started doing research on it and I spent some time around the shelters and—well, it was partly about me. This woman moves to LA to be helpful to her family, but finds her family members are busy with their own lives. So she tries to find other people to help. Anyway, she winds up getting involved with the homeless. I call my pilot, *Needy*. And now the first draft is finished and various friends of mine are reading it. And having the

Speaker's Bureau to think about and my pilot to work on were projects I was passionate about.

Linda: It's like you always find something to get excited about, a place to use your gifts as a writer and researcher and a generally curious and creative person.

Elaine: As my daughters say, it's my way of transferring life into art. Also, I think that it not only gives my life structure, but also it attracts other people to me, transforming my life into art.

Linda: Especially the tough parts. While we're horrified at the moment and depressed and feeling stuck, later on, we can look back, with perspective, and laugh. It's like the Mark Twain quote, "Comedy is tragedy plus time"—I may be paraphrasing, but that's the general idea.

Elaine: Right. But one has to be willing to expose themselves. If you're a writer, if you say, "Oh, I can't write about that," you're thinking, *I'm not good enough, it's not good, nobody will be interested, or other people will be upset*, then you're finished! If you're willing to get past those barriers and say, "No matter what, I want to write," then you're okay. And I think if you can write honestly and universally, then people will want to read what you've written. But one has to be willing to expose oneself. I mean, almost everybody has self-doubt. It's just a matter of getting past it—You know the book, *Feel the Fear and Do It Anyway*, by Dr, Susan Jeffers?

Linda: I love that book!

Elaine: I think if you let your fear be your guide, you'll end up not doing anything. Because fear of embarrassment or failure and letting these things stop me is like a death.

Linda: Some element of perfectionism can be a good quality. And I know you have a lot of discipline in your life too. You go to bed early and get up very early, you exercise...

Elaine: And I try to keep some balance in my life. I know how to use Facebook. And I use social media to build up community, to share other peoples' events and build up my friends, reach out to people and give them a way to reach out to me. I was at an event a couple of weeks ago and a woman was sitting in front of me, and I said, "You look familiar." She said, "Are you Elaine Soloway?" And both of us realized that we're Facebook friends.

Linda: I think your natural curiosity and your interest in learning is infectious. You don't seem to spend a lot of time feeling sorry for yourself.

Elaine: No, I rarely feel sorry for myself. I always felt that every one of us has some challenge in our lives. I never say, "Why me?" Should you live to be my age, you see a lot of things. Nothing that's happened to me doesn't happen, in one way or another, to everybody else in life.

Linda: Sometimes it occurs to me, that if one did have a life-partner, it might actually get in the way of working toward a goal—you know, wanting to please them, making wonderful meals or grooming time and expense—mani-pedis, trying too hard to be attractive or pleasing.

Elaine: And it's hard to do both. It's very hard to keep a man happy and to keep yourself happy. I mean, that was why Tommy and I were so compatible, because he had his own interests. He had his friends and his bowling and golf. He didn't need me to entertain him or keep him company all the time. So, we both did what we enjoyed and we enjoyed our time together sharing our respective days.

Linda: At this time of life, many times, one partner wants to pursue something and the other might feel neglected or competitive. Or one is retired and the other is involved in either paid work or volunteer work or learning something new.

Elaine: I like change in life, which is why I've moved so much. I like the challenge of finding new doctors, finding new maps. But, I just feel blessed that I like that about me.

Linda: It's interesting that you would be so unafraid—or afraid and you do it anyway.

Elaine: I think I was a fearful child, but my daughters have taught me audacity. Besides "Transparent", Faith, my older daughter, has written "Jesus Has Two Mommies" and all of her lesbian schlock operas. So, I have learned from them to lose some of the fear. Their lives are exposed.

Linda: I think the thing that makes me angry for those of us, especially women, who are older, is that we have dreams, too. And many of us are made to feel as if it is too late for us to fulfill any dreams we might have.

Elaine: You just said something interesting, you said you have dreams. I don't remember having dreams, I want to do this, I want to be that. I'm a dabbler. I try things and then they're not really dreams of mine. I don't have ambitions; I have experiences. Because, to me, dreams are something far off. Whereas, I prefer to develop a series of goals. To me, dreams just don't seem to have action plans associated with them. Like with the pilot, my goal was to do it in six weeks. Even if nothing happened with it, it would have been okay, I'd be fine with that.

Linda: So, rather than a product or results emphasis, yours is more of a process emphasis. Some people may say of something they're dreaming of, "When I get to the end of the rainbow, this is what my life is going to look like, and if it doesn't, I've failed." Instead, you seem to be saying: "Life is an adventure." I think you are an adventuress. It's like that quote from Helen Keller, "Life is either a daring adventure or it is nothing at all."

Elaine: I like that. . . . I believe that all people have creative sides. People can paint and write and sing and dance and write poetry. It's a shame we don't teach people how to let their creative sides out, because I think that's an intrinsic part of us. Like hair color or something, we are born with a creative side. But somewhere, we're taught that you have to have our projects appreciated by others. We get talked out of it. I think you have to learn how important creativity is for our soul, whether no one sees it or it's not on TV. That we, ourselves, need that part of us; that that part of us is for our soul. We need to make art in some way.

Linda: I know your sense of adventure and your positive attitude have taken you to a lot of projects that have been really worthwhile for you. There's something very alive about being a risk-taker. And even if you get no response or a negative response, you just pop back up and try something or somewhere else. I think you're very independent.

Elaine: Well, I'm 80 years old and I can walk and I can do a lot of the things I'm interested in. And I have two daughters who love one another and I have family and good friends, which is something not everybody has. I've been very fortunate—and during the tough times, I try to remind myself of that and be grateful. Also, I advise women to get a dog; they are wonderful company and one has to take walks. You meet lots of other dog-people, too.

*Frontotemporal Degeneration is a disease that typically causes deterioration in the ability to think, speak and/or move, until it eventually leads to death, People with this disease typically decline quickly over the 2-3 years and may live up to 6-8 years, dying of related problems, such as aspiration pneumonia or injuries due to balance problems.

CHAPTER THIRTY-SIX

Mary Miller: Life After Grief Tsunami

Mary Miller, in her seventies, has been a good friend to me for almost twenty years. She lives in a cozy condominium just outside Milwaukee. I knew her when she was a cheery and focused Catholic school principal with many friends, Then she left that school and began to work in the inner city with kids from challenging environments, trying to share her love of learning. These were not just children who were educationally-challenged, but kids from poor and often dysfunctional homes. The school itself had bullet-holes in the windows.

In her personal life, when people asked her, "Why hasn't a lovely woman like yourself ever married?" She answers with her typical humor, "I've made some pretty good choices in my life."

There was a point when she faced several of the grief issues that older women deal with and she became depressed. Being a therapist who reads and studies depression as well as a depression-survivor myself, I thought Mary's journey might enlighten and prepare other sager women to have an easier time of it, should they go through what she did.

Mary: "I had four main worries at the time I became depressed. First was my job, which I couldn't do anymore. I felt like I lost my passion for teaching and this job wasn't helping me get it back at all. I was just barely getting to work and just keeping body and soul together. I was depressed and anxious and, though I was getting help for it, I wasn't feeling much better. I would walk into that dark, dismal classroom and open those doors and think, *I don't know how many more days I can do this.* I wasn't fired, but my depression became so severe, I had to leave.

And because I couldn't make it work, and I did everything I could, I had the second worry, the money worry. This was because I expected to work at least another few years before I qualified for Medicare. I needed Medicare, because of some health problems I could not afford to treat without medical insurance.

The third concern was that I was in a relationship that wasn't working for me. I loved this man, but he really didn't get me, or understand depression. If I continued seeing him, I would have had to put on a false face and I didn't think that would be healthy for me.

My fourth worry was just thinking about getting older. Where would I live? How would I live? I had always been an independent woman, but if I wasn't working, didn't have health insurance, couldn't afford my condominium anymore, what would become of me?

I felt my world was falling apart. I didn't feel like I was an effective teacher and I had been a really good teacher for a long, long time. And I just kept slipping away. I went from being a school administrator at a really good school to an urban school, where kids weren't so motivated and the environment was depressing. It's hard to teach kids who aren't responding to your teaching.

Linda: Why did you leave your position at the really good school and take a job at an inner-city school?

Mary: I found the school was changing in ways that made it like a dysfunctional family for me. So I left and found other work in the inner city, but when I saw I couldn't effectively teach there, it was a terrible loss.

Linda: How did your family and friends deal with your depression?

Mary: My family cared, but I don't think they understood what I was going through. They did what they could, calling and bringing a meal or stopping by, and I think they wanted to help, but I don't think they knew how. I didn't know how to help myself, but I was doing all I could.

I was very blessed. My therapist, who'd known me for a long time and was seeing me without charge, told me she never saw me this depressed. She said she thought I needed to take a leave of absence.

I did take a leave of absence and I went through two outpatient programs. They helped some, teaching me tools to help me not isolate and to take care of myself and not blame myself. After all, part of the cause of depression is sensitivity and chemistry and feeling stuck in your situation. And I was seeing a psychiatrist, who was doing her best.

I wanted to get a second opinion, because I wasn't feeling better and it had been a long time. But I didn't have energy enough to make that change. The depression depleted my energy. However, I had people in my life. My cousin, who's a nurse, and a friend, who's a psychiatrist, looked at the meds and they both wondered how I was still walking around on so much medication.

Finally, a nurse-friend who worked in a psych unit talked to me about another doctor. So, I went to a nurse practitioner who was supervised by this doctor. She was looking at and very slowly tweaking my medications. And she asked me, "Have you ever considered suicide? Do you have a plan?" And I told her, "No."

As I walked out of her office, I said to myself, *I lied to her.* So, when I got home, I called the office to tell her the truth: "Yes, I have been considering suicide and I do have a plan." Then I called my therapist who suggested I go to the hospital.

And then you were coming to stay over, and I decided I wasn't going to go because you were coming. But we talked very openly about it. And I even asked if you would sleep next to me because I was afraid I would do something. And you did.

And the next morning, you said, "Mary, I think you should go to the hospital, because I don't feel good about you being here by yourself." And I think I was pretty compliant.

Linda: You were really ready. I really wanted them to recheck your meds with another opinion, and I knew the psychiatrist at the hospital we went to was a geriatric psychiatrist, so he might better understand the meds in terms of people our age.

Mary: That's right. I knew that there must be an answer to this. I felt like I was working as hard as I could. And I was just relieved to be going inpatient, because it gave me hope. Now, somebody who was an expert was going to take care of me. I still had insurance, and I stayed in the hospital for six days.

Linda: You tried everything, everything your doctor said to do, everything your outpatient groups taught you. If they said, do one spiritual thing a day, you would do it. One social thing, you would do it. One problem about living in an I-can-do-it-myself society, was that we come to believe that we are weak if we ask for help.

You were always such a disciplined person. I think you took the same discipline you used at work and at home and you applied it to this depression, only with more balance. You began to rest when you needed to, not overdo so much, change plans when you were too tired. And you began to set limits with friends who might have asked too much of you at that time or might not have been nurturing for you.

Mary: One of the words that comes to mind is "allowing," allowing myself not to be "the nice girl" all the time. Allowing myself to go to the physical therapist and tell her that the exercise routine she prescribed did not fit in with my lifestyle.

Instead of listening to everybody, I allowed myself to say, "This person says I should do this much exercise, and this one says I should do something else. The heck with it, I'm not doing all that. I don't care if it takes some years off my life, I don't want to live like a gerbil in a cage!"

Linda: What I saw was that you did a combination of letting go and trusting yourself and your helping professionals and friends, as your confidence returned; being able to pick and choose what strategies and people worked for you.

Mary: I felt like a leper, at one point. I felt like I couldn't get close to people and as if people were distancing themselves from me. I would go through these lists of things that I was supposed to do and I would try to check them off: I had to keep my diet healthy; I had to exercise; I was supposed to connect with others socially. But I would temper my list with my own instincts, like not doing too much in one day and, instead of watching more serious movies, I would read and watch fluff. And the seasons were changing; the light was coming back—and for me this always helps.

So when that April came, between the medication changes and the changes in me—I broke up with my boyfriend, I left the job that gave me the feeling I wasn't a good teacher, that I wasn't making a difference—It was like I rose from the dead. I got my life back.

Linda: And, a step at a time, you really did.

Mary: I did. And I started to volunteer and things came back gradually. I think from being in Overeaters Anonymous for years, I learned that I could replace old habits and I could struggle through new ones. I could "Act as if" and go to meetings and work the steps. But now I was letting go. The program gave me some structure. I began attending more meetings and writing about my feelings and reaching out to others more by making phone calls. I think the shame that I felt about my depression kept me from doing those things. I have to be careful not to spend too much time alone; I do need that social contact.

Linda: Yes. My own experience with depression is that one gets very self-involved, but it doesn't feel good, it just makes us feel worse. It seems like, as in 12-Step programs, it's really the service to others and compassion to ourselves and others that give us back purpose, making our lives meaningful—and for these things, age is irrelevant.

And then, here you were, starting with one thing, volunteering at the library a few hours a week, then joining a conservation group, and continuing to walk either outside or inside the local shopping mall for exercise when the weather was bad. And, in addition to a number of old friends, you came to meet new people through your activities.

You seemed to get to a point where you said to yourself, "This is my challenge and I have to accept it," and you baby-stepped along until you felt more like yourself.

But the whole time, you never stopped taking care of yourself. You always took a shower or a bath, always looked well-groomed and attractive. You ate in a healthy way, cooked things for yourself. These are all good signs. Some people, when they are depressed, get to a point where they can't get out of bed. They lose their energy and can't even do the things they need to do that will, in time, help them to feel better.

Mary: Yes. In our crazy society, the harder you work, the better you are. And I don't believe that anymore. Because I think I was working too hard and I think I burned out.

Linda: It seems like you've put much more balance in your life. I see that you're cooking and shopping, as you did, even when you were depressed. It's just you aren't overdoing it; you're enjoying it more.

And you are not self-involved, you have a number of causes you care about and work for. I wonder about whether part of your depression wasn't grieving some things you were letting go of –your vision of you and your boyfriend as a couple, your identity as a teacher, your security of always having worked and been self-sufficient—and then the fear that comes with ageing in our society: What if I don't have health care? What if Social Security doesn't give me a dignified and secure way to live for however long I live? Where will I live, if I can't afford to stay in my home? These social and environmental problems have been studied and shown to be huge causes of depression.

I even wonder if your depression wasn't a message that saved you from a relationship that might not have been the right one for you and a warning that saved you from a job that gave you a disempowered feeling. You were a teacher who was passionate about teaching, but this job gave you a feeling that, no matter how hard you worked, you couldn't be effective in these particular classrooms with these particular kids.

Mary: I enjoy doing—I feel like when I was first teaching, it was like a gift that was given to me and I was so glad to share it with somebody. And that's what I feel about my mental health now. It's like a gift, like a hell that I've come through, and I want to make sure that if other people are overdoing it, like I saw myself doing, I don't want them to go through that. So, I caution people not to work too hard. That's why I offered to speak at the psychiatric hospital that I felt helped me so much, because I think doing this helps me to gain perspective and not forget what I came through.

Linda: It's true. More than just a role model, you've become an activist: writing letters, making phone calls, and following your strong feelings with action.

Mary: Lately, I call or write our political representatives when I feel passionate about something they are doing, and not just to criticize, also to thank them. And I got in contact with the woman from the '53206' movie.

Linda: 53206, what is that?

Mary: That's a zip code in Milwaukee. There was a documentary film that showed that the 53206 zip code has the largest proportion of African-American men in the world who are incarcerated.

I went to see the movie, and I got the business card of this woman whose husband was incarcerated. I talked to her after the movie and I ended up calling her to suggest she contact WUWM producer Bonnie North there, because I thought Bonnie could be a source of change by publicizing the situation of the woman's husband and others like him.

Linda: I see you empowering yourself and trying to empower others about issues you care about.

Mary: I try. But I also try to keep my life balanced. Like now, I'm playing tennis with a group of mostly younger women.

Linda: And didn't you start a group?

Mary: The group I started is actually based on Julia Cameron's book, *The Artist's Way: A Spiritual Path to Higher Creativity.* It's a small group and we use our creativity to enrich our lives. For example, we made lamps that were decorated with symbols that were meaningful to us. The projects we did were to help us use our creativity to remind us of what held meaning in our lives.

Linda: It sounds to me as if you used your own creativity to overcome this depression: you limited your friends to those who could be supportive in an effective way; you replaced your passion for teaching with your strong feelings about causes you care about.

Mary: I even wrote a letter to our Archbishop about women being acknowledged for their contributions to the Church, as teachers and administrators and volunteers.

One of the things about right now, is that, most days, I feel very satisfied. I am grateful for my friends and I can be happy working in my garden. I really don't need to have more money; I don't need a man in my life—not that if the right man came along who made my life better, he wouldn't be welcomed. But I just love the things that I have in my life. I am just so full of gratitude for the people I do have.

The depression, which was the most painful thing I've ever suffered—held a sense of shame, like I was weak. But it was a real wake-up call to appreciate each day, to set limits with toxic people and embrace the supportive ones. I think going through that awful time actually taught me a lot and made me a better person. Our experiences help us to be the people we become.

When I look back, the result of these hard times brought gifts that I could never have imagined.

Linda: I think most people, especially women, fear that we will end up dependent and we don't know who we would depend upon. Going through what you did, I wonder how you handled that?

Mary: I was very scared when I had to retire early due to my depression. It wasn't until my 50's that I took savings more seriously (that and I earned more, so saving was easier). I planned to retire at 65 or maybe even later. When I had to leave work, my financial planner went over my expenses with me and bluntly told me I would have to lower my expenses. When I left my job, I had no income. I had to live off of my savings.

I heard of a disability lawyer who was known to help people who could not work with applying for Social Security Disability. I made an appointment and dragged myself there with my brother for support. I was so ill and foggy at the time, I wasn't sure I would remember or understand the consultation. But I took careful notes and filled out some forms and I did as told. I was able to get Social Security Disability until I was eligible for my regular Social Security.

I also got another miracle. The woman from my employer's Human Resources Department called to tell me I was eligible for long term disability. I had already applied for short-term disability through the company and was denied.

When I began to have a fixed income, I listed all of my basic expenses first, compared that to my income and then planned on how much I had to live on for the month. A few times, I had to go into savings, but only when big items came up.

Because I worked hard and feel like I did the best that I could, I had to trust that I'll be okay. I shop rummage sales, lower-end grocery stores and I got a used car when my car started breaking down . But my life is very good. I am much healthier and much happier.

I don't know if I'll be able to live on my savings until the day I die. Just like all of us, I don't know how long I'll live. Will I need help from the government when I am older, I can't say. But, for now, I am doing my best, staying as healthy as I can, realizing that, with God's grace, I have come through hard times, and all I can do is do my part.

CHAPTER THIRTY-SEVEN

Dr. Renee Garrick:
The Healing Power of Spirituality and Community

I first met Dr. Renee Garrick, in her sixties, when she was one of the facilitators in a series of hypnotherapy retreats I was part of. I felt she was very accepting, positive, and loving. I saw her as a gentle soul other trainees reached out to. I saw her, first hand, using her gifts to teach and supervise. As well as being a group facilitator and supervisor for hypnotherapy, she is an ordained minister and has a private counseling practice. Whenever people in our internship group felt stuck, Dr. Garrick (everybody calls her Renee) was one of the first teachers called upon for assistance. There is just something about her that beckons to others, welcoming questions and sorting out differences.

Once, she facilitated a hypnotherapy training at a house I was renting, and it was held on a Jewish High Holy day, but even when I realized that, while I wanted to honor the holiday, I didn't feel drawn to a house of worship to do it. I shared my concerns with Renee and she encouraged me to do whatever felt meaningful to me. So I meditated and wrote all day.

I know I wasn't the only therapist or trainee who consulted Renee, and I wanted to find out what it was about her that drew us and how she would advise us to greet our sager years.

Linda: So, Renee, I've seen you as a very loving and spiritual role model for others. I am curious about how you get through the tough parts of life, like illness or death.

Renee: I know in the grand scheme of things, and I really believe this, that even on the rainy days of my life, those experiences that were challenging and not fun to go through, that actually those difficulties had also been opportunities for me to grow, to explore, to evolve and step into who I am and what I'm doing now.

Linda: Could you say more about this?

Renee: I look at a couple of years ago in January, when my mother made her Transition. It was not expected. She was certainly older, had challenging health concerns, but nothing even remotely looked as if she was going to make her Transition.

Linda: I've heard you use this term before, Transition, could you explain why you don't call the end of life, Death?

Renee: I prefer naming, identifying a person's passing or dying as making their Transition, moving from one phase of life into another phase of life, evolving from the physical to the non-physical. Because I believe there really is no death; that our spirit is the manifestation, the collection of energies that has consciousness.

And when did that consciousness begin? When was it born? It's the same as energy. Energy isn't created and it isn't destroyed. It just moves from one form to another. It's like moving water into an ice cube, it didn't die, it just changed form.

When an ice cube is put into a heated space, it becomes steam. It's still a form of water, it still has the same molecules and atoms, although its physical formation is now different. I believe that our spirit does that, going into a body, and then changing into another form. So, I don't say someone died. I might say "passed", but rather, they Transitioned, they graduated. They moved from this form of life to another form of life.

My mother's Transition happened suddenly, in January, where I needed to leave a day just to get to her. And I'm grateful that the way things worked out, that I was able to get there, because that was the agreement that she and I made with each other, that she wanted me to be there.

And I believe I was away for two weeks. Afterwards, when I returned home, I literally pulled into my driveway, into the garage, and there was some kind of odd sound, an odd odor. And I learned that my pipes broke and burst while I was away. The water was still running. So, there was a significant amount of damage to my home. Well, the firefighters and the construction company said that there was so much damage and the water when the pipes burst was so forceful, that perhaps it was a blessing that I wasn't home. That if I had been standing, for example, at my kitchen sink, the force of the ceiling that fell in the kitchen, well, it could have fallen on me. And, so, when I look at it, did I want my mother to have made her Transition, goodness no. But, if I had been in my house, I might have been badly injured or I might have Transitioned myself. But, not only did my not being there save me, but the damage later created a pathway for me to make some repairs in my home that I might not have been able to do otherwise.

Linda: So, even in the most difficult times, it seems as if you have a larger perspective. Your mother's unexpected Transition, and your being away because of it, first, may have saved your life, and your burst pipes, while at first seeming disastrous, ultimately allowed something more positive to happen, in that you were able to repair your home.

Renee: I look at all of that and find ways to create a place of gratitude. And, if I can't find gratitude in that moment, I try to have faith in the purpose for whatever happened, until I can move to that place of gratitude. It's as if I were building a bridge to get there; to really embrace that notion of a purpose for everything, which seems, to me, to be a universal truth.

Linda: So, when the challenges come, you are seeing and feeling them, but also having faith that they will ultimately create space for something good.

Renee: I just believe that we're only governed by what we allow to come into our realm of consciousness.

Linda: Are you referring to ego here?

Renee: I believe that if I limited myself, allowed ego or fear or someone else's mindset to override what my soul's journey could have been, I would have missed a great deal. And, without the experience I gathered through years, I couldn't have been at the same level spiritually.

Linda: What would you advise us to do to further our own spiritual journeys?

Renee: One of my teachers, years ago, would offer us these assignments, like to sit under a tree, because trees are ancient lines of power, whose roots run very, very deep. And trees get a deep view, because they connect and mingle with other roots, who connect and mingle with still others, so there's this network of shared wisdom. This teacher would have us pick a tree we liked and to ask, "What are the most important things for me to know or do now?" And, then, wait for the response. Sometimes, it's more than just knowing; it's how do I put that feeling into action?

I could go on and on about key times in my life where experiences helped to shape my spiritual journey. I guess I took all of that and mixed it together, creating a really fragrant, tasty, textured and beautifully colored marsala, that I get to eat and share at other people's tables now. I wouldn't have been able to do that if I hadn't had some years of life under my heart, under my belly, in my consciousness; they are like blocks under my feet.

This faith seems to also take the sting our of whatever I'm going through, at least for a moment. And, that way, I can move through life in a place of balance and wholeness. No matter what is going on, I know I will move through it. I get a "knowing," an overwhelming feeling of hope and inspiration. Like, Okay, I'm going to move to the next step and what's that going to be for me? And I can find joy and hope in that.

Linda: That's such a beautiful way to look at life. Eric and Joan Erikson's Adult Stages of Life theorized that in our mature years, there was a time of what they called, "Ego Integrity versus Despair." In other words, in our sager years, we could appreciate our life's accomplishments, feeling fulfilled and accepting, or else we would likely descend into despair. Joan Erikson, co-creator of her husband Erik's Adult Stages of Life, said, "Conflicts and tension are sources of growth, strength, and commitment." It seems as if even in your own dark times, you are aware of this tension.

Do you think there is a way to prepare for growing older with wisdom and appreciation, rather than falling into despair? What has been helpful to you in your growth?

Renee: Spiritual practice and Community, yes. When I was preparing to purchase my home almost twenty-five years ago, a teacher once told me he was a little concerned that I would cloister myself away and become a hermit, but that this would probably not be the best for me because part of my purpose in this life is to really be out in the world, to teach, to guide and to support.

Earlier in my life, I was involved in many groups and organizations, just doing everything, connecting with people, because I love being in the midst of activity and organizations and life. But I now see in later years, silence and alone time becomes very valuable. I can put on favorite music, pick up a book, sit out in nature.

I find that while I can have a spiritual practice by myself and it's meaty and deep, when I engage in or share my practice with others, it grows exponentially. The people around me really are a lifeline, giving me an opportunity to expand and experience something different.

Linda: Is there any specific practice you do?

Renee: There's a practice I do in the morning, a way that I greet my soul and the Creator. I do that every morning before I get out of bed. It's a way I connect with myself and I've done versions of this for many, many years. I meditate twice a day. Once in the morning— though, honestly, I don't do that every morning. My meditations may be in the meditation room that I created for myself. Or they may be outside in nature or wherever I can be still and listen. Or I may provide myself with "sound energy" as a spiritual practice.

Linda: What is "sound energy"?

Renee: I use sacred sounds, such as chants or other spiritual music which have high frequencies or vibrations. This seems to clear and shape the energy frequencies within myself.

In the same way, there are ways I close out the day. These practices can be anything from asking myself, "Whose life have I impacted today? Who caused me to smile and who did I cause to smile? What could I have done differently? What did I learn that was new? What might I want to do next time that I did not do this time? Maybe I was not in the highest form of myself today, and how might I do something different? This might mean creating a way to make amends. The evening offers me an opportunity to reflect upon my day.

Linda: So, you reflect on the day, but you don't beat yourself up.

Renee: I'm moving toward not doing that, yes. I was once pretty good at that, because I wanted to get it—I hate to say that awful P-word, Perfect. Perfectionism comes from our shadow side. So, I guess I've learned not to do that, but to hold myself accountable and keep the highest vision of myself and look at what prevents me from being that.

Linda: I think it was Brene Brown, who said, "If you want to be admired, be perfect. If you want to be loved, be vulnerable."

Renee: Yes, well now I try to watch out for my own perfectionism. I try to end my evenings by saying goodnight to the Creator, to the mother of us all. To consider what to have gratitude for and how I can best express that. This doesn't have to be a long, long list; it can be a few minutes. I try to have a closing to my day.

Linda: Do you have a community with whom you work spiritually?

Renee: I have several groups I belong to, where we learn and grow together and where we study together and have discussions. We may or may not be similar in our spiritual understanding, but, especially because of our differences, these exchanges open up opportunities to learn and grow even more. And several groups that I belong to do spiritual practice together.

Linda: Does your practice and your teaching help?

Renee: Yes, absolutely. I use those and other processes and workshops to delve into those aspects of healing myself, releasing any trauma, releasing any shock,* releasing the adverse effects of these parts of myself and teaching others how to do this as well.

Linda: It's interesting that you say that. For myself, I went to hypnotherapy, initially to help my clients, but I learned a lot about myself that I hadn't expected, and that helped me to grow in so many ways.

Renee: I find people use these groups and trainings to stop running from those parts of ourselves that we've thought of as, air quotes here, "wrong" – in other words, our dark sides.

Renee: I do think that Community is very key. I tell my students sometimes, you can be so heavenly, where you're no earthly good. You know, you're spending all your time in meditation and reading, but how do you put that into practice? How do you live it?

So, I find it's important to me, to spend time with friends who may not be doing exactly what I'm doing, but in their hearts and souls, they are every bit as spiritual, in that they are trying to be the best versions of themselves.

I have this group of friends, my book club, who've been together almost twenty-four years. And we've always said that we're like Sacred Sisters. So, we get together on a Saturday, and we go out to a beautiful restaurant and we eat and we share with one another. And, once, we looked at a table across from us at a couple who both had their cell phones out, texting away. And we watched the lack of conversation, eye contact, laughter and joy in their eyes. And I thought, I never know when is the last time I'm going to see these beautiful souls I am sitting with or any of my beloved friends or family. So, I've grown to that place of really wanting to make these times together sacred and purposeful, to really connect.

Linda: So, you create a sacred space for the people in your life.

Renee: Yet that place of community doesn't always have to be with people I study with, or people that I worship with, people I teach and learn from. That sense of community can be anywhere and everywhere. It can be going to the grocery store and having a conversation with whoever is there, helping a little lady reach up to a high shelf or sharing a recipe with a gentleman. When I'm connecting with others, that's Community.

*Shock: from "Overcoming Shock" by Diane Zimberoff and David Hartmann, a term used for the traumatized mind and heart, which is one of many things which are treated in Wellness Hypnotherapy

CHAPTER THIRTY-EIGHT

Barbara Leigh: Hard Times As Lessons

Barbara Leigh, in her seventies, is the Cofounder/Artistic Producing Director Emeritus of Milwaukee's Public Theatre. At forty-one, on her way back from a performance in Prescott, Wisconsin to Milwaukee, Wisconsin, the car she and other members of the performing company were in hit a patch of ice on a bridge and jumped the embankment. The accident left her partially paraplegic. Her spine was affected, leaving her paralyzed from the waist down. Some of the use of her legs came back little by little, so she has been able to walk using two canes. Through creativity, meaningful work, and her own persistence, Barbara has used her life and her training as a clown and a mime to inspire others.

Recently, after forty-five years, The Milwaukee Public Theatre company shut down, but Barbara has not stopped working and creating and doing. Entering her apartment in a lovely elevator building in downtown Milwaukee, the colors, the décor, and her own cheery demeanor make the wheelchair she sits in the least important fixture in her home.

Linda: Barbara, how did you get through the loss you had, the partial paraplegia? The adjustment must have been overwhelming.

Barbara: Well, I think, fortunately for me, my tools were developed long before the accident, and it was those tools that really helped me to survive and make the most of it.

Linda: Could you say more about those tools?

Barbara: My work as a mime and a clown made me always open to discovery and learning. My mime teacher always said, whatever you're performing, whatever you're creating, especially something that's invisible, the character has to be done with the utmost respect, respect coming from the Latin "spectare," "to look," and "re," or "again." Also, I spent so much of my time as a physical theatre artist, I exercised all the time and did a lot of work isolating parts of the body. So I was very familiar with breathing and posture. Working as a mime clown was the best preparation for trauma.

It took about from about forty-five days to two years for my legs to start working again. I was in the hot tub and I was cold, so I told my right leg to go down. And it did! I was so excited! The physical therapist wasn't there, but my friends were. And I told my left leg to go down, but my left leg is a little slower than my right. After about six weeks, I could walk very slowly with two canes.

Linda: When I listened to your Ex Fabula* reading, telling the story of the accident, I thought, some people would be decked by what happened to you. They might consider it the end of life as they knew it.

Barbara: One thing that was important was that I had huge, huge community support. I didn't have time to go down. My hospital room was constantly filled with people, giving me all kinds of encouragement and little gifts and fun cards. My friends put posters on the ceiling. And the staff at Froedert Hospital was so wonderful. Also, I think I've always needed to have what I considered to be meaningful work that brought me through the time of the accident and I expect will bring me through anything. So, having passion for my work helps me to push beyond the other stuff. Also, I'm very persistent.

Linda: How do you think you developed your persistence and positive thinking?

Barbara: Actually, my mother was a terrific role model for me. She was an actress and a wonderful storyteller herself. She had an amazing range of vocal expression. She worked in Chicago, directing and producing shows at the Allerton Hotel. She cast my father, an aspiring playwright, in one of the shows, which is how they met. The two of them had theatrical ambitions, so they moved to New York. But it was wartime and she became pregnant with me, so she moved back to Sheboygan, where her parents lived.

But moving didn't stop her. She developed these amazing one-woman shows about women who really made a difference.

Linda: Who were some of her inspirational women?

Barbara: There was Indoc Poc, for example, who started a school in Korea; Anna Allacora, who was a spy for Lincoln during the Civil War. She told the story of Helen Keller. And she did her dramatizations mostly for women's clubs all over the state. And she was her own agent. She'd just change her voice, saying, "This is Charlotte's agent. I'll see if she's available."

And there's something else really amazing. She was seriously, seriously injured in a car accident when she was somewhere in her twenties and her left knee was completely shattered. They were thinking, back then, that they'd have to amputate. But she was very fortunate, because she was taken to the one hospital in Chicago where there was a bone specialist who was actually able to save her leg. And, as soon as she could walk, she was in the play, *The Barretts of Wimpole Street*. Wow, I hadn't thought about her handling of her own injury as part of her as an inspiration for me, but I guess it was lurking in the back of my mind.

Linda: So your mother was a model of a survivor with a positive attitude…

Barbara: Actually, so was my father. My parents were in their 70's and starting to feel a little like they needed some purpose in their lives. At that point, I was co-director of a mime theatre and I said, "Why don't you start a theater company?" And, a month later, my father said, "Barbie, Charlotte and I have decided to start a theatre company." At first, it was senior citizen theatre, but under Milwaukee Public Theatre Company's umbrella. And then about a year later, they said, "We'd really like to have our own nonprofit." And they went ahead and started *Theater Within You*. And they did lots of radio talk shows to discuss aspects of aging. Their motto was, "You can be practically ageless."

Linda: You had terrific role models! I know you mentioned humor as an important part of your life after your accident.

Barbara: Yes, whatever you're going through, keeping your sense of humor is tremendously healing.

Linda: Do you think anyone can develop their sense of humor?

Barbara: Most people have a glimmer of a sense of humor. You have to find your own level of what's funny to you. Books like Norman Cousins' *Anatomy of an Illness*, where he found that ten minutes of genuine belly laughter have an anesthetic effect. He was the editor of the Saturday Review, who became deathly ill. And when doctors told him there was no cure for his disease, with the help of friends who brought in a film projector so he could watch funny movies, like The Three Stooges and The Marx Brothers, he decided to try to heal himself. And he lived. And on Bill Moyers' television documentary on the art of healing, the message was that the more you can be a part of your treatment, the better for your health.

Linda: So being empowered to be active in your own recovery is important. You've mentioned friends and community as extremely helpful in your life.

Barbara: I have to admit that, at first, my experience of paralysis was terrifying. I was brought to the hospital after the accident and I was scared and in pain. And I saw my legs were spasming like wild horses out of control. My first instinct was denial and anger and frustration and sadness. I thought my creative life was over.

But I was very fortunate. My friends, family and the Froedtert staff wouldn't let me forget who I'd been. They collectively helped to transform my environment. Gradually, they showed me that there were still some choices open to me. And, eventually, I was able to begin to apply the creativity that had always been so much a part of my life. Lucky for me, my sister made sure the hospital team included me and my family and friends. Together, we actually did become an amazing network of support.

Linda: Anything that stands out to you?

Barbara: My leg spasms only got worse if I was upset, so I had to learn to relax and slow down to gain any control. But I also couldn't sleep at night; nothing was comfortable. Some friends brought me a continuous play tape recorder and tapes of beautiful, relaxing music.

Later, I took a creativity course and learned about how the brain works with different frequencies, and how, when we are awake and trying to cope, we are in beta. If we can relax a bit more, we enter a slower alpha state, which is ideal for creating and healing. Most of the nursing staff seemed to enjoy it, too. Although I remember asking one nurse if she used breathing/relaxation techniques and she said, "I have enough to worry about without trying to relax."

I had dancer friends who gave suggestions of exercises I could do and my physical therapist incorporated them into our routine. I began to use my old mime skills, using muscles in isolation. And these helped me to learn things like transferring, turning over, getting dressed.

My favorite nurse had a great sense of humor. She told me she had the secret ambition of being a clown, so I taught her how to juggle. I'd play my accordion, while she wafted scarves. Later, when I was working on one of my shows, I put bladder control into the show. Like this:

Welcome to Incontinental Airlines Flight Number One. There is a Flight Number Two, but that is usually delayed. We are about to take off, so please make sure your seats are in a secure and uptight position. We're expecting moisture and a lot of turbulence along the way today. Please pay attention and note as I point out the entrance and exits (points to mouth and below).

There will be no bowel or bladder control on today's flight. In the likely event that you do encounter a full bladder, a catheter will descend from the ceiling panel. Please insert the device as illustrated on the card located in the seat pocket in front of you. First, cleanse the area, using an iodine swab, then open the sterile package and squeeze a small amount of KY Jelly on the catheter tip. Don't touch that catheter!

Now, don the sterile gloves, making sure you don't touch the gloves with your dirty little hands while you're putting them on.

For those traveling with small children or children of any size, for that matter, please insert your own catheter first before assisting others.

In the unlikely event of large liquid volumes, your seat bottom converts into a flotation cushion.

Please observe that the Captain has turned on the "No Dignity" sign. Don't expect that to change for remainder of the flight.

On behalf of the Captain and crew, thank you for flying Incontinental.

Linda: I love it!

Barbara: So, I gradually began applying humor to my legs. I noticed that they had different personalities. My right leg seemed more controlled, whereas my left leg was totally wild. I named the right one Frisky and left, Feisty. In an exercise given to me by my occupational therapist, she suggested that I make something like a model airplane. I asked if I could make a pair of puppet legs instead. She enthusiastically helped me, bringing in a pair of panty hose, some stuffing, some fishing line, some stiffening used for making casts. We put my shoes on them and those legs were one of the most important tools in my healing process,

There's a body of research on the therapeutic value of smiling. Dr. John Diamond wrote a book called, *Your Body Doesn't Lie*, in which he tells us that, "Smiling helps strengthen the thymus gland, an important contributor to the immune system, because the smile muscles and the thymus gland are closely linked."

Linda: Pema Chodron, the American Buddhist Nun, says that a half-smile gives the brain a positive message which actually makes us feel better.

Barbara: I think one can assist in their own healing, using humor, creativity, meaningful work, support systems and good role models and finding ways of avoiding too much stress. Do your yoga, your exercises, your breathing, and relaxation. If you work, find escape routes too, so you're not working all the time.

Linda: Has it been hard to ask for help from others?

Barbara: I'm not proud; I'll take help. I think it's really important to share responsibilities. If there's any way you can remove yourself from the center of everything and get competent people to work with you. . . .

Linda: Is that how you did it, in terms of the theatre company?

Barbara: The only way we really survived was through the talents of our artists and the support team I had, which was amazing. People are often glad to help. It's just amazing how wonderful people are.

Linda: Barbara, if you had something you wanted to advise other sager women, what might you say?

Barbara: For me, I've got to keep at it! I walk so slowly that I often use the wheelchair. But it's a double-edged sword, if I don't use my legs, I will lose the use of them. So, I walk in the pool, I do yoga, I do exercise, too, a lot of stretching and strengthening. You can't expect the physical therapist to do it all.

For me, it's been really, really important to be part of the world. I've been very active in helping to make positive change. I just finished doing this film which is a retrospective of the forty-five years of Milwaukee Public Theatre Company. The film was fun and it was an opportunity to reflect and do some closure. Keeping your sense of humor is paramount, staying active, doing positive things with and for the community. Keeping your friends—friends are so important. Most important, I've found, is staying open to all the possibilities, not focusing on the impossibilities. I'm learning Spanish again. I'm singing in a choir. Oh, and I have a new man in my life. It's very exciting.

Linda: How did you meet?

Barbara: I met him at the Unitarian Church when I accidentally ran over his foot. He's seventy-six, like me. And he's just been diagnosed with Parkinson's. I've been his cheerleader. And I've learned a lot about Parkinson's, in turn, which has been helpful to me. And when you reach this age, you know a lot about relationships; you've had some experience. My most important message is, Don't buy into the stereotypes about being older; the key is to stay open.

*ExFabula: Latin for "from stories," ExFabula is a series of presentations of storytelling workshops and community collaborations in Milwaukee, where people tell their stories aloud and connect. In this "live" storytelling mode people begin to communicate and feel heard.

CHAPTER THIRTY-NINE

Mary Pender Greene: Re-wiring and Balancing

Mary Pender Greene, now in her sixties, is a sharecropper's daughter and one of eleven children She was for many years Chief of Social Work and then Assistant Director of Jewish Board of Family and Children's Services in New York. She was, at the beginning, the only black woman administrator at the world's largest volunteer mental health social service agency. She introduced the idea of diversity to her agency well before it became politically correct. Mary also came to hold the position of President of NASW, the National Association of Social Workers. She is a therapist, a coach and an innovator, and the author of *Creative Mentorship and Career-Building Strategies: How to Build Your Virtual Personal Board of Directors.* I interviewed her in her home in Brooklyn, New York, to find out how she was faring after "retirement".

Linda: Mary, what would you advise women to do to prepare for aging?

Mary: Well, as the saying goes, "Life is not a dress rehearsal". So, we have to be conscious about our choices. In the future, some choices will no longer be options—such as having children. Time is limited. And if we're just working, putting off fun and socialization and relationships for later, putting all your energy into work, the older you get, the more difficult it may be to make new friends. After all, when you are younger you are in situations where everyone's looking to connect, like school or work. Those are natural settings for building new relationships. It's not impossible to connect later on, it's just more complex. Also, cultivating and maintaining intergenerational friendships is especially important as you age.

Linda: How can women who haven't prepared for growing older, or may find that the plan that they had—maybe travel or retirement with a partner, may not be possible or as satisfying as they imagined it to be?

Mary: I believe that using your intellectual abilities is something that never ends as long as we live. So it's important to remain curious and be open to new ideas, whatever our circumstances.

Linda: But sometimes unforeseen events, like illness or caregiving a partner or the deaths of friends or one's partner, may leave us feeling stuck and wondering how to handle the rest of our lives. Have you had any struggles in growing older?

Mary: I find one thing I've had to struggle with is my body changing. I used to have a very small waistline. And, now, no matter how carefully I eat, it doesn't seem to make a difference. So, there's a part of me that mourns the loss. I was also surprised at my energy changing. Sometimes, I'd say to myself, *What's wrong with me? I never used to get tired like this.* I've had to come to terms with the idea that it's unrealistic to continue to be the me-that-I've-always-known. I'm coming to accept being the best I can be today.

Linda: How do you handle that acceptance?

Mary: I remind myself that there's are tradeoffs for being the me-I-am-now, rather than the me-I-was-when-I-was-younger. For one thing, I had a lot less emotional sophistication when I was younger. And another is, I trust myself more and need less validation from others than I did when I was younger. My body may have been firmer and younger, but I'd never trade the wisdom I've gained or the feeling that I can trust my gut, my instincts, even if I don't get validation from the outside, for the waistline or the youthful energy of my younger years.

Linda: What do you advise a psychotherapy or counseling client who feels stuck or hasn't prepared for the years beyond middle age?

Mary: I had a client who was having a conflict at work, and rather than work on the conflict, she decided to retire. But, later, she came to feel that she made a mistake. My work was in helping her pick up the pieces.

Linda: How did you do that?

Mary: I asked her to consider when she last felt passionate about something. In her case, it was when she was working in art, but she couldn't make a living at that, so she chose to work in the helping professions. She worked very hard, but lacked passion for the job. A part of our work was helping her reconnect with what brought her joy.

Linda: How did you talk to her about reconnecting?

Mary: We talked about her taking some classes that could help her get back into her art, as well as other aspects of her creativity,

Linda: I find that creative people are most often able to be creative in more than one way. For example, Paul McCartney was a brilliant songwriter and singer, but in his later years, he's become a prolific painter. And though you are still doing coaching and psychotherapy, you have a consulting business and have written a book on your ideas about mentoring. Tell us more about what led to the book and its ideas.

Mary: Well, I call it re-wiring. I think the core of it is that I am so excited about the wisdom that comes with aging. I had no clue suddenly everything would click in and all of the things that I've done, and all of the things that I've experienced would give me insights I didn't have earlier. And I get so charged with the idea of looking at younger people and about how cumulative wisdom can really make a difference. And that's really at the core of the book, too. It's offering mentoring moments to many people, rather than being the sole mentor to one person.

Linda: How did your thoughts about re-wiring begin?

Mary: This started happening at The Jewish Board in my early years there. Way back then, I interviewed all potential clinical staff. So the policy basically was, if you interview somebody and you don't hire them, send them a note thanking them and saying you chose someone else. On occasion, people would ask me, you didn't choose me, what would have made it different? And I started by giving some people insights about some of the things that they said in the interview that were not helpful. And also, when I was Chief of Social Work and then Assistant Executive Director, many people in all of those offices used to come to me with one problem or another involving their supervisor or staff. So I got to be sort of the troubleshooter for a lot of folks.

What it actually did for me, though, is it helped me think about how to be helpful to somebody, without being their mentor per se. Because, then, mentoring in my mind was you choose somebody, you stay with them throughout their career; you help them develop. But what I realized is that I was offering mentoring moments to many different people. And I then started talking to others about offering mentoring moments as well. As a result, it was about paying it forward. That no matter who you are, no matter where you are, there's somebody that's got some wisdom that you don't have.

In the process of this, it occurred to me that, "Wow, I know a lot of stuff!" I realized that what I knew could be useful to others.

Linda: So, how did your book grow out of that?

Mary: I was doing a keynote address about mentoring moments, and creating a virtual personal board of directors. And someone in the audience was from Oxford Press, and approached me to ask me if I wanted to write a book. I was just about to leave The Jewish Board. I wasn't quite out the door as yet, but I was about to go. And so the timing in all of it just fell into place.

The other thing that happened too, was when I was President of New York's National Association of Social Workers. I met people from all over the country. I realized that being at The Jewish Board in New York all of those years exposed me to many different experiences, because it was so big and so diverse.

And it was also complicated and hard and difficult to negotiate. I was a woman of color in the midst of a lot of white men. I had a strong interest in broadening the organization with regards to how they functioned and how they were viewed by the larger community. And the CEO and the Deputy were white Jewish men who believed in me. They supported my suggestions about diversity, equity and inclusion before it was in vogue. They encouraged me to bring my full self and my wisdom. They wanted me there, and I felt I belonged. It was my professional home for many years.

Linda: So you always found ways to work with ideas you were passionate about.

Mary: There is something about being able to bring your best self to whatever you're doing, and to explore things that you have passion for. Some of my colleagues, who worked in places where they were not able to bring themselves fully to work, retired and still don't feel as if they're living their best lives. Several stopped taking care of themselves, stopped going out, and watched a lot of TV. If we don't pursue our passions, especially after retirement, we can feel bored, disconnected and unproductive. I believe that many of these people had shut down in their younger years and failed to develop personal passions, which can be crucial in one's older years.

Linda: Can you give an example of someone you know?

Mary: A woman who I would say is one of my virtual personal board members is probably in her 90's. I hired her to do a special project. And she was doing fine, until we became computerized. She was maybe 75 at that time. But she believed she could not learn computers. And what that meant is that I no longer could offer her an opportunity I once was able to offer her. She subsequently moved further and further away from doing leadership development and training, things that she loved and was excellent at. These are things somebody more mature really can do very well. But if the institution you're working with is moving to virtual platforms, you've got to learn those things.

Linda: So, you've got to be willing to keep up, to learn new skills.

Mary: Yes. I've done lots of training and being able to see the bigger picture requires help. And you've got to see how you can manage within the institution and be able to take care of yourself while learning, growing and contributing.

Linda: Many women think about others, but sometimes forget about themselves.

Mary: Absolutely. So realizing that made me feel as though I wanted to be able to share that thought with others. So, I stopped following the rules as such. Most institutions have the practice of not giving authentic feedback to interviewees, potential staff, because of the fear of getting sued. But I bump into people now who say that I met them at an interview and I told them they needed to go back to school or that it wasn't appropriate to talk about outside interests too much in an interview. People want to hear about the job that you're interviewing for.

I was often out of the box, because I would sometimes say to people,

"Are you sure this is the career that you want, because what you're saying about your stated interests don't match with this job." Even though our contact was brief, I run into people who tell me what I advised was very important to them. That's part of what made me feel like there were things I could write about that could be useful.

Linda: You spoke earlier about relationships, what kind of relationships do you find are important?

Mary: I think it's so important to have people that you can be honest with. I have no relationships where I can't be authentic or real. Now, I'm not saying I don't say hello, but I'm talking about the idea of investing my time and energy.

The colleagues that I kept relationships with over time, I started first of all referring some private patients to them, because I didn't have enough time to see everyone. I started giving people coaching assignments that I couldn't do. And then it became people could do the coaching, but they couldn't manage the relationships with the institutions. I had experience in talking to CEOs, speaking to boards, communicating with the people who ran organizations about issues or negotiating with them around contracts.

I say that as an example of being open to possibility. I expanded my role doing private practice, to include taking on more coaching. I saw lots of individual adults, mostly women, who were struggling in their work environment. So that's what I thought I was going to do.

And my business in coaching kind of grew. This was not what I had in mind at all, because I was focused on couples and women especially, but it grew because I was open to possibilities.

Linda: It seems like your direction just naturally took on a life of its own.

Mary: It did.

Linda: And what did you learn? Was it different working with the men than coaching women?

Mary: One thing that I learned in the process is that most people need the same things. People all want love, they want to feel good about themselves, they want to be able to be in a relationship where they can be heard and be themselves. The idea that you're going to get married and live happily ever after is such a bunch of nonsense, without work. Also, that without telling somebody what you need, they're going to read your mind because they love you. So I was helping people to stop and consider the realities about their lives. Probably because of my own relationship.

My husband, Ernest, is my anchor. He's a great guy. And he's very different than me, and that's a part of what I talk about. Most people don't choose somebody exactly like them and stay with them, because they make you crazy if they act exactly like you.

Linda: So, people probably work best in complementary relationships. I think you are saying that if you aren't doing things you are passionate about and you don't have important relationships, when the work part of life drops off—say your workplace downsizes and your position is eliminated, you need to have other important aspects of living that give you support.

Mary: You have nobody else covering the other parts of life. And if either person is not negotiating for what works for them, both as a couple and as a person, the relationship can't work. Well, the other thing I need to say, too, is that my parents had a really good relationship with each other.

Linda: You said they were sharecroppers with eleven children, of which you were the tenth.

Mary: Yes. So when we came to New York, I was twelve years old and my siblings were older. The thing is that I always witnessed them truly valuing each other. They were best friends to one other and that really made a difference. It helped me to know what close looked like. All of my siblings live nearby, and so I still, at this point, have all of them within ten minutes of me. My younger brother is furthest away, in lower Manhattan. I know how to be in a relationship because my parents and my siblings are all close to one another.

Linda: It seems like, when you talk about your family, that they were mentors for you around having good relationships. And, your siblings all helped one another. Do you think that there is a more positive view in Black families than in white ones? Sometimes it seems that there's more of a sense of community in people of color, even because of discrimination—maybe a sense that "we've got to stick together to get through this life."

Mary: It's hard for me to answer that, having to do with the fact that family is such an important piece for me. And I think that my family is unique in how big it is. And I see this as a gift. Other people might not see family in the same way. And many of my coaching clients, as well as psychotherapy clients, had families who were not so supportive or loving and connected.

So it's hard to know. I have a very racially, ethnically mixed group of clients. And I have people who have family that support them, and others who have families who don't.

It's really clear to me that no matter who you are, you want and need support. And I have many older people who really focused on their career and did not develop their family. And so no matter what racial or ethnic group they came from, if they got to be fifty or sixty and never had children or never married, they are often in pain about it. But they can still develop those kinds of supports through friendships and community. It is practically a universal that people all want and need support, especially as they age.

I think the work that I've done really helps me to see the human condition that exists in every group. People want love. People want to belong somewhere. And when you're working in the beginning, you can be so busy succeeding that you don't do the connection part. So, when I'm meeting with coaching folks about their getting that next job, even if they have not come to me talking about anything personal, I'll ask, "What are you doing for fun? Do you have time for a relationship? Is there somebody that you're sharing your life with? Is this really going to be okay for you when you're older, and there may be fewer choices about the things that you're not paying attention to."

And then sometimes when they've made a wrong choice, it didn't work out; it's not all over. I'll talk to them about the fact that it's absolutely fine to make a mistake and then make another choice. And that even if you choose the wrong person multiple times, all you need is one at any given time. So you choose another one. If you know that you're the kind of person who wants to be in a relationship, it's important to be able to pay attention to that social part of you. What are your interests? What fun times do you have? How well are you taking care of yourself? What are you doing with your spare time?

Because I find that, even if a person desires a relationship, no one is interested in someone who's waiting to find them. It's not about finding the right person, it's about being the right person. So focusing on yourself and doing things that bring you joy is key to connecting with like-minded people.

Linda: So, no matter if you've made a good choice for yourself or one that hasn't turned out to be a good choice, you should stay open to and pursue interests in your own life.

Mary: Being open to options is what it is. If you are honest with yourself, are you happy with what you're doing? If not, here are some options, and here's how to create some options. So the book is also about creating options. Often, people's ideas about a mentor is *I'm going to find this person and I'll have a soul mate that's going to help me work on my career and my life, forever.* And that's not the way it works. You need multiple people.

And sometimes, it's mentoring moments, like you start talking to someone sitting next to you at the airport and they recommend a book, share ideas that interest you and you might want to pursue. And so it's all about being open to opportunities.

So every morning, when my feet hit the floor, one of the first things that I think about is being open to what the day brings.

Linda: What kinds of things do you do for fun? What other interests do you pursue?

Mary: I mean, I love audio books, especially biographies. I watch CNN for what's going on in the political world, because I feel like I need to. I go to plays and concerts, and take dance lessons with my honey. But, you know something else that I do, that I hadn't thought of until you just asked me – I spend time with other like-minded folks. I tend to stay away from events where twenty-year olds are. If I'm going to go out dancing, I want to find a place where there are people my age.

Linda: It's as if, since you had a family that was close, you learned first-hand how to be in relationships and how important that was.

Mary: When my oldest brother graduated high school, he came to New York to be with my father's sister. And then two years later, he sent for the next one, and two years later, the two of them sent for the next one, and when it was time for my sister to graduate high school, it then meant it was just my parents and me and my younger brother, and we could not run a farm. So the nine of them got together, and instead of sending for just my sister, they sent for my parents, me, and my younger brother. And we all came together from North Carolina.

Linda: Everybody pitched in, so there you had that network. It's so important to have good relationships with your family and to have them nearby.

Mary: Yes, whenever I needed something, they pitched in. But now if anybody needs something, it's been a part of my life to pitch in.

Somebody's getting married; somebody's going to school. Whether they are immediately here or not, we make collections for books, marriage, babies, funerals, or whatever it takes to address unmet family needs.

Linda: It sounds as if you always had that support.

Mary: And my book is about the idea that you're paying it back. "Paying it forward" is the term I like to use, but, yes, I was born in a very functional group and I went on to study and teach the skills I first learned in my family. And I continue to learn and to use these skills in my business and my personal relationships now.

CHAPTER FORTY

Elinor Tolpin: Age is Just a Number

Elinor Tolpin is my former college roommate, Sue Kaplan Tolpin's mother-in-law. Sue met us at Elinor's home. At first, I thought Elinor might find it easier to be interviewed alone, but I found later, I was grateful that Sue was there, as she brought up some strengths that Elinor might have overlooked, had she not been prompted. Elinor lives in a retirement community, where she, in her late nineties, might very well be one of its oldest residents. She and her husband moved there thirty-five years ago. Elinor travelled the world with her husband, Sam. Souvenirs from their travels are on display in pristine glass cases all around her lovely condominium's living room. The apartment is large and looks as if it were meant for a couple or family, but Elinor has lived here alone since her husband died over thirty years ago. We began with my asking her what she believes are the secrets of long life.

Elinor: I've always had a very positive attitude. And I go back to my father always saying to me, do the best you can do. And I think I have followed this my entire life. I've always had this great desire for learning and books. I started to read at an early age, and I was very much encouraged by my mother because of this.

I don't think I could survive now if I wasn't a positive person. You know, as you grow older, and I've noticed it especially the last couple years, you find certain things happening. You may be alone. This is the big problem, being alone, and sometimes you're frightened at what could happen to you, when you're by yourself. I do have a special Life Alert that I keep in the house, because I have fallen. So, I learned the hard way. But whenever I get depressed because nobody's around, I always go back to my gratitude. I'm a very, very fortunate person.

Linda: So, when you're feeling lonely, you look at the glass half full.

Elinor: I'm very fortunate. I had wonderful parents, who always encouraged me. Whatever I did, it was my decision to make. They made me very independent. Even though they might have thought I was wrong, I made my own decisions.

Linda: That's pretty forward-thinking for those times, huh?

Elinor: I was married at eighteen. And it was wartime, so we got married and I continued going to school. I had already finished two years at the University of Illinois, and I was majoring in history. I loved history. And fortunately, I was always a good student. My husband was in chemical engineering. So I said "Gee, I don't know anything about chemistry," so I stayed away from all that. My husband said, "Take it." And I said, "But I can't." He said, "Sure you can." And I he told me, "If you get in trouble, you can come to me, but I'm sure you can do it." He gave me confidence, just as my father did. And I took the one class, got an "A," and I just took to it. This changed my whole life because I became a chemist.

I was going to go back into the chem lab to do research, but it's a nine to five job, five days a week. A nine to five job, five days a week was hard with children at home. I didn't want to leave my children. So, I was volunteering in the schools. They had the science fair and, after I helped with that, the principal said to me, "Why don't you come and teach here?" And I said, "I don't have a teaching certificate." So he told me, "We are desperate for science teachers."

So I went back to school, at night. I still had the children, you know. At night, I would take a class here and there. And when I had my certificate, I taught science. And I taught for almost twenty-five years and loved it.

Linda: So, with a little encouragement, you took a leap and carved out a whole new career as a chemistry teacher.

Elinor: My husband was a chemist. And then he had his own business. His family was in the pottery business. They did china decorating. So he worked with them. Then after I started teaching, unbeknownst to me, he went down to the Board of Ed and he had all of his credits, chemistry, physics and math, just what they needed. So he signed up as a substitute teacher.

And that year, in February, business was really slow. And the school called him in. He told the principal, "I've never been in a classroom before. I don't know what to do." But the principal said, "Come on in, we'll show you. Here are the books." And they liked him so much, they had him come back for two weeks. And that just kind of started a bug. He substitute taught for a little while, and then he said, "Why don't I go and take the exam to be a certified full time teacher?" He went back for that certification and then got a Master's in science education. So, he started teaching too. He downsized his business and kept it, but he loved the teaching.

I had eighth grade science students. My students would graduate, and by their second year, they had him. They went from Tolpin to Tolpin. And it gave us a different way of life, too. We were able to take vacations we couldn't take before.

Linda: You had holidays and semester breaks off.

Elinor: Yes, we were able to do these things as the kids were growing up.

Linda: Do you think your lifestyle contributed to the length of your life? Like those vacations, exercise, good eating, things like that, or do you think it was just, as some might say, "being blessed" or maybe luck.

Elinor: It's a combination. My mother was, kind of a health nut, as far as food was concerned. Way before it became popular, she stressed eating raw fruits and vegetables. I always ate healthy. And after I was married, and started a family, I prepared healthy meals, too. Fresh salad every day, fresh fruit every day, very few fried foods. And to this day, what do I eat? Salads. Also, I was always very active. I did a lot of walking. I didn't have a car at my disposal. And even when I got a car, I still did a lot of walking. To the mailbox, to the grocery store, to wherever I was going, I loved walking. And then later on, when aerobics came in, I was older then, but I joined aerobics classes. Even now, I try to walk every day, but not as much.

Linda: Did your parents live long, or their parents?

Elinor: No, my father died of a heart attack at sixty-six. My mother died at seventy-two, which is young these days. At that time, I thought it was old. So as far as genetics is concerned, I didn't have long life in my family.

Linda: You think you've lived a long life because you took care of yourself?

Elinor: Possibly, or maybe I was just lucky. But, fortunately, my heart has been fine. And no cancer, *kineenehora*,* as they used to say. And fortunately, no Alzheimer's in the family.

Linda: You mentioned that you're older than some of your friends.

Elinor: I'm older than all of my friends.

Linda: Does it make a difference? I mean, how do you deal with that?

Elinor: Well, about three years ago, I really got depressed. I moved here having all of these friends. And within a year, my three closest friends, one I knew since elementary school, one from college, all of them died. Now, not only was I missing my husband and my friends, but I had no one to go places with. So my daughter-in-law (Sue) said, "You have to get younger friends." I said, "How can I get younger friends? Who's going to go with me anymore?" So Sue told me, "You don't look older than they do, just don't talk about your age."

Elinor: With my friends now, nobody knows how old I am. I'm afraid to tell them. Because there is a definite prejudice about older people. I can hear it sometimes in the conversations. Some of the people in my bridge club will say, "Oh, my poor friend, she's eighty years old and we have to be careful with her."

Elinor: Well I would say – that there is this tremendous, I don't know if the word prejudice is right, but the feeling about older people is that others kind of overlook them.

Linda: One of the reasons for this book.

Elinor: Yes, it seems to some that you don't exist. There are even some doctors, you'll come in and, you're done, why bother? You're old, you know.

Sue: They don't see you as a long term patient.

Linda: And you may outlive them. You've probably outlived a lot of them.

Sue: She has. She's outlived younger doctors.

Elinor: So, in my social life, I don't tell them my age. I've gotten into this bridge group. I never say a thing.

Linda: On the other hand, I see you as a role model.

Elinor: Well, one of my closest friends is your age. Barbara knows how old I am. I met her when I was teaching and this was her first teaching job. I kind of mentored her for a while, and we became very, very close friends. I remember when she dated her husband for the first time. But none of my new friends know my age. Sue told me, "Mom, you have to make new friends, younger friends."

Linda: It's not healthy to be isolated all the time.

Elinor: Well, I'm really very careful. You know, I'll say "my grandchildren." Every once in a while I'll say "my great-grandchildren."

Linda: But I know you said you're a very positive person. And I notice sometimes as people are growing older, they think about death more often. Do you ever think about that?

Elinor: I try not to obsess about that. I think about living and positive things.

Linda: It sounds like you were always a pretty wise person, whatever age you were. Have you noticed anything that the additional years have given you.

Elinor: Well, I'm coming back to maybe an attitude or philosophy. I used to be of the philosophy that you had to learn something new every day. Whether it was a new word or something that's happening in the world. And I've always been a very curious person. I love reading, I like to learn about things. You know, not only fiction, but non-fiction.

Sue: Did you tell Linda how wired you are? I mean, she knows how to use Apple Computer, iPads, and iPhones.

Elinor: When they started with the computer – like I said, my husband would say, "Go ahead, you can do it." I always had that you-can-do-it. So, when I retired – well, I wasn't exactly retired, I became a volunteer. And Before I knew it, I was president of ORT*. And I had to write the monthly newsletter. I was typing it, and I had to send it out. And one day, my husband walks in with a computer. I said, "What did you do? It's so expensive." Especially at that time. I said, "I don't know how to use a computer." He said, "That's all right. You're smart, you'll figure it out." That was always Sam's answer to me. He said, "I can set it up. " That part I couldn't do, but I could follow directions. And he set it up, and I don't know, I followed the directions. That was it.

Sue: She uses everything, texting, and e-mails and all of it.

Linda: How many people can say that at twenty or more years younger than you?

Sue: Well, tell Linda about when you went to the audiologist, and they gave you this thing, because they said that you would be one of the people that would be able to understand how to do it.

Elinor: This is one of the things we might have to adjust to as we age, losing the sharpness of our eyesight, our hearing.

Sue: Boy, her mind's so sharp, though. Her memory's better than mine. I'm always asking, "What do they call that thing?"

Elinor: (Showing me the device.) This is a Bluetooth. What happened was, my daughter-in-law Gail said to me, "Mom, you're not hearing too well." I said, "I think I hear fine." She said, "No, you aren't, because when you're turned around, and I talk to you, you don't answer me." So I found an audiologist. And she said, "We have something new. Do you want to try it?" I said, "Sure." So she set up this Bluetooth and showed me how to do it. And then she said, "I want you to report back to me on that, because you are the only one I'm giving this to. "

Sue: Because she's computer literate. That's the reason, right?

Elinor: Yes. Do you know, the audiologist even came to the house.

Sue: Did she really?

Elinor: I mean, I don't know anyone else that would –And she said to me, "Because of you, we're using this now." She said, "You gave us all the data." That's because of my background. I could write down data. And I she never charged me for anything.

Linda: Wow. Hearing aids are expensive now too.

Elinor: Yes, but maybe because I did all the research part, whenever there's anything, she will take care of it for me. And I get a check up twice a year.

Linda: And that was because you're computer literate.

Sue: How many people her age even use an iPhone? Really.

Elinor: True. I think people just avoid learning it, or they think they can't. They're afraid of trying it.

Elinor: Well to me, the phone is like a lifeline. I'm not one that has to be talking all the time. I prefer where it's quiet, I sit down if I have a conversation. But I feel if something goes wrong, I have my phone. A couple times, I'll go downstairs in the car, and I realize I don't have my phone, so I run upstairs, because I think, what if I'm in an accident? How would I contact someone?

Linda: I was thinking about what you might advise women, in order to prepare for aging, whether they're as fortunate and as healthy as you are, or whether they're not. What would you say to them in their younger years to prepare?

Elinor: Well, the first thing I would say is learn how to be independent. Women of my generation, and maybe some of your generation were brought up in a way that their fathers would take care of them, and then their husbands would take care of them. And, it was, "Don't worry your pretty little head." I would definitely say, that every young woman should learn how to be independent; she must be able to take care of herself. I do all my finances myself. And I learned how to do this, and I had a husband who believed that I should learn how to do these things. And I'm very grateful for that.

But I know women much, much younger than myself who have gone from being dependent on their fathers and husbands to being dependent on their sons.

After Sam, my husband, passed away. It was the end of the year for income tax. So I called the accountant, the same accountant we had gone to, and I always went with my husband for the income tax. And so when I came in, he says "Elinor, I have another man who specializes…" – and this really hit me – "…in widows." [She groans.]

So I go to this other accountant, the one our accountant recommended, and he introduces himself. Then he says, "All right, I'm going to explain it all to you. You have debits and you have credits." And I say, "Stop right now. I know what a debit is. I know what a credit is. I have not only done books with my husband all these years, I took a course at Northwestern, in accounting.". And he looked at me in shock. He said, "My wife doesn't even know how to write a check." And I said, "Shame on her and shame on you. Because it is your responsibility as a husband to make sure your wife knows."

Elinor: He didn't mess with me after that. But I have found that many women don't want to do this.

Linda: But it's so important to know about your finances.

Elinor: Oh, who wants to do it? I wish somebody else would do it for me. My advice is to be independent. And to live a healthy life. You know, don't eat all this junk. I mean, maybe once in a while.

Sue: She's a good role model for moderation. She never pigs out.

Linda: And you've got a good energy level too, which is great.

Elinor: Yes I do.

Sue: And if people ask her to go someplace, she rarely says no.

Elinor: Another piece of advice is if you're going to get married, find someone who thinks you are special. My husband, Sam died over thirty years ago, a week after his sixty-sixth birthday. But he was the one who always encouraged me. To him, I was very special.

Linda: Yes. And if that doesn't work out, then what?

Elinor: Well then you have to be special enough in yourself. You have to have enough self-confidence so that your whole world doesn't depend upon that relationship.

Sue: I keep thinking, when you're talking about this, I keep thinking of this friend of yours, Sylvia, who was afraid to be alone.

Elinor: Actually, I always thought Syl was a very independent person. She taught at an open college, she was a writer; she was attractive and had a nice personality. But, after her husband died, very suddenly, she just didn't want to be alone. And this guy latched on to her. I think they went on one or two dates, and he told her, "I'm not going to see you any more unless I can move in with you."

Sue: That would have been a red flag. And he moved right into her condo.

Elinor: I thought she was independent, but evidently not. She supported him. He moved in with her and he never paid a penny. Maybe they would split the bill for the groceries. And when they would go out to a restaurant, to a movie, to the theater, they split the bill half and half, even though she was paying all the household bills.

Linda: So, you can end up with somebody, and your life can become worse than it would have been if you were alone.

Elinor: Exactly, And, then, when she got sick...

Linda: Did this guy take care of her?

Sue: Are you kidding? Her son came and got her.

Linda: So, it's important to be independent. Emotionally, especially.

Elinor: Oh, yes, emotionally; to have enough faith in yourself that you don't have to depend on somebody telling you that you're wonderful. My sons sometime think I'm Superwoman too, that I can do anything. Tom (Sue's husband, Elinor's oldest son)....

Sue: I know, he can be oblivious, sometimes.

Elinor: All of a sudden my air conditioning in my car was not working. I have a twenty year old Volvo. And I'm driving over to give Tom his birthday present. And all of a sudden, it's hot in the car. I'm not getting any air conditioning. So, Tom says, "No problem. You go to the repair people and pick up the Freon and buy a funnel and you open up your hood. This is my son, Sue's husband. I said, "Really

Tom?" He said, "You can do it." But like my husband, Sam, he says, "Of course you can do it. You've always done everything."

Linda : They have a lot of faith in you.

Elinor: Exactly, having a positive attitude about yourself is important. But be honest with yourself. I'm not the most beautiful person in the world, but I'm passable. You know. I'm not bad, but I'm not the gorgeous person who everybody's going to turn around when I walk in. So, I learned to develop a positive personality. You learn how to get along with people.

Linda: Do you think the years and experiences have made you wiser? Do you think having lived through the Depression and World War II, you have a wider lens?

Elinor: I think so. Because many times now, when there's an instance of something happening – maybe in the news – I can analyze it in terms of what I've experienced before. And I think this gives you a different perspective.

Linda: So because you've been through the Depression, World War II. . . .

Elinor: My grandson, Brett, and I were talking about the Supreme Court. And I said when you revisit history, not that I remember that this happened, but I remember in reading history, FDR came in with all these programs. The CCC, which was to help the young men get jobs. Helping our national parks, doing all these things. It came back to me. I hadn't thought about this in years. But when Roosevelt's attempt to get favorable rulings on his "New Deal" was knocked down by the Supreme Court, FDR proposed adding justices to the court. While his plan to add justices met with opposition, Justice Owen Roberts shifted in his opinion on The New Deal, giving acts like Social Security and other economic regulations his vote on the Court. This swing vote from Roberts and the threat of adding justices to the Court was enough to switch the Court to a pro-New Deal position. So, you can't predict what is going to happen, but if you look at history, you can find precedents for times we thought, *We'll never get through this.*

Linda: So, knowing history or precedents from the past help you stay positive about the future.

Elinor: You try to do the best you can. And one thing that keeps me going is having Tom and Sue here, and Brett and Marina (Tom and Sue's son and daughter-in-law), the great-grandchildren – you know, that's a special gift. And as I say, I'm really, really fortunate.

Marina says, "Why don't you come over during the week?" And I say, "The kids go to camp." She says, "Then, after camp." I don't stay that long. I stay an hour, an hour and a half. But this just boosts my morale, just being with them.

Linda: And it's wonderful to be loved. Especially when those little ones are so loving. Sometimes, just taking a short time in their week to connect with us, they may not know it, but it can mean so much. It sounds as if your list of living long in a positive way might be: eat healthy and exercise, maintain your curiosity, stay social, be independent and keep strong ties to family and friends.

Elinor: That and try to maintain a positive attitude.

*_kineenehora_-A Yiddish word, said to protect from "The Evil Eye." A Jewish superstition.
**_ORT-_ Organization for Rehabilitation through Training, started in 1880. a Jewish global education network, but not limited to Jewish people.

CHAPTER FORTY-ONE

Epilogue: Thank You for Coming

So, you've met my Annie, encountered my better half, learned my back story, seen several *Psychobabble*s, and, I hope, been able to assemble your own INCH bag, inspired by the women I've interviewed.

In the over five years it's taken me to write this book, some things around ageism and women are slowly showing signs of change in our culture: Maxine Waters is still going strong as a United States Representative in Congress and her congressional colleague, Nancy Pelosi, is Speaker of the U.S. House of Representatives; Leslie Stahl is a featured reporter for CBS' "60 Minutes"; Whoopi Goldberg and Joy Behar are both co-hosts on *The View*, the interview/talk show; Dame Helen Mirren continues to star in films and has been featured in Revlon ads; and Mae Musk, in her seventies, has resumed her past career as a cover-girl and model.

Though these women are well-known and started their careers long ago, for the rest of us, in general, I still see women fearing growing older in a culture which reveres youth, especially in women. I guess, as I shared at the beginning of this book, I was always searching for a way to grow older well. And what I learned was that many factors come into play.

I know that some things are not within our control, such as illness and loss, even financial security. But it helps to have tools such as: self-compassion and self-care; independence of spirit; willingness to take risks and be flexible; to find meaning in life and projects that hold personal meaning; and to maintain one's creativity, humor, friendships and family connections.

Having a good attitude, whatever the dominant culture presents or ignores, and gratitude for what we do have seem to be the most important tools we can use throughout our lives, most especially in aging. As psychiatrist and Holocaust Survivor Viktor Frankl theorized, all can be taken from a person, except one's attitude in any given circumstance.

And, if all this seems like juggling too many balls in the air at one time between family, friends, work, passionate projects, financial acumen, eating-well and exercise, all of which take time, I'd like to add one more tool to your I'm Not Coming Home (INCH) backpack—balance. In writing this book, the reason it's taken me this long to complete it is that I have tried to attend to the rest of my life. I visit my children and friends, pay careful attention to my work as a therapist, keep up with my own preventative health care, such as taking medication and supplements as needed, prepare and buy organic healthy foods, keep up with doctors' and dentists' appointments, use support groups and get enough sleep. If only I could get more disciplined about flossing!

As you've seen, each of the women you've met here, including me, have survived life challenges by learning to have less of the self-absorption of youth and focusing instead on connecting, teaching, and inspiring those around them.

It can be depressing to be stuck in the idea that you're nobody if you aren't rich and famous. Since most of us *aren't* rich and famous, does that mean we've failed in our lives? I think not. Maybe, despite the perks, the rich and famous have at least as hard a time ageing as the rest of us do.

All along the way, writing this book, I fought my own negative voice that said, *who cares about you or your life or opinions? Who do you think you are, Oprah?* And, again, I'd love to have the security and the power to do good in the world that Oprah has, but I would not have wanted her early life struggle; or earlier in her career, as a Black woman who didn't fit the stereotype of a TV personality, trying to make it in television.

I think many of us suffer from fantasized comparisons of ourselves to others. But, as a therapist, I've come to learn that even those whose looks, resources, health, or fame we wish we possessed, all have had their own life challenges.

For myself, I've lived with the fear of growing older and being alone and poor. There have certainly been times I've been alone and times I've been poor. But, ultimately, I always met with a synchronistic miracle—like my radio segments in my mid to late sixties, my sons' finding themselves in meaningful work and love, my grandson's birth, my meeting the love of my life when I'd totally given up on romantic love. So, for me, and for so many more women than I've had room for here, there are still dreams and surprises.

It's been both painful and great fun sharing my challenges as an older woman and the earlier moments of my life that shaped me. And it's been great fun to interview inspiring women and to learn that whatever fate has in store for us, we can use its lessons to grow.

There are so many ways to inspire and contribute. The ways I've most enjoyed my life most are the ways I've given to others. I hope I've been a role model to you, as well, as a seventy-five year old first-time author of a book that takes on the stereotypes of age for women.

So, I say to you now, as my Bubbe (grandma in Yiddish) Alice used to say to us kids when our parents bundled us up to leave her apartment, "Thank you for coming and thank you for going."

Still, I will miss you.

THE END

Acknowledgements

Black Rose Writing/ Creator Reagan Rothe and Design Director David King for creative assistance and believing in this book.

Kathie Giorgio and Allwriters" Workplace & Workshop for support and editorial assistance.

Ron Gould Studios for author photo and super-support throughout the completion of this book.

Barry Lewis, Attorney at Law, for legal assistance.

Stuart Stein, Attorney at Law, for legal assistance.

Dr. David Drapes, for years of phenomenal therapy.

Also, many thanks to Donna Stein, Lisa Zimbler, Laurie Barry, Bette Carter, Josette Day, Olympia Dukakis, Karen Forman, Marty Forman & Jack Forman, Geena Goodwin, Lorraine Hale, Melanie Jones, Janice LaRouche, Kaylan Pickford, Francine Ross, Johann Hari, The Wellness Institute. And for all of my terrific cousins, who have encouraged me along the way, some of whom are mentioned in chapters of this book.

About the Author

Linda Benjamin has been a clinical social worker for over thirty years. She was Supervisor of Program Development at WNET/Thirteen in New York. She hosted a live radio program in New York City. Linda wrote and aired her humorous radio segments, *Psychobabble*, on Milwaukee's NPR. She has published articles in *The New York Times*, *Chicago Woman*, and *The Woman's Newspaper of Princeton*.

Note from the Author

Word-of-mouth is crucial for any author to succeed. If you enjoyed *Girls' Guide to Aging with Grit and Gusto,* please leave a review online—anywhere you are able. Even if it's just a sentence or two. It would make all the difference and would be very much appreciated.

Thanks!
Linda Benjamin

We hope you enjoyed reading this title from:

BLACK ROSE
writing™

www.blackrosewriting.com

Subscribe to our mailing list – *The Rosevine* – and receive **FREE** books, daily deals, and stay current with news about upcoming releases and our hottest authors.
Scan the QR code below to sign up.

Already a subscriber? Please accept a sincere thank you for being a fan of Black Rose Writing authors.

View other Black Rose Writing titles at
www.blackrosewriting.com/books and use promo code
PRINT to receive a **20% discount** when purchasing.
purchasing.

Made in the USA
Las Vegas, NV
16 November 2021

34571773R00144